REBUILDING
LIBERALISM

REBUILDING LIBERALISM

Social Justice
with
Individual Freedom

GUY STANLEY

DUNDURN
TORONTO

Printer: Webcom, a division of Marquis Book Printing Inc.

Library and Archives Canada Cataloguing in Publication

Title: Rebuilding liberalism : social justice with individual freedom / Guy Stanley.
Names: Stanley, Guy, author.
Description: Includes bibliographical references and index.
Identifiers: Canadiana (print) 20190080639 | Canadiana (ebook) 20190080663 | ISBN 9781459745117 (softcover) | ISBN 9781459745124 (PDF) | ISBN 9781459745131 (EPUB)
Subjects: LCSH: Liberalism.
Classification: LCC JC574 .S83 2019 | DDC 320.51—dc23

1   2   3   4   5   23   22   21   20   19

We acknowledge the support of the **Canada Council for the Arts,** which last year invested $153 million to bring the arts to Canadians throughout the country, and the **Ontario Arts Council** for our publishing program. We also acknowledge the financial support of the Government of Ontario, through the **Ontario Book Publishing Tax Credit** and the **Ontario Media Development Corporation,** and the **Government of Canada.**

Nous remercions le **Conseil des arts du Canada** de son soutien. L'an dernier, le Conseil a investi 153 millions de dollars pour mettre de l'art dans la vie des Canadiennes et des Canadiens de tout le pays.

Care has been taken to trace the ownership of copyright material used in this book. The author and the publisher welcome any information enabling them to rectify any references or credits in subsequent editions.

The publisher is not responsible for websites or their content unless they are owned by the publisher.

Printed and bound in Canada.

VISIT US AT

dundurn.com | @dundurnpress | dundurnpress | dundurnpress

Dundurn
3 Church Street, Suite 500
Toronto, Ontario, Canada
M5E 1M2

For my children and grandchildren
and for
Charles D. Tarlton

CONTENTS

Preface   9

Introduction: What Happened to Liberalism?   13

1 Classical Liberalism's Failure: No Theory of Civil Society   41

2 The German Historical School   92

3 The Rise and Fall of the Welfare State   128

4 Rebuilding Liberalism: Where Do We Go from Here?   174

Acknowledgements   200

An Abbreviated Literature Review   203

Notes   206

Bibliography   237

Index   267

PREFACE

THE PROMISE OF LIBERALISM is not only political and economic freedom, but also social justice: liberalism is three dimensional. Those who say otherwise are probably unfamiliar with the history of liberalism from the end of the Napoleonic Wars to our own day. That history shows that while liberalism has guidelines, it comes with very few instructions. Mostly, it is a product of advances in some areas and retreats in others, until a coalition forms of people who care as much about the quality of their society as they do about their own individual advancement. When such a coalition is in charge of governance, then three-dimensional liberalism can be realized.

The story laid out in these pages suggests how difficult it was, historically, to get to that point, especially when the powerful were prepared to override every concept of fair co-operation in favour of their own economic and political benefit. Mainly, such gains were made when influential circles were seized with the belief that a fairer and more ethical community could be constructed, and when they had the influence to mobilize the necessary ideals. In the cases of nineteenth-century Germany and twentieth-century England, national survival — and the political situation before and after wars — played crucial roles. In the cases of France and the United States, it was the experience of a generation or more of bad governance together with an understanding that the national circumstances had evolved to the point of a new, truly liberal possibility — a national movement toward a progressive representation, after decades of misrule by greedy oligarchs.

Successful liberalism and unsuccessful liberalism alike are products of history, the interplay of ideals and ideas, of adult humans in conflict and co-operation. In particular, the idea of the liberal state and the special role occupied in the liberal state by civil society are among the keys to achieving liberal freedom with social justice. Another point of emphasis is that very little if anything in liberalism is automatic — markets are not always fair, democracy is not always adequate to the demands of statecraft, society can become so divided that the political centre necessary for successful liberalism becomes impossible to establish or sustain. Liberalism is no better than the people who are responsible for it. The only points that are certain are that (1) when liberalism works in all its dimensions, then society advances not only itself but also the horizon of possibility for humanity; and (2) when liberalism is hijacked by the interests, then the four horsemen will suddenly make their appearance and rather quickly people will speak of a coming dark age.

The book now before you was written with the aim of showing how liberal ideas emerged within a social and historical context, in particular the challenge of industrialization. The main argument is that the abstract liberalism of ahistorical principles — especially the principles of small-state, classical liberalism — offer no reliable insights into how free societies are achieved. Nor are the assurances of self-regulating interests of any kind worth much. Instead, the history of liberalism is the history of real individuals who understood what it meant to be free as individuals and who struggled to create free societies that would continue the Enlightenment program, mindful that humans are not just economic agents but moral ones as well. The takeaway is nothing more than that freedom with justice has to be earned — except perhaps to remind us as well that it is available, despite some learned arguments to the contrary.

This book thus joins a rising chorus of opposition to the prevailing Western ideology of neoliberal market fundamentalism. It nevertheless respects a conservative hope of finding actual, "timeless" principles behind liberal systems. I believe a number of these are indirectly illustrated in the history covered here: such principles as responsible government; transparency sufficient to permit public accountability; full access to economic, social, and political rights as citizens; protection of the weak and vulnerable; noble rather than mean action; equality of access to, and treatment before, the law. These principles and others like them are common to fair and open liberal democracies, but are violated regularly by neoliberal regimes. In particular, neoliberalism has no use for civil society — to the point of denying its existence — and demeans the professional public servants whose role is to serve society, assuring that all public policy serves the public good.

INTRODUCTION
What Happened to Liberalism?

LIBERALISM IS IN CRISIS. Worse, it seems to be breaking down in the countries where it used to be strongest: Britain and the United States, where populism is in power; and Western Europe, where the ultra-right is growing in strength in angry popular response to the past thirty years of governance.[1]

In a sense, one might think this is just business as usual for liberalism, which talks of social justice while too often implementing its opposite. If one is of a certain age, then one would remember one's parents' tales of the Great Depression and would have experienced the stagflation of the late 1970s and early '80s, and its wage and price controls, and later the currency crises of the 1990s and the "tech wreck" at the turn of the twenty-first century. These marked the decades before the Great Recession of 2008. And these were just some of the economic crises. The societal scandals are arguably worse and far more persistent: high rates of relative poverty, disproportionate imprisonment of racial minorities, ruthless exploitation of the vulnerable, particularly in labour-intensive sectors like agriculture, food processing, and the sex trades. Then there are the newer issues around climate change and the West's obsession with oil, to the point that it is changing the chemistry of the planet, with the disastrous effects on coastal areas and islands that we are beginning to see regularly.

Internationally, since the euphoria over the fall of the Berlin Wall, we see Western governments undertaking wars of aggression in the Middle East and aiding authoritarian forces of popular repression around the world. And when they try to do the opposite, as in Libya, there is no follow-up, to the detriment of peace in the entire region. And then there is the migration crisis, the thousands of migrants — mostly young people, the flower of their home countries in search of a better life — drowned each year in the Mediterranean with no coordinated action to resolve the underlying problems. This on top of the well-publicized issues of stagnant Western middle class salaries and the enormous rise in the wealth of the richest 1 percent: in the United States they now control over half the assets by value in that country. This is not the liberalism one knew in the postwar years and that helped defeat the tyranny of Soviet communism by holding up a mirror of freedom with justice.

There is a new element in this as well: the rise across much of the world of a tide of popular resentment against the West and its frivolous opulence in the midst of so much human distress. Resentment does not actually capture the feeling. There is a better French word: *ressentiment.* It expresses not only the outward resentment against an enemy or situation, but also a bitter self-hatred, a sense of personal failure for not having done more, despite its impossibility, a reaction to the waste of one's life as one watches, helplessly, a bystander in one's own fate.[2] This seems to be an emerging trend among young people who make up the vast majority of the populations of the developing world.

The great problem facing the West today is that it has succumbed to a simplistic ideology — a caricature of liberalism — that seems to paralyze reflection and make it impossible for liberal regimes to adapt to experience except by making things worse. That ideology is not liberalism, it is neoliberalism.

Today's liberalism — neoliberalism — makes a fetish of markets and individualism. Neoliberalism not only is based on Jeremy Bentham's utilitarianism, but has embraced a version that is Bentham on steroids.

Bentham, the father of utilitarianism as a doctrine of governance, hoped for an adjustment toward the middle: to the contrary, the neoliberals' version has achieved an unprecedented accumulation at the top of society and a corresponding disaccumulation and household debt at the other end of society. Nevertheless, markets, according to neoliberals, are self-stabilizing, automatic optimizers. Neoliberals don't believe "society" exists in any way other than as an aggregation of individuals. Neoliberals think monetary policy alone can pull countries out of a deflationary slump if the country will only ruin itself with austerity. Neoliberals think multinational corporations have equal or superior legitimacy to national governments. Neoliberals also hold that foreign direct investments are contracts underwriting current business practices and, therefore, that host governments should have no right to challenge them — to the point that even friends of free trade oppose recent trade deals.

Every one of those neoliberal postulates has been refuted in practice. In 2008, so-called self-stabilizing financial markets crashed and without government intervention would have pulled down the global economy. Monetary policy was unable to promote a recovery, such that eight years later the least "austerian" economy was outperforming the most ardent. The International Monetary Fund (IMF), which bowed to its board of rich neoliberal governments to support severe austerity in Greece, had to backtrack on that strategy, saying its costs outweighed the benefits. And as for the highly touted hyper-individualism the philosophy promotes over collective public policy, income disparities are higher than they have been since the Gilded Age of the Astors and their socialite friends in the 1880s. The great exceptions to these results are the authoritarian Asian regimes of the north Pacific, as well as to Singapore and the Scandinavians. It should surprise no one that under these circumstances Brexit — the popular outrage pushing back against European Union bureaucracy and its support for austerity — won in the 2016 referendum, and now Britain, the second most powerful economy in the European Union, may be leaving the organization. Neoliberals should perhaps begin to wonder if destabilizing the European Union, Europe's most ambitious attempt at finding joint solutions and a common expression of its culture, is really in the interest of the West.

The bottom line is that leading Western democracies are beginning to feel they may be in serious trouble. The middle class decline is opening opportunities for extremes on either side: mass or populist solutions favouring the nation or property over the constitution, in some cases without meaningful popular elections. Caesarism, if not outright tyranny, seems to be lurking just around the corner.

Well, one might think, liberalism has always been in some kind of crisis. In some places where the crisis grew particularly acute — such as Central and Southeastern Europe in the 1920s and '30s — it failed to overcome and perished. Knowing the result — the most ferocious war in history — we need to ask ourselves: Is this a movie we need to see again?

Here's the problem: liberalism is about political freedom. Almost by definition, liberalism is inherently unstable because it aims to create a stable society from that most destabilizing of elements — human freedom. The Russians are right when they point out that authoritarianism has a longer, more continuous history of governance: but that is not a mark of success, rather the opposite. Now, however, the crisis is coming home to the liberal "heartland," which can also be called the West: liberalism's most enduring achievement.

Some (myself among them) believe that political freedom in the West has been in trouble for some time, ever since the triumphal arrival of neoliberalism in the late 1970s and early 1980s to preside over the dismemberment of the welfare state. For, under neoliberalism, a doctrine or philosophy that was once a vehicle of political freedom and social emancipation — and that may still look that way from countries ruled by dictators — came to symbolize financial oppression, economic and social precariousness, and the dashed hopes of an ever-brighter future to millions living under that philosophy, especially in the North Atlantic countries of its birth.

It ought to be fairly clear that neoliberalism is a mistake that flies in the face of liberal history and hopes. It ignores the aspirations and efforts of earlier generations of liberals who strove to complement political freedom with social justice. It may come as a surprise to neoliberals to realize that for most of its history, liberalism sought to meet that challenge. Feudalism, which liberalism strove to supplant, already gave more or less carte blanche to a ruling class to have its way with the rest. Removing the strict moral imperatives for the well-born to have a care for the poor is not liberalism — it is just a licence to destroy.

Yes, to be sure, it has occurred more than a few times in modern history that the 1 percent has claimed ownership of everything by demanding "freedom" for itself and no one else — most famously after 1880 when the barons of the newly industrialized West claimed a kind of vulgar nobility of extravagance. By the end of the nineteenth century, they faced the consequences: attacks on their legitimacy by New Liberalism in the United States, Fabian socialism in the United Kingdom, and by social democracy in France and state socialism in Germany, supported by the mobilization of the millions of working people who now populated the cities. Already the new urbanism had shown the superiority of municipal socialism and co-operative enterprise. Now organized to share power nationally, the working class parties and their middle class allies would force the rich to pay their share and contribute to better education and a range of social services. This was the tide that lifted all boats — if only because in effect it gave a boat to everyone. Was it liberalism? It was not classical liberalism, which was widely believed to have failed. Yet its novelty, an expanded state along Hegelian lines, never abandoned core liberal values, such as rule of law, enforceable contracts, and democracy. As for capitalism, that was also accepted, but subject to regulation and state interventions to alleviate its worst excesses.

Yet, somewhat counterintuitively, the gains and the general understanding that supported them took about a century or more to develop. It took the experience of the Great Depression before the fragility of markets — especially financial markets — was understood and accepted. How and why did it take so long? And if the answers offered by democratic, limited socialism were so powerful, how is it that they ultimately lost public support? The questions deserve answers. But one should also express a certain wonder that social democracy achieved much at all, given the onslaught of the anti–New Deal, anti-Keynesian attacks it endured. Over the thirty years between 1945 and 1975, under the welfare state, middle class living standards improved, educational and employment opportunities opened up, and excluded classes of citizens found themselves victorious in their fights for recognition and public acceptance. The *ressentiment* that was increasingly aimed at the bourgeoisie and its civilization at the end of the nineteenth century had begun to disappear by the mid-twentieth century, as the welfare state unfolded and the colonial wars of liberation ended. Capitalism, despite its history of squalor and oppression, even began to look attractive.[3]

THE LIBERAL IDEA OPPOSES NEOLIBERAL POSTULATES

Ultimately, liberalism is about ideas — ideas on how to reconcile freedom and justice. Readers today may wonder about the significance of political theory, especially the history of ideas in political theory. The grandeur of the liberal project has been trivialized in the struggle with organized greed and selfishness. But for those who grew up during the Cold War, political philosophy — in particular the clash between Soviet Marxism and Western liberalism — was a battle of ideas between two nuclear superpowers and therefore an argument that could have terminal consequences. Despite a number of close calls, that obviously did not happen. Eventually, Soviet Communism collapsed, and liberalism prevailed in the West.

The liberalism that accounted for the "victory" was not the neoliberalism of today. It was the Keynesian liberalism of what J.K. Galbraith called the "new industrial state" that won the day — despite the strange fact that it actually collapsed before Communism and had already been replaced by neoliberalism ten years before the Berlin Wall came down. So why do I claim that the Keynesian new industrial state won? Because that was the version of liberalism — with its thirty years of growing affluence, its buoyant middle class, its steady levels of near-full employment, its dazzling consumer technology, and its growing economic opportunity — that seemed so attractive to the postwar generation in the relatively grim economies and drab, oppressive structures of everyday Soviet life, despite the economic security those economies offered.

Liberalism, the characteristic Western operating system since the American and French Revolutions, prevailed in the Cold War over central planning because it offered individual freedom, rising prosperity, and effective democratic government. What a contrast to today's neoliberalism, the handmaiden of massive financial fraud and of speculation ruling over investment!

As for political freedom, the economic crisis of 2008–12 demonstrated the relative ease with which democratically elected governments could be suppressed and technocratic regimes imposed on the basis of financial theories. At the same time, the threat of terrorism since September 11, 2001, demonstrated the ease with which long-established constitutional guarantees and international law could be set aside by a panicky executive power. The ordinary workings of democracy no longer seem capable of effective public stewardship in the face of either growing social crises or the environmental challenges posed by climate change.

It is a testimony to the power of neoliberalism that the near-automatic reaction to these problems is generally to look for mere economic explanations for the Great Recession of 2008–12, to try to make sense of anti-Western terrorism by analyzing comparative gross domestic product (GDP) and demographic data, and to confront climate change by denying for as long as possible the role of humans and their use of hydrocarbons for energy. The possibility that there might be a connection with liberal thought and the philosophical evolution of the West — in particular the rise of postmodernism — has not received anything like the amount of attention devoted to economic and behavioural political answers. It looks very much as though liberalism has thrown away every tool other than those of behavioural politics and economics, and that the very ideals of postwar liberalism no longer offer a useful formula for organizing a free society.

By contrast, the main argument of this book is that liberalism has lost its way and needs a makeover that includes a closer look at its roots. It is there that one will rediscover what it means to live in a free society. Surprise! It is not a society in which individual autonomy is the only collective value and in which market performance alone determines who "wins." There's more to it than that. Indeed, individual autonomy and *"tout m'est dû"* ("winner take all") entitlement is the opposite of what liberalism traditionally means. These lead — as we can see with our own eyes — not to freedom but its opposite: tyrannies big and small throughout society and a worsening material outlook for just about everyone.

Even neoliberal authors recognize that the West's current crisis is a crisis of ideas, even if the ideas they address are the familiar failed ones of economic austerity.[4] The theme of the essays that constitute this book is that today's neoliberal triumphalism is actually a confession of liberalism's limitations as a theory of political and economic guidance. Liberalism has very little to offer in the face of the traditional political challenge it poses for itself: how to reinforce society as a "fair system of cooperation."[5] It also offers little comfort to anyone concerned about the power of technology, in particular the three world-historic revolutions now under way: globalization, climate change, and the digital revolution. Worse, the persistence of neoliberalism as a dominant approach to pressing public problems leaves the West helpless before the more effective and pertinent political systems of Asia — more effective because they are able to face up to real problems and deal with them as political systems, at least for now.

NEOLIBERALISM'S FATAL ABSTRACTION

Unlike the Cold War, the current issues are not about which political systems are "better." Rather, they are about which systems can grasp and respond effectively to the main challenge of securing fairness in communities divided legitimately over fundamental differences, and also to the challenges of technology and the three tech revolutions. Why? The answer is that neoliberalism has reduced the social sciences to a narrow, financial view of economics and is blind to social issues. To put it a different way, neoliberalism has embraced the limited tool kit of positivism and its shrivelled idea of "explanation" as the only useful way to analyze the world's political and social difficulties. The tech revolutions on the horizon challenge earlier ideas of what it means to be a human living with other humans on this planet and cannot be correctly and fully evaluated without a grasp of what it means to be an individual living in society. Yet the crucial problem of "meaning" cannot be addressed by positivism alone. Positivism provides an explanation the way an algebraic function provides a "solution": rearranging the variables according to the laws of mathematics generates a conclusion. But the conclusion is dependent upon the initial variables: it does not provide actual understanding of a human situation. Positivism evaluates technology, for example, as a tool. It asks questions such as: Is it effective? Can using it make our activities more efficient in the light of our attainable goals? Does it lower costs?

To get to an understanding of technology and the totality of its impact, one must go beyond the economic variables to analyze its impact on people and how they live. Then it will become apparent that besides its direct economic benefits, technology also has the power to destabilize society and to create a new feudalism under an oligarchy composed of the 1 percent of the population that make up its highest earners. This is not a new insight — it dates back to the early nineteenth-century critique of industrialization. But it cannot be computed in the neoliberalism policy machine. If something adds to "efficiency" — even if its social costs are far greater than its economic benefits — neoliberalism has a hard time grasping such facts. Our addiction to hydrocarbon energy is a case in point. Excessive sugar in the popular diet, the long-term effects of monoculture agriculture, the promotion of a sedentary lifestyle through such things as office design, urban design, our addiction to the automobile, and so on: these are additional examples.

RECOVERING THE WEST'S COMPARATIVE PHILOSOPHICAL ADVANTAGE

Historically, the West has outperformed the East only when its political ideas generated effective leadership. Moreover, "outperformed" did not include economics. Until the Industrial Revolution, the West was generally behind the East in wealth accumulation and luxuries. What we had — and what we still (barely) have that they did not, and in many places still lack — what the West had, then lost for a thousand years, then a scant two hundred years ago began to recover, was individual freedom and dignity. That, plus industrialization, changed the game for a while.

It used to be widely accepted that the real source of a people's wealth lied in its ability to mobilize its intelligence. And now Asia, always more populous than the West, has discovered an effective way to do that — in some measure by bending many of the insights stimulated by liberalism to serve collective goals. The philosophical challenge for the West, then, is to emerge from the dead end of neoliberalism and its nihilistic companionship with postmodernism to consolidate and reinvent its public philosophy on a higher level. That is, a level in which atomized individual humans rediscover the essence of their humanity such that they can steer the three tech revolutions in directions that enhance mankind and its relationship with Earth and all its creatures. One of the great historical achievements of liberalism was to free up positive science; its greatest failure (as I argue here) is its failure to expand human consciousness to an equivalent understanding of itself and its place in the world's natural system.

Political philosophy is generally considered — if it is still considered at all — as a subordinate type of thought that corresponds to political party ideologies and the occasional judicial pronouncement on some constitutional matter. However interesting some specialists might find it, it is now almost entirely abstracted from reality. Concepts like "the rule of law," "accountable government," "independent judiciary," "bureaucracy," and so on have become characters in a morality play, ostensibly more real than the underlying physical and historical actions they reference. What is "law" if it is not a snapshot of current social combats? Is it law or economics that designates fiduciary responsibility as a higher management responsibility than, say, worker safety? Why is private property better protected than, say, employment? When we say that certain postulates together underlie "liberal" institutions, shouldn't we add a word or two about the social disequilibrium that results? If the result is toxic for the many as opposed to the few, are these abstractions, then, really the essence of liberalism? I would say not: rather, liberalism is debate, discussion, the flow toward justice, equality, and the realization of human potential. The meaning of those terms are at the core of liberal philosophy. But neoliberalism has instead turned its back on its rich history and excluded these ideas, subordinating liberalism to its anti-historical, abstract view of economics, which in turn has become a branch plant of financial accounting. Basic concepts of political philosophy, such as the state, the citizen, property rights, human rights, political representation, political values like justice and identity — all are headed to history's scrap heap of human sense and meaning. Today, what counts in politics is economics redefined as financial power. Everything else is smoke.

Thus, sovereign debts are enforceable, full employment as a democratic program is not; risk has its place, but is almost entirely to be borne by borrowers, not lenders (however determined); cost and efficiency are balance sheet items, while wasted human potential has no place in accounting; and constitutions are secondary to financial priorities. Monetary policy is a legitimate, if ineffective, tool to use in a deflationary crisis; fiscal policy, an effective tool, is not legitimate — because of a theology that says "efficient" markets are self-correcting. Human beings in this set-up are supposed to respond to "signals," like electrons in a magnetic field, controlled by distant authorities deaf and blind to any information other than the dials on the grid.

The political repercussions of these fundamental economic and political misconceptions are already disturbing. In the United States, the hub of the world financial system, corporations are people for the purposes of political contributions, and money is a form of political speech and therefore "protected" — whereas, say, reporting on animal cruelty and taking unauthorized photos of animals in food plants is, in some U.S. states, equivalent to terrorism. Financial manipulation that caused the implosion of the global financial system is a corporate crime to be punished by fines on the company rather than criminal penalties on any of the individuals involved, whereas a poor black guy caught with a pizza he can't prove he bought may face life imprisonment, depending on his "priors" (under so-called three-strikes legislation). Much of this is the unquestioned law of the land as decided by the learned justices of the U.S. Supreme Court, as indeed was *Dred Scott v. Sandford* in 1857, now regarded as one of the worst decisions in the court's history. Will *Citizens United* turn out to have been our generation's version of *Dred Scott*?

One thing is certain: injustice will grow as economic prosperity withers. In a world in which "the people" cannot use the state to jump-start a failing economy and bond rating agencies penalize any debt as dangerous to investors, economic growth beyond inventory replacement becomes impossible. Nation-states are condemned to a new normal in which banks create company debt to be converted into share buybacks that boost prices and bonuses for the captains of industry. But industry no longer has much time for Western markets because household incomes have stopped growing — in contrast to Asian markets in which technocratic planning continues to achieve growth rates well in excess of those in the West. Commentators may see this as an economic problem. But if economics is a science based on evidence, and the evidence shows the policies adopted cannot work, why have they persisted for ten years or more? The answer must be political choice.

Oddly, Western political philosophy has not evolved in response. On the contrary, the neoliberal mantra continues to circulate in the mainstream media — although it began to be challenged in the Canadian elections and the U.S. Democratic primary campaigns of 2015–16. But as yet, no alternatives have emerged to replace the neoliberal consensus.

Political philosophy as we know it in the West began in fourth-century Greece. We still read texts of Plato, Aristotle, Thucydides, and Xenophon, to name but a few. We do so in part for their content, but mostly because these ancient texts reveal to us a culture of astonishing capacity for reflection on some of the most important questions of what it means to be human and on the meaning of living in society. Such intensive and extensive reflection is a "bursty" phenomenon in Western intellectual history. Fourth-century BCE Greece is an island of originality and depth (admitting some individual exceptions in the Middle Ages) until the early modern period and the development of modern political science with Machiavelli and subsequently others around the English Civil Wars, the European Wars of Religion, and the French Enlightenment of the late eighteenth century, through which our modern ideas of the state were formed.

One might say that these bursts were occasioned by existential political crises — the crisis of Renaissance Italy, Europe's inability to handle the Protestant Reformation peacefully, and the French government's inability to make both absolutism and mercantilism function synchronously. But there were other crises — such as those Rome faced in the first and fourth centuries, which failed to find an adequate response in political theory, or the period between the twentieth-century wars, in which the main innovations of political theory — fascism, Nazism, and Stalinist Communism — were violent and monstrous. Or again in our own era since the economic collapse of the West in the tech wrecks of the 1990s and the Great Recession of 2008, in which political philosophy has been stunningly silent except for the reiterated failed mantras of neoliberalism. The takeaway conclusion for consideration is that for most of the time and for most political cultures, political philosophy is not able to play an originating role. Yet in the West, liberalism did have an answer to the monstrous tyrannies of the 1930s and '40s, namely Keynesian economics, allied with a humane version of the neo-Hegelian superstate, which was put together under the New Deal and Allied postwar planning. After the Second World War, it became more generally known as the welfare state.

Why did the welfare state "fail"? Neoliberals can only supply a dubious economic argument: debts and taxes were both too high, regulations too restrictive, so that growth effectively stopped. The argument misses the larger, civilizational picture. For the meltdown of the welfare state was, after all, the stalling out of the most successful liberal political-economic system ever seen. Its demise requires more than an accountant's steely pen. The chapters that follow advance a cultural explanation linked to social change and the transformation in the main currents of modern philosophy from the Enlightenment to the collapse of Soviet Marxism. The principal cause is that the purpose of the welfare state — its teleological goals, its raison d'être — became collateral damage to the dead-end Western philosophy reached by the 1970s.

By then, most of the key ideas underpinning the liberal state no longer compelled belief. Reason, sympathy, liberty and freedom, consciousness, truth, beauty, and public duty no longer mattered sufficiently to maintain the liberal state's success. What remained of its liberal content were the formalities of its legal system — in particular its "rights" claims. These had become dominated by modern "positive rights" doctrine in the service of new claims by experienced rent-seekers in single-issue groups. These succeeded in opening financial markets in particular so that speculative finance held sway, allied with a new technology that drove (and continues to drive) its own self-serving digital revolution. This gave big finance and its industrial allies the power to reorder and transform not only the economic landscape but the social and political landscapes as well.

THE CHALLENGE OF POSTMODERNISM

How liberalism lost its way so thoroughly is a complex story that follows the twists and turns of Western culture and philosophy since the eighteenth century. The cultural despair associated with the First and Second World Wars is sometimes taken as having destroyed the generally optimistic liberal values of the eighteenth and nineteenth centuries, in particular by the hijacking and perversion of these values in the totalitarian regimes of the twentieth century. The fact of totalitarianism ruined the credibility of European humanitarian ideals. Philosophy pared itself down to individual authenticity and the implicit dictatorship in every grand theme. As one of the slogans of the 1968 student demonstrations put it: *"Pas de replâtrage, la structure est pourrie."* Now ennui was the revolt of the authentic self, its antidote authentic self-assertion; truth was henceforth grounded in one's being, no longer in principles. As a consequence, Hegel's hope for a universal consciousness of understanding and Kant's hope for a moral law based on reason no longer applied. Yet these had been the foundations of liberalism.

As a British philosopher recently put it, drawing attention to the interwar destruction of the idealism historically rooted in liberalism:

> Who now believes that the truth will make us free? Even optimists limit their hopes to economics and politics, disclaiming any broader vision of human redemption. Francis Fukuyama's end of history is not the glorious consummation of Hegel or Marx, but a vista of endless banality. Contemporary liberals are faced, whether they like it or not, with the unpromising task of erecting a philosophy of political hope on a foundation of cultural despair.[6]

That postmodern challenge has generally been ducked by recent liberal political philosophers. As a general proposition, liberalism as a political theory has received considerable discussion but little scrutiny of its principles and operations by liberals since the end of the Cold War. This is perhaps not surprising in that neoliberalism represents a victory of sorts for the anti–New Deal commentators. Those are the ones who between the 1950s and 1970s claimed to be defending liberal principles while hammering the social conscience of the welfare state.[7] Perhaps even more surprising, the philosophical community — which has been generally extremely critical of neoliberalism — is only beginning to advance alternatives. In contrast, climate change activists have put forward a number of books challenging the current global order and proposing intelligent changes.[8] The low uptake has testified to the "capture" of our current debate, thereby underlining and confirming Margaret Thatcher's "TINA" claim: There Is No Alternative. The contrast with the 1930s is striking.

SOME CONTEMPORARY CHALLENGES

This work goes in a different direction. The underlying theme is that the crisis of liberalism today is linked to the crisis of meaning in modern sociology and philosophy. This manifests as a scientism that suppresses critical awareness of one's situation based on a capacity for historical and sociological interpretation. Postwar Liberalism's increasingly exclusive embrace of positivism became increasingly an exercise in suppression of what C. Wright Mills calls the "sociological imagination,"[9] which nevertheless had triumphed by the nineteenth century's end, bringing with it a different, more comprehensive, view of the state and its responsibilities. Sadly, not even the more socially aware liberalism of the post–New Deal Keynesian era could altogether escape the twentieth century and its dark currents. Its successor, neoliberalism, a second-rate, timid philosophy that tragically holds the individual to be in opposition to society, triumphed in part because of the decline of critical sociology, and in particular its failure to probe thoroughly the persistent social problems arising from capitalism.

As a result, neoliberalism suffers from a kind of arrested development that renders it ineffective in confronting some basic challenges of advanced civilizations. Worse, these shortcomings leave it completely unready for the challenges of civilizational change, such as those indicated by globalization, climate change, and the digital revolution.

The major problem of neoliberal ideas is that they do not control their own consequences. The liberal claim that spontaneous order optimizes, and planned order can only suboptimize because of the opportunity costs of regulation, is factually incorrect. In fact, one can identify at least six obvious objections to that liberal claim:

1. **Pareto's constant, Mosca's ruling class, and the challenge of political sociology:** The rise of sociology beginning with Saint-Simon and Comte, followed later by Émile Durkheim, Vilfredo Pareto, and Gaetano Mosca, revealed that the liberal societies of the nineteenth century — despite their rhetoric of freedom — reproduced many of the characteristics of the *ancien régime:* a near-permanent ruling class, and near-permanent disparity in income and household wealth. It revealed as well that material inequality was the

complement of permanent political inequality, despite constitutions and talk of the "rights of man."[10]

2. **The impact of the multidivisional business corporation:** Thorstein Veblen's close observations of the business corporation showed the decisive role of large-scale industrial corporations in the modern economy.[11] The subsequent analysis of Berle and Means showed that shareholders of public companies had ceded effective control to management.[12] Instead of the liberal model of business, the modern corporation had become a private bureaucracy, able to dominate markets and impose its plans and priorities on society. In the postwar period, the work of J.K. Galbraith drew attention to the new industrial state, the evolution of the liberal order into a near-seamless managerial elite, linking business and government into a technocracy of capitalist planning rather than an economy based on competitive markets and entrepreneurship.[13]

3. **Status and function:** A particular issue in liberal regimes is the bifurcation of status and function. The *ancien régime* guaranteed status irrespective of function. Liberal society derives status from function, and its functions are generally unstable and dependent on markets. This means that social structure is in play simultaneously with the economy and that economic changes threaten the social status quo. An alternative economic approach is that of cameralism,[14] an approach akin to estate management. German cameralists created Bismarck's social insurance plan that guaranteed working class retirement; the resulting solidarity propelled Germany's rapid rise to great power status based on industrial leadership. The cameralist approach was later adapted by the Japanese to ensure that modernization could be achieved with minimal disruption to Japanese traditions. As Japan emerged to become a world-leading manufacturing power, Japanese firms achieved significant advantage by guaranteeing workforce status in the plant, while North American industry continued to treat its workforce as a disposable commodity to be used as a business cycle control mechanism with all the risks and uncertainty that implied. The resulting financial costs of labour peace hamstrung the North American automobile industry in the face of Japanese competition.[15]

4. **The challenge of meaning in history and economics:** This point adds to the previous one. Cameralism — the progenitor of a form of economics that ultimately characterized the German historical school — is attuned to the issue of the developmental stages of liberal society. Liberalism, especially the Austrian variety of which we shall read in chapter 2, is blind to the significance of historical development. Its insights are universal and invariant in both time and place, inspiring the one-size-fits-all approach to policy, and thus development of such one-size-fits-all solutions as the Washington Consensus on economic development. The disastrous consequences were evident in the West's financialization of development problems as "monetary crises" and the harsh advice meted out to troubled less-developed countries in the 1990s. Development economics now challenges these one-size-fits-all views. But they remain responsible for many of the economic imbalances that persist even after the crisis of the Great Recession.

5. **"Spontaneous" order — powerful mythology and its destructive misunderstanding:** The eighteenth-century critique of the *ancien régime* was based on a discovery of "natural order." Philosophers and even some high officials in the cabinets of the last two pre-revolutionary French kings (such as Turgot and Choiseul) observed that free markets alleviated food and other shortages of supply much more effectively than any set of official decrees. The doctrine perhaps reached its highest expression in the work of Adam Smith, who noted that mankind had advanced via the development of three "conventions": language, markets, and money.[16] This insight was developed throughout the nineteenth century, gaining additional momentum through the (mis)appropriation of biological analogies from Darwin and Spencer, and the development of marginalist price theory. Yet science shows that natural evolution applies to species, not individuals. Experience confirms Carl Menger's insight that the marginalist price theory weakens under general affluence. Since then Friedrich von Hayek, a key figure in the rise of anti-Keynesian neoliberalism, took the idea of spontaneous order to a higher stage of belief.[17] These ideas nevertheless seriously understate the importance of the state in making economic order function efficiently.

Today, with the development of complexity theory and the theory of criticality, the flaws in the neoliberal concept of spontaneous economic order have become only too evident. The new ideas underline the importance of public policy for enabling institutions to handle risk and control the drive of markets and other types of organization to critical levels followed by collapse.[18] One of the important issues was raised by a brilliant young philosopher killed in 1915, Emil Lask.

6. **Lask's anomaly:** Emil Lask (1875–1915) was a nineteenth- and early twentieth-century philosopher who influenced thinkers as divergent as Max Weber and Lucien Goldmann. Lask's anomaly holds that systems cannot be viewed simultaneously as wholes made up of parts and as parts that make up wholes: both views are valid, but the observer must choose one at a time.[19] By the middle of the nineteenth century, liberal philosophy had become organized around parts and rejected the perspective of controlling wholes or "totalities." "Watchman state liberalism" treated the reality of social circumstances as subjects outside the reach of public policy. Liberals thus believed that states could not deal with issues such as social justice as a goal of public policy. In other words, it was held that the liberal state's inability to correct for harmful social consequences was a function of the freedom permitted to economic agents. Liberal thought on this point was well summarized by Margaret Thatcher: "There is no such thing! There are individual men and women." But Lask's anomaly actually means something quite different: that focusing on the macro picture will change the state of the micro picture, and focusing on the micro picture will change the state of the macro picture. Another way of putting this is George Soros's idea of reflexivity — an idea that can be traced back to Durkheim — which is to understand how the parts affect the whole *and* how the whole affects the parts, in a dialectical relationship. Getting this right through a continuous stream of adjustments is one way of describing liberal politics and social learning. This, in effect, was the same as the British Fabian view that came into vogue just before the First World War and led to a vast improvement in working class conditions, including the entry of a working class party into parliament.

The Challenge of Liberal Consensus

Associated with the inconsistencies and contradictions in liberalism is the reality of liberal democracy's fragility. More specifically, it must confront the challenge of consensus. In a famous essay, the libertarian Ayn Rand attacked democracy's "ruling consensus" as arbitrary, exclusive, and economically dysfunctional.[20] She neglected to say that without some form of consensus, democracy breaks down. Indeed, the collapse of consensus is often the first step on a short path to tyranny or even civil war. Rand's concept of consensus was that around laissez-faire — a consensus that history shows is tantamount to "the cynic's golden rule": those with the gold make the rules.

The ideas of James Buchanan and John Rawls concerning the building of consensus for a just or fair society offer a profound diagnosis of the problems of getting the necessary "overlapping majorities" when the economic program is in contradiction to the political program of individual liberty and property rights.[21] The dimensions of the problem itself are canvassed in Isaiah Berlin's famous "two freedoms" essay, opposing all government redistribution in pursuit of social aims, in essence restating David Hume's position of inviolate selfishness.[22] Remarkably, this essay marked the limits of consensus in favour of "redistribution" in the welfare state. Perhaps we can blame the Cold War in which capitalism was in competition with state-directed "socialism": the fact accepted before the First World War that capitalism creates a vulnerable population that cannot support itself seemed to have become a taboo in elite discussions after the Second World War.

Hayek's *Constitution of Liberty* — which became one of Margaret Thatcher's articles of faith — recognized a need for minimum social redistribution in an industrial state, but offered only as generally available state-sponsored social insurance.[23] Specifically, targeted assistance was eschewed as an invitation to socially divisive rent-seeking. A contrasting approach, put forward by John Rawls in *A Theory of Justice,* suggested a politically constructed order designed to ensure a progressive narrowing of the inequality produced by the pro-cyclical effects of "spontaneous" economic growth in which the rich get even richer while the poor can never hope to close the ever-widening gap. The failure of Rawlsian political "constructivism" to end division over this issue is all too evident in the disabling political divisions currently hamstringing the legislatures in the United States and inspiring the ineffective austerity measures in Europe and Canada. Yet despite these and other formal political models (such as, for example, Arrow's impossibility theorem), there is another level of argument that resolves that issue in favour of social liberalism; it turns on the issue of foundational ethics as a criterion of political action. Does liberalism, or any democratic, market-based system, raise or lower mankind's civilizational aspirations and attainment? Hippocrates' "Do no harm" and Kant's moral law — that every maxim to be valid must be acceptable as a universal law — require that full consequential knowledge be available. This is obviously an impossible condition, a counsel of perfection. Liberalism accepts the challenge and offers a better way forward in this regard.

Liberalism is the custodian of the only new knowledge creation system known to man — experimental science and competitive technological innovation — in which consequential knowledge is part of a discovery process: that is to say, not known in advance. Liberalism can take society forward. It can also learn from experience and correct its flaws based on evidence, as long as it remains an open theory based on testable propositions and does not retreat into a defensive community of belief.

In particular, this raises the contextual problem of how a given system can transform itself into a better one, while handling the risks of evolving something worse. It is especially puzzling since any market-like system at its starting point contains the level of knowledge required to sustain itself, but no more. How then can it advance to a superior state on its own, endogenously, with no external "Lycurgus" (who, it will be remembered, was recalled from foreign exile to legislate for the Spartans) to provide new answers?

The answer is conscious evolution through the learning — individual and social — that competitive markets encourage. Learning involves coming to terms with new data and their meaning. It is why only liberalism — properly conceived in its fullest sense — speaks to mankind's unique and peculiar nature: the driving, urgent desire to know more and understand better. This property, which emerges from the emphasis on individual liberty, is particularly important for the future of mankind. But it implies that liberalism must absolutely overcome (at a minimum) Lask's anomaly and the challenge of consensus while enhancing freedom. Can it be done? Not without a lot of fresh thinking and a deeper understanding of liberalism and its relationship to society.

The Modern "Crisis" of Philosophy and the Concept of Freedom

From the early modern period through the Enlightenment, freedom meant autonomy to accept or reject community norms in return for accepting personal responsibility for one's actions. Liberalism measured the space between the individual and the norms, trying to find a balance. Postmodern freedom has dropped the responsibility clause altogether. Community norms are anthropological only — with few if any claims on the individual. (Hence, for example, a paradigmatic CEO asks: "Show me where it says I can't do XYZ.") This kind of thinking is often (wrongly, I think) traced to Nietzsche as the will to power. The principal idea here is that only the subject has valid claims. Others, well, they're the "others" … with no valid claims on me.

The upshot of these flaws in liberalism is extremely dangerous: namely, liberalism's claim to scientific authority for ideological positions. Consequences when that kind of liberal economism infuses a society as normal thinking include a slow death of democratic politics, an incapacity to handle economic problems at the macro level, and a "vision thing" that inhibits imaginative solutions to institutional and governance shortcomings. Today, as in past eras, this kind of liberalism ultimately amounts to permission for capital to control political power, pursue monopoly, and abuse market power, while labour is thwarted in its ability to offset the exercise of capital's power. For example, just as it was denied the right to organize for almost the whole of the nineteenth century, organized labour ever since the 1980s has faced new obstacles. In a kind of eternal return, today privilege for financial capital is baked into neoliberal arrangements enacted since 1980: examples are the tightening of individual bankruptcy laws, easing of rules for private financial political contributions, restricting the public lending rights of central banks, increasing the scope of investor protection for multinational companies in trade agreements to the point they impinge on political levers of economic development, and changes in taxation regimes that privilege income derived from capital over income earned through labour.

Despite these shortcomings, the full body of liberal theory offers a great deal more than its past and current errors might suggest. Above all, liberalism is about personal liberty — an ideal that has propelled social change from the eighteenth century to now. Historically, liberalism — in Peter Gay's words, the "science" of freedom — represented a clean break with the past for mankind. It installed the individual as the master of his or her own fate and thus, on balance, eventually left everyone better off. The improvement was not only material — it was above all social, transforming the lives of humans as social beings. Liberalism eventually reinvented the state in such a way as to enable human beings to flourish according to their own lights as long as they respected the law — which, as citizens, they made together. This did not come easily. Classical Greece and Rome gave birth to certain ideas that inspired modern liberalism. But they offered nothing to match the well-developed legal and political infrastructure of the modern state that liberalism produced: a comprehensive system of discovery and protection of human rights; a democratic, verifiable electoral system; and a justice system that works to protect the rights of the accused and to bring the guilty to justice based on actual proof and the decision of an impartial jury — where the ancients relied on clans and families of the victims to bring criminals to trials and enforce justice.

The accomplishments flowing from liberalism despite the errors stemming from its economics are impressive. It accelerated the Industrial Revolution and the transformation of Western civilization from a scientifically ignorant agricultural base to a historically unprecedented technological civilization. Moreover, when that civilization was threatened with complete economic collapse followed by world war, it was the promise of liberal prosperity with justice that rallied the Western forces of victory and then organized thirty years of growing prosperity. Under that liberalism, social or Keynesian liberalism for the most part, there were no serious, system-threatening bank crises, and living standards rose across the West.

On the political side, if one can make such a distinction, expanding freedom overcame persistent barriers of race, gender, sexual orientation, and poverty, and expanded constitutional protection of freedom in line with the U.N. Charter and the U.N. Universal Declaration of Human Rights within the Western liberal bloc. Such was its momentum that it carried over into the former Communist bloc during the 1990s, and even made some inroads toward bringing democracy to Russia. The state that supported that achievement was the most advanced political construction in history — the pinnacle of liberal and Western political achievement. Unfortunately, it could not endure its own creation of prosperity.

Since the 1990s, as neoliberalism has replaced the earlier variety, it re-incorporated classical liberalism's errors into public policy. Result? Freedom's rise has flattened and is even going into reverse — not only on the Western periphery, but in NATO countries, as civil society erodes and people become preoccupied with personal matters and retreat from political activity other than demonstrations. The re-emergence of anarchism, repurposed as Middle Eastern terrorism although committed mainly by anomic elements of domestic society, has recently added reactive "patriotism" to the calendar of Western popular movements.

This situation is, or ought to be, serious enough to compel a careful re-examination of liberalism as a public philosophy whose goal of a society with freedom and justice ultimately led to the establishment of social science, not just economics. Freedom is liberalism's greatest contribution to humanity. Inescapably, freedom in society is a balancing act between individual autonomy and innovation against collective norms and traditions. The boundaries of this zone of constructive tension are not always obvious and are always debatable. Yet it is within this zone that society conducts its exploration of the meaning of the public good, the good life, or the "pursuit of virtue." Freedom requires that the determination of the space given to this zone be based mainly on practical wisdom rather than science and/or technology, as Aristotle underlines in his *Politics*. That requires the protection of political speech and a continuous public deliberation that involves the whole of adult society: indeed, defending that space and maintaining its effectiveness is the principal challenge of democracy. In the speed and scale of the modern world, that also requires a public sector capable of handling large quantities of excellent social research.

Today's neoliberalism is failing as a viable implementation of important liberal goals. It has left us in a non-liberal, morally shrunken world, in which justice is whatever the strongest interests say it is. Our situation is not exactly new. It is, for example, the world described by the Sophist, Thrasymachus, for Socrates, over two thousand years ago, when asked by his friends to lay out his vision of justice.

> I am speaking, as before, of injustice on a large scale in
> which the advantage of the unjust is more apparent; and

my meaning will be most clearly seen if we turn to that highest form of injustice on a large scale in which the criminal is the happiest of men, and the sufferers or those who refuse to do injustice are the most miserable — that is to say, tyranny, which by fraud and force takes away the property of others, not little by little but wholesale, comprehending in one, things sacred as well as profane, private and public; for which acts of wrong, if he were detected perpetrating any of them singly, he would be punished and incur great disgrace.... But when a man besides taking away the money of the citizens has made slaves of them, he is termed happy and blessed, not only by the citizens but by all who hear of his having achieved the consummation of injustice. For mankind censure injustice, fearing that they may be victims of it and not because they shrink from committing it.[24]

As Thrasymachus points out, not only does this form of "justice" put one's property at risk, but it also enslaves the citizen. This is achieved in our day by economic austerity, which reduces the possibility of freedom for all but the most comfortable because it imposes economic insecurity. It also reduces individual political freedom by promoting instead the particular interests of the powerful over those of the general population. It also reduces political freedom by opening the door a little wider for financial power — political will backed by money from the oligarchs — to override even science and informed judgment for decades with regard to climate change and the impact of poverty, for example.

In a nutshell, this neoliberalism reversed a near-half-century of equality between industrial labour and capital established as a result of the twentieth-century wars. Instead, it put capital back in the driver's seat, free of any significant restriction, bolstered by re-establishing its former alliance with political power as in the nineteenth century. Social science research — not just political philosophy — shows that this is a recipe for social inequality that leads rapidly to political inequality and misery, with the result that freedom's zone shrinks to a narrow public space vulnerable to revolution and oppression.[25]

Where This Book's Argument Goes and How It Gets There

The key to understanding today's neoliberalism is to understand what happened to classical liberalism over the last two centuries. In this account, we examine the implementation of industrial liberalism in Britain from 1815 to 1860. The story is that of utilitarian ideology confronting the social disaster that characterized the 1840s. Britain's cultural response became a general template for social adjustment to industrialization. We then examine a contrasting story in which the state steers the industrialization process, Bismarck's Germany from 1870 to 1894, and the role of German historical economics and the *Verein für sozialforschung* (Association for Social Research), also known simply as the *Verein*. This group, among its other achievements, laid the groundwork for modern sociology. Then we look at the rise and fall of the welfare state to show how liberalism's greatest achievement led to its defeat and replacement by neoliberalism, with all its shortcomings.

Neoliberalism accepts and encourages the postmodernist tendency to divide us from any collective past, to reduce history to genealogy, science to technique, and education to job training — as there is no civic culture left to learn. Neoliberal ideology denies liberals the ability to look at the structure of society, to estimate its position in history, and to critically examine the varieties of men and women who prevail in society at this or any other time. In so doing, neoliberals deny the validity of the "sociological imagination,"[26] clearly unaware that it is part of the legacy of classical economics and its shortcomings. The failure to bring economic and sociological perspectives together is a major reason for the West's current stagnation. Although neoliberalism denies it, liberalism does have the tools to resolve this crisis.

The welfare state was liberalism at its highest development. It stabilized finance and employment, and generated broadly shared advances in both material and cultural development. If it did not overcome all the problems of capitalism, it nevertheless provided the political space for addressing them. In particular, it advanced individual freedom on many fronts while providing the social services the majority need to ensure their prosperity. Its record, which stands in stark contrast to that of neoliberalism, suggests that material progress based on reason, rules of law, and respect for human rights can achieve the goals imagined by what one might call the Enlightenment program. But despite its success — far greater than the achievements of classical liberal capitalism — it also generated a wave of popular hatred that eventually destroyed much of is achievements, leaving us with today's neoliberalism. The question then is how to recover.

How to Rebuild a Vibrant Liberal Social Culture

The liberalism of the welfare state — mild, democratic socialism, where it was not actual social democracy — placed an emphasis on education for general culture that ensured a greater resilience than the narrow skill-building favoured by neoliberals. Neoliberalism consciously encourages the destruction of tools that enable individuals to develop a larger understanding of their life and purpose other than as employees or entrepreneurs. The canvas of existence for neoliberalism is not the problem of Being or of Understanding. Rather, it is the pursuit of economic purpose and the accumulation of assets as the highest expression of humanity and human civilization. The one who dies with the most toys wins. It sounds amusing, but it is tantamount to a civilizational suicide pact for the West.

An important related angle is the advent of "management." Management's source of authority is derived from the power of ownership rather than the contribution of labour, despite the fact that in our economy labour also brings to its task an irreplaceable quantum of specialized knowledge and skill. The concept of management as we know it might well be considered a failure of liberalism, in that the majority of workers claim they hate their jobs, or that psychological depression and "burnout" are widespread. How many neoliberals recognize that it is one of history's leading liberals, John Stuart Mill, who emphasized the benefits of co-operatives — that is, alternatives to top-down control by owners over workers — and the benefits of workers assuming control? Among other things, this insight addresses a yawning discrepancy in liberal society, in which work has an economic function but much less (if any) social status.[27] Rediscovering the virtue and value of labour is essential to liberal society's recovery from a technological trend toward the capitalization of everything, through the expansion of "property" concepts, such as patents, copyright, and trade secrets for routines that complement human labour and may soon replace it.

The focus of this work (or essay) is on what the history of liberalism can show us about liberalism's ability to adjust itself to the culture it produces:

namely, the recognition that civil society has status as the core of the socio-political community and that it forms a community of needs that cannot be fulfilled solely by private transactions. In that respect, it points to the importance of expanding the role of social sciences in liberal decision-making, as it is at the level of a self-conscious society that the new opportunities will present themselves for reopening the public square to society as a fair system of achievement, compassion, and political equality — all of which promote a more developed consciousness that neoliberalism allows.

Two new elements enter the picture at this point. One is the concept of design as applied to business and social organizations. These organizations create and distribute wealth with idealism, or the common good, as a third strand. The application of design enables groups to articulate the performance goals they want their economic and political systems to achieve, and in consequence stipulates the organization that will have the necessary performance characteristics to achieve them. The second element is the emergence of management as a social and economic function that can generate local optima within larger, more general systems. Networking technology such as social media will allow the construction of social groups and alliances so as to minimize dependence on interactions with groups that subtract value and obstruct success. Is this just basically Newspeak for what John Stuart Mill finally came to understand — that worker-owned co-operatives provide a better opportunity for ordinary people than the traditional capitalist organization in which everyone works for the rentier? Yes. It probably is. The difference is that the force of technology is now more clearly understood. Part of the contemporary problem is distinguishing between creative destruction and destructive creation, and allowing the former precedence over the latter.

Systems are controllable only if they are designed to make their control possible. Politics and economics can ultimately correct each other's worst mistakes. But (as Kant underlined) the imagination and the will have to be brought to bear. A liberal political system can correct and stabilize the liberal economic system. However, it has to work on principles of social service, technical design, consensus, and adjustment — not the neoliberal ideas of exclusivity, repression, and accumulated private wealth. Among the consequences that flow from that conclusion is the problem of neoliberalism's rejection of sociology in favour of a "scientistic" obsession with mathematical economics. It has passed mostly unnoticed, but the social science that underpinned the welfare state has all but disappeared in a confusion of scientistic methodology. The generational effort devoted to creating a sociology of the scale envisaged by Comte has all but capitulated to neoliberalism's narrowly positivist academic hegemony.

As a result, policymakers are left blind when it comes to developing a full understanding of current problems and solutions. This is an error with potentially civilizational consequences. Neoliberalism, like nineteenth-century Manchester liberalism, lacks the necessary tools for understanding the challenges of a humane, advanced economic order. Out of Manchesterism's failure, however, arose a different, orthogonal approach to economics, one that we would recognize today as sociology. Most of that story has been lost, yet its achievements for civilization were remarkable and deserve to be more widely understood. For one thing, they are at the root of Germany's startling recovery after the Second World War, and its ability to reconcile capitalism and social justice in its social market economy. This book lightly sketches the outlines of this problem and explores the ideas behind Germany's "ordoliberalism," as it also explores the roots of the welfare state's decline. Our conclusion is that rebuilding effective social liberalism requires a return to a social science envisaged as a science of humanity, in which *Verstehen* or imaginative understanding lies at the root of investigation, and hermeneutics — grounded interpretation — is at the heart of methodology. People are not atoms, and individuals have minds of their own that work in unique ways. It is the task of social science (including history) to probe and explain the human phenomenon of society and to make it intelligible to all based on reason and critique, the main tools of the *Geisteswissenschaften*, or moral sciences, as the social sciences used to be called.

More broadly, the struggle of civil society to rehumanize the state and the economy, if successful, will involve the rediscovery and reconfirmation of some old liberal values: that *liberté* is unachievable without also honouring *égalité* and *fraternité*. And, yes, truth — especially based upon the evidence of performance, not dogma — opens the path to political freedom.

Bonne lecture!

CHAPTER 1

Classical Liberalism's Failure: No Theory of Civil Society

TO UNDERSTAND WHAT IS WRONG with liberalism and how to fix it, it is useful to start with a specific question. A critical question that remains almost unnoticed in all discussions of classical liberalism is this: Why did it fail to develop a theory of civil society? The usual discussion of nineteenth-century Britain revolves around parliament, the Industrial Revolution, the struggle for an expanded electoral franchise, the hardships of the working class, and the emergence of what has come to be known as Victorian England. The problem with this conventional analysis for those interested in liberalism is that the focus on a political elite overshadows the larger, more complicated phenomenon of the formation of an industrial civil society, the first such in Europe and perhaps in the world.

EARLY WRITINGS ON CIVIL SOCIETY

The concept comprises the whole of adult society which, for the most part, is not involved in the day-to-day affairs of government but which (1) pays attention to them and (2) makes its views known — ultimately by exercising its sovereign power in democratic elections. The creation of civil society is a crucial part of political development, which, if it is to complete itself in a robust democratic polity, must accompany economic development. It is upon the latter, however, that our contemporary approach places almost all the focus. The advantage to the concept of civil society is that it underlines the collective public dimension that concepts like "class" or "individual" reduce to a question of particular interests. In other words, civil society is that part of society for which public goods are produced and by which they are consumed, and which is able to express itself outside the regular political machinery of parties and parliament. In action, it is an extraparliamentary entity.

Paradoxically, perhaps, the most extensive thinking about civil society in Europe at the beginning of the nineteenth century was done by Germans — at the time, a people without a country. Most German-speakers lived in feudal principalities grouped under Austrian leadership as the Confederation of German States, of which Prussia was the largest next to Austria. Prussia's capital, Berlin, rivalled Vienna for predominance. The philosophical imagination of the German idealists — mainly allies of Berlin — went furthest in the analysis of the state, civil society, and the moral implications of both.

Liberalism is (or was) the philosophy of freedom. But how was freedom to be instituted? By the end of the eighteenth century, after two revolutions, and the early nineteenth century, after nearly twenty years of war against Napoleon, the varieties of freedom available amounted to three: the practical example of the United States under its constitution and Bill of Rights; the British example of economic freedom, under the laissez-faire utilitarianism of Robert Peel's Radicals; and the philosophy of the German idealists, whose achievement in speculative philosophy was antipodean to Germany's striking lack of political achievement. Paradoxically, despite the lack of tangible German political achievement before 1848, it would be the German idealists whose solution ultimately proved the most viable. Beginning in the eighteenth century, they identified and most deeply explored the key to instituting freedom successfully: adult human consciousness. Without consciousness of what oppression means, of what it means to stand up against oppression or even just dogmatic authority, and without reason and imagination to fuel the understanding that freedom is the basic requirement for a life worth living, humans will not sustain freedom. Instead, they will be distracted by concerns of material well-being, honours, and rewards. It is the ability of adult humans to sustain philosophical values that support the consciousness of freedom that makes freedom possible and attainable — not the reverse. The story of liberalism in the nineteenth century is the story of how that eighteenth-century insight was eroded by industrialization and other forces, only to return and reimpose itself at the beginning of the twentieth century.

Some of modern liberalism's deepest roots lie in the turmoil of the seventeenth century. Liberalism incorporates the challenges that Bacon's *Novum Organum* and Galileo's *Two New Sciences* posed to the rule of faith as an explanation of nature and of the prevailing social order. The achievements of the new empiricism, from Galileo to Newton, accompanied the nascent ideas of modern liberalism in Hobbes and Locke, among others. These came after the revolutions provoked by Protestantism — intellectual and social revolutions such as the translation of the Bible into national languages, and political upheavals including a century of religious wars, culminating in the Peace of Westphalia in 1648. Shortly thereafter, both Hobbes and Locke emerged as social contract theorists, challenging the divine right principle upon which royal absolutism rested. There followed the so-called Glorious Revolution of 1688, in which Britain deposed its last Stuart king, James II, in favour of the Protestant William of Orange, husband of the deposed king's daughter Mary. The event fused English fortunes with those of Holland, one of the most advanced commercial states in Europe, whose earlier rivalry with England had provoked three short wars between 1652 and 1674.[1]

The following century was one of economic and intellectual developments that made England, along with Scotland, the most advanced economy and the main philosophical power in Europe. French intellectuals from Voltaire to Montesquieu to Rousseau flocked there for instruction. Leading thinkers from Scotland, such as Hume and Smith, attended French salons, in which the Americans Jefferson and Franklin were also welcome participants. By the eighteenth century, liberalism had become the main theme for reform of the *ancien régime* in France, then England's greatest rival and the Continent's leading military and cultural power.

Many prominent themes coloured the conversation about politics and government during this formative period. Among the most important was the theme of secularization — owing to the widespread popular rejection of religion and its sectarian divisions after the wars of religion. Western intellectuals sought a way of separating religion and politics — in other words, to create a political science in the sense of an organized body of analyzed experience that would establish the limits and procedures for popular self-government, without altogether abandoning the ethical perspective of the ancients. By the eighteenth century there was consensus on two things: that reason was the only legitimate basis of government, and that the mercantilist theories of economics, which dominated early modern economic thought, were failing. Everywhere the question on people's lips was the question of political change and what would be its appropriate dimensions. It was in this climate that modern liberalism emerged.

Although there were many variations, from Voltaire and Montesquieu to Rousseau, as well as the Encyclopedists d'Alembert and Diderot, one important theme united them all. This was the power of the conscious individual's reason to understand, and in particular the need for freedom so that humans might exploit their reason — exercised within a framework of laws — to better their condition. Eighteenth-century liberalism was a mixture of unresolved questions about natural law and natural rights theory, of democratic principles that placed sovereignty not in the divine right of kings but in the will of the people, and legal principles that respected the right to property ownership and lawful contracts. In addition to these political ideas, liberal thinkers also argued for ending the economic regulations imposed by mercantilism. They insisted years before the publication of *The Wealth of Nations* (1776) that markets organized by buyers and sellers according to the forces of supply and demand would ensure higher quality products and lower prices. In France, they were particularly concerned with supplying the major cities with ample and affordable food, which royal regulation struggled vainly to accomplish. That this liberal brew signified that national governance everywhere would face important challenges was generally understood. But few expected revolution and the geopolitical upheavals that followed. Ironically, perhaps, today it is a measure of the unquestioning acceptance of the basic propositions of liberalism that the opening lines of the American Declaration of Independence seem almost a cliché. Yet they effectively summarize the most powerful threads of the liberalism that "turned the world upside down."

> We hold these truths to be self-evident, that all men are created equal, that they are endowed by their Creator with certain unalienable Rights, that among these are Life, Liberty and the pursuit of Happiness. — That to secure these rights, Governments are instituted among Men, deriving their just powers from the consent of the governed. — That whenever any Form of Government becomes destructive of these ends, it is the Right of the People to alter or to abolish it, and to institute new Government, laying its foundation on such principles and organizing its powers in such form, as to them shall seem most likely to effect their Safety and Happiness.

Jefferson and his coauthors illustrate the power of the liberal political ideas originating in England and further reflected upon in France. The main ideas can be found in particular in Locke's *Second Treatise of Government* (1690) and his *Essay Concerning Human Understanding* (1689). There are also echoes of Rousseau in the overall emphasis on happiness achieved through radical political change. But these ideas represent just one layer in what one might call the action stack of liberal political concepts. They assume a number of prior propositions about the rational mind and the legitimate boundaries of reason and metaphysical ideas, among other major themes; they set aside the even more fundamental concepts of Hobbes about political order, although there is an echo in the reference to the consent of the ruled. So compact is the expression of these ideas that we need to look to outside observers to understand what lies behind them.

Such a comprehensive investigation and synthesis of the main currents of foundational Enlightenment thinking was provided by Immanuel Kant (1724–1804) in his three critiques, written in the decade after the upheaval in North America and completed as the French Revolution was getting under way. The first of these, the *Critique of Pure Reason,* develops a picture of the liberal mind that reconciles the philosophical controversies of the eighteenth century into a sophisticated theory of representation. It sets the table for the major philosophical battles of the nineteenth century, from Hegel to Schopenhauer and Nietzsche. From these ideas and their associated controversies there emerged by the 1940s the political theories that took liberalism to a new plateau, from which it could set out to reconcile the social conflicts of the preceding century. That new plateau involved the development of a concept of overarching political consciousness that would be capable of transcending the limits of the individual pursuit of private interest, or "happiness," in the language of Jefferson's Declaration. Even now, coming to grips with this level of consciousness is perhaps the main challenge facing liberal reconstruction, a clear sign that the "liberal revolution" remains unfinished in certain regards.[2]

Karl Marx and the poet Heinrich Heine both thought Kant the official philosopher of the French Revolution. Hannah Arendt explains why:[3] Kant was the first philosopher to break with the idea promoted by Parmenides of the unity of thought and existence — to be is to think; what is thought exists! Kant's analysis of reason showed that this was not true. A human being can analyze and synthesize experience or data about the physical world. But the mental — *noumenal* — world only exists on the level of ideas. Mankind therefore can be "the measure of the world," but remains subject to the physical reality of existence. Only through reason can we come to understand the independent moral structure that is open to human freedom to choose. Taken together, Kant's system of philosophy underpins with carefully constructed logical arguments the essential postulate of liberalism: that mankind must find its way by balancing what is known and unknown according to the light of reason.

Kant's analysis of "practical reason" is similarly interesting for liberalism. To the horror of a younger generation of German philosophers, including the young Hegel, Schelling, and, later, Schopenhauer, all of whom longed for a German version of the French Revolution, Kant's "second critique," *The Critique of Practical Reason*, seemed to reverse the advances toward the modern era made in the first. In the "second critique" Kant seems to uphold the premodern view of a three-tiered universe — God, royalty, and mankind. His break with the past is shown by his argument for mankind's moral autonomy via a supreme moral law that compels compliance by the force of its logic, in contradistinction to divine law. This law, Kant intriguingly proclaims, *must* be upheld by all free men who act on the basis of reason. Indeed, he suggests, it is their *duty* to do so. That law is the following: to choose no action nor make no law that would not be tolerable if made a universal law, applicable to everyone. Elsewhere, in his *Groundwork of the Metaphysics of Morals* and the *Science of Right,* Kant also sets out the proposition but in different terms: it is unethical to treat humans as mere instruments to achieve a goal.

Kant's categorical imperative, his moral law, is an intriguing proposition that deserves careful consideration by liberals. For Kant is saying that the project of a free society operating under reason is to treat its citizens as they would wish to be treated, and that it will act in the world as a political entity that treats others as it would wish to be treated itself. Indeed, the condition of freedom's preservation is the mutual respect that moral law commands at home and abroad. This is an endorsement of individual freedom that is rooted ultimately in the concept of the individual as a moral entity — a rebirth of the fundamental tenets of ancient political thought. With Kant, mankind's morality is rooted in reason and its logical consequence, the categorical imperative to live by universal and timeless principles. Many people, myself included, regard Kant's work as the supreme expression of Enlightenment reflection. Yet he differs from contemporary neoliberals in important ways that are perhaps worth noting.

Kant succeeded in providing a ground for liberal "reason-based" ideas at the leading edge of eighteenth-century epistemology and moral imagination. But he clearly opposed exploitive capitalism and the use of human beings as economic factors. In so doing, Kant reminds those of us inclined to see economics as a branch of mathematics or physics that economics, as a study of human choice, is in the end a moral study. Kant's concept of economics is that of a moral science designed to improve individual capacity to understand and live by the universal laws of morality — fair dealing, mutual respect, and so forth. He was not a utilitarian; he condemned utilitarianism with the same vocabulary used by the ancients to condemn Epicureans: it is more appropriate for animals than humans, it provides pacification through sensual gratification rather than reason and moral reflection, and it dissuades us from undertaking great aims that would advance civilization. It is not a stretch to suggest that Kant would distinguish utilitarianism as a science of biological behaviour, whereas he accepted the ideas of Hume and the Scottish Enlightenment as philosophy.

Kant's achievement did not long remain unchallenged as a foundational guide for Western thought. Not long after the French Revolution, the world assigned a different meaning to reason and in no way accepted that human affairs were governed by timeless principles. The Romantic period rediscovered history with a capital *H*. Kant's critical philosophy was almost immediately attacked by Georg Wilhelm Friedrich Hegel (1770–1831), whose own massively original and difficult system of Romantic idealism supplanted Kant for most of the nineteenth century. If Kant was Bach, Hegel was Beethoven. Where Kant is crisp and precise, a model of Euclidian or Cartesian straight lines and right angles, Hegel's system presents a dynamic, constantly changing, almost biological reality. Its basis is the unity of opposites, a vast reworking of Kantian categories related dialectically so that each suggests its antithesis.

Hegel had no patience for Kant's distinction between *phenomena* and *noumena*. In Hegel's system, Being begins with Becoming and ends in Nothing. Each being contains its opposite as the seed of its own destruction while striving to understand infinity. The history of mankind's understanding is that of Reason struggling from faint beginnings to emerge at the end of time, and History as the unity of the particular or individual understanding with all-comprehending Absolute Reason. Hegel's ethical concerns dismiss Kant's moral law and the tension between will and obligation, between nature and duty. Hegel's system sees the struggle for perfection as the evolution of "ought" from a representation of morality to its incarnation in Man through Reason. At that point, Man's will and God's understanding will have come together. The willing adult individual will feel at home with God in the light of Absolute Reason. Hegel's message of mankind's advance through successfully negating the negatives in its condition over time somehow exactly suited the sense of onrushing movement and power experienced by millions as the industrial world began to transform Europe and North America.

At the end of the nineteenth century, Benedetto Croce summed up Hegel this way: "Aristotle stands in the previous development of Hellenistic thought in the same relation in which Hegel stands to the whole philosophical development up to his own time, from the Hellenistic, even from the Oriental world."[4] Hegel claimed to show that history has a purpose, and that purpose is the emancipation of mankind from its flaws to become a better creature in a more fulfilling civilization. Even capitalism's forging of an alienated working class as industrial capitalism deepened its hold failed to change the positive Hegelian outlook. Kant's attempt to confine rationalism to its epistemological limits was clearly not to Hegel's taste: what is real is rational and what is rational is real, he wrote. Parmenides was back, disguised as History.

Hegel thereby "corrected" Kant's assumption that human philosophical and scientific insights and discoveries amount to permanent, ahistorical truths. Everything human, Hegel believed, is historical, and it improves or decays over time. Kant, indeed, offered Hegel his most powerful ammunition, in a way, by arguing that space and time are preprogrammed (or, as we might say today, hard-wired) elements of human consciousness that enable us to analyze our surroundings and our situation. The universe itself may be timeless and space may indeed be dimensionless — it is humans who impose these categories of space and time as analytical tools. Hegel uses time and the horizon of human activities through time to construct a philosophical theory of history based on the objective power of reason and the gradual human development of consciousness. As humans become increasingly able to synthesize self-consciousness with objective consciousness, the dialectic between them will end with human consciousness rising to an understanding of the historical force of Absolute Reason incarnated in a global government. His survey of history runs from the ancient world to nineteenth century to the advent of Napoleon, whom Hegel saw as the incarnation of Reason as modernity. Indeed, for Hegel, Napoleon personified history's rational broom sweeping away the cobwebs of superstition and tradition that kept the Continent subject to obscurantism and absolutism.

Hegel's arguments are no more than speculation, however masterful and intriguing. In presenting us with a unified and unifying historical process, Hegel is striving to overcome the Kantian division between the *noumena*, or things-in-themselves, that make up our subjective feelings and opinions, and the *phenomena* of nature and objective reality. Hegel's thought is hardly science. Rather, it is a hugely ambitious challenge to future generations to continually progress in their understanding of the human condition in order to reconcile the "great antinomies," such as justice and freedom, subject and object, universals and particulars.

Hegel's theory of history is a plot line for mankind's conscious moral development. In it, the great "villain" or menace to human destiny is the allure of triumphant subjectivity — individualism — that crowds out the general considerations needed for the survival of mankind as a collectivity and for overcoming world-historical challenges. Hegel is ultimately optimistic, despite the night flight of the owl of Minerva away from sinking civilizations and toward rising civilizations. Clearly, in Hegel's concept of history, narcissistic individualism is one formula for civilizational decline faced with competition from other civilizations that are prepared for greater sacrifice to achieve a common good. Hegel's theory of history leads to a theory of civic consciousness that enables the persistence of the general will, as described by Rousseau.[5]

In a famous exchange with Hegel, Johann Gottlieb Fichte (1762–1814) — an admirer of Kant even as he disagreed on many points — explored the possibility of a global politics united by personal interests and market forces. In his *Grundlage des Naturrechts nach Principien der Wissenschaftslehre* (*Foundations of Natural Right*), Fichte argued that international trade coordinated by free markets under a legal regime that preserved property rights and enforced contracts would generate societies (or a great society) through the growing dependence of individuals on the economic coordination the market provided.[6] In reply, his friend Hegel — in a work with a similar title, *Naturrecht und Staatswissenschaft im Grundrisse* — agreed that such a society could be created, but stated further that its level of consciousness could never advance beyond that of its members' individual interests.[7] Such a society would develop a limited understanding of itself based on individualism. But it could never become fully rational — that is, fully conscious of itself — by market forces alone. In other words, it would never be able to recognize or accept the effects of market society on itself. Nor would it be able to develop the institutions necessary to control the effects of the market on society, because the predominant subjective individualism of its members would prevent that. A society monopolized by market transactions, in other words, would be incapable of developing a mind broad and deep enough to control itself. It would therefore eventually collapse of its own weight into anarchy and even chaos. Hegel in effect builds a layer of social self-consciousness atop the layer of individual incentives — a form of political awareness that supports reflexive social policy, that is, a level of awareness of the total effects of individualism upon the collectivity as a whole. This extra layer of reflection is generally absent from the more classically liberal philosphies that leave unchallenged the view that a society that is the sum of its competitive interests is automatically fair and just. Experience shows that Hegel was more right than Fichte — or Bentham — but it took almost the whole of the nineteenth century before liberals began to recognize that Hegel's insight might be correct.

Taking these thinkers together, we should remember that they are reacting to the challenges of their age in which liberalism emerged as the vehicle of modernism imposing spectacular, even devastating, change on an old order — an order that thought it had achieved stability and permanence after the wars of religion by revitalizing the feudal combination of religion and aristocracy. How? By preserving the principle of divine right and vesting the state with all the levers of power, subject only to the advice and consent from time to time of the clergy and the noble aristocratic orders.

The concept of liberalism that opposed the old order was liberating but destabilizing, and the new order it promised was a mystery to all but a successful merchant class habituated to markets and finance. Hence the number of important explanatory and advocacy works it generated, such as Adam Smith's *Wealth of Nations* and François Quesnay's *Physiocratie*, to name but two. But it was clear that the power of feudalism on the Continent was still significant at the end of the Napoleonic era, with the pushback everywhere to re-establish the prerevolutionary ideas of legitimacy and royal succession.

In England, however, liberal ideas developed entirely in opposition to Continental thinking. Manchesterism, the liberalism not of Smith, but of David Ricardo, Jeremy Bentham, and James Mill and John Stuart Mill, rejected the idealist challenge to the development of human consciousness beyond the ability to calculate and pursue individual interests. Utilitarianism to its adherents is a philosophy based on the calculation of alternatives rather than idealist imperatives. Bentham's utilitarianism is designed as a system of laws that creates inducements of pleasure or pain rather than explorations of virtue or the discovery of universal law through reason. It is a theory of human control that eliminates consciousness as an important factor, especially in managing large organizations such as a city or a country. Utilitarianism is a pitiless behavioural science, not a social science that links consciousness and society. The modern French philosopher Michel Foucault calls it a socially learned system of "governmentality" that enables masses of people to live lives of colourless conformity with the directives of the state.[8]

Benthamite utilitarianism is fundamentally a system of social control in which prices replace argument, and calculation of pleasure and pain — physical reaction — replaces moral imagination. In the language of computer science, one might say that utilitarianism offers an algorithm for controlling human action. Acceptable actions — result: pleasure. Unacceptable actions — result: pain. Hobbes's wish for a robot to dispense certain justice saw its achievement in Bentham. Pre- and early Victorian England established foundations for a Benthamite civil society, but, in a powerful dialectic, it also developed some other, more understanding, dimensions that with mixed results sought to relieve much of the harshness of pure utilitarianism.

In evaluating these developments, it helps to have an idea of what problems they were tasked with addressing. Here is a tightly written description of the horrors of the Industrial Revolution, of conditions that were not expected by the champions of a new, "free" society running mainly according to economic laws and with minimum state interference:

> With the advent of the invention and use of machinery in the manufacturing industry came changes in the needs of men which were later to cause the rise of democracy throughout the world. From the seething cauldron of the Manchester and other slum districts, filled with disease, filth and immorality, was to arise, in England, the spirit which had expressed itself but a few years before in the fury of the French revolution. Men and women were taken from the peace and security of a rural cottage in which they wove the cloth and spun the yarn, and forced to learn new trades or to operate great machines which ground on and on, hour after hour, in the dust and cloth laden air of the

poorly ventilated factories. Some could not adjust themselves and went down early in the sacrifice to the god of
progress. Others struggled to live and by so doing saw their
children, their wives and sisters literally starved to death,
chained to their machines to prevent the possibility of escape. Crimes of every conceivable kind were committed by
people, packed like herds of animals, in quarters containing
no sanitary arrangements and where drinking water was to
be had only from the stagnant pools in the open sewage
ditch between the rows of vermin-infested buildings.[9]

The failure to create a civil society in pre- and early Victorian England
is the crucial development by which subsequent versions of liberalism have
ever since been marked. The working out of social relations bore little re-
semblance to what the liberal thinkers like James Mill, Jeremy Bentham,
David Ricardo, Thomas Malthus, and even John Stuart Mill imagined
would occur. That working out is the subject of the second part of this
chapter. Spoiler alert: it was an incomplete process, which, despite the best
efforts of many, failed to address the fundamentals of the problems that
the process disclosed. The British failure formed the basis of the German
"swerve" toward a sociological rather than a utilitarian orientation when it
became their turn to confront similar issues.

THE ENGLISH EXPERIENCE

The English philosophical radicals, as they were called, envisaged a society
of abstract utilitarian individuals, more similar than different, energetically
labouring in pursuit of individual material comfort, their activities aligned
productively by market forces under the competent, all-seeing panopticon
of middle class government. In order to break clean of all the persistent cobwebs of history and its feudal entanglements, Bentham's utilitarianism treated each individual as a representative unit, without ties of any kind, coldly
calculating the relative advantages of the actions facing him or her and that
were open to choice, the aim being to maximize advantage (happiness, pleasure, good) over disadvantage (pain, punishment, negative consequences).

True, conceptually, for political analysis, individuals were grouped in the utilitarian view according to social background — that is, class. Within the classes, however, were only individuals, and the term "class" was merely a reference point for placing someone in a vertical pecking order that remained more feudal than modern. The radicals never imagined anything, for example, resembling Hegel's theory of a single civil society connected to the state and which constituted a "community of needs," nor of a dialectical interaction of civil society with itself and the state in an ongoing exercise of social creation. Yet that is what actually happened in England, eventually, after a century of uneven progress.

For the generation that first addressed the problem of "the condition of England," the issues and their nuances were unprecedented. Fear of what industrialism had unleashed combined with the memory of the French Revolution and the Terror. Despite the inclusion of the middle class and the new industrial districts in the Reform Act's expansion of the franchise (1832), middle class governments remained under the influence or even the control of the landed interests until midcentury, if not longer. Much of their understanding of their situation and their legislative agenda was disconnected from the social changes occurring in the street, the factory, and the appallingly shabby working class districts of the industrial towns. As a result, the extraparliamentary social and political movements generated in those spaces shaped the country and contributed to the process of creating a civil society.

Parliament, when it acted deliberately along the lines of its utilitarian philosophy — as for example, in the 1834 amendment to the Poor Law — clearly failed to grasp the humanitarian dimensions of the poverty that accompanied England's "spontaneous" industrialization. Utilitarian belief in the power of treating people as instruments — a violation of more traditional ethical principles — generally proved harmful or irrelevant to grasping what was, after all, a social problem. The civil society that formed during this period was eventually able to address many of the problems that originated with the utilitarian policies of the early nineteenth century. But even today, British society is scarred by those original mistakes. And liberalism, which has generally failed even to acknowledge that civil society is more than the people who make it up — that it constitutes a collective entity with a distinct social function — continues to produce disasters similar to those of the 1840s, albeit now on a world scale instead of just within a single country.

Instead of working toward a social theory of any kind, classical liberalism rested initially on its three pillars of utilitarian legal theory, Ricardo's economics, and James Mill's theory of government.[10] The latter was essentially a justification of middle class rule as a replacement for the aristocratic, landowning proprietor class, with no added principles other than those of strong representative government. Nothing about *liberté, égalité, fraternité* — perhaps because the memory of the Terror and Napoleon was so recent in people's minds — and just as little about "the rights of Englishmen." Instead, the elder Mill justified his theory with the claim that the middle or professional class was the one whose position required it to have the interests of the whole nation at heart, that it was large enough to serve as a check against potential tyranny of the aristocracy or monarch, and that the wisdom of its views could shape the views of the working class. Continuity was implicit in that the Hanoverian parliament would continue to rule, guided and steadied by middle class professionals who would see their task through the lens of a strong dedication to utilitarian values and possibilities.

Implicit also was the continuation of "virtual" representation of the lower middle and working class by their "betters." Explicit was a rough partitioning of power in which the middle class professionals would find common cause with landowners and factory owners against the working classes if they felt it in their interest to do so. Above all, parliament would be the centre of national society because it was at the centre of national politics — while at the same time the political nation did not include the working class elements of the country. There was never a suggestion that in a representative democracy it is civil society that in the last instance controls the political process, if only to ensure that public policy addresses the public interest. In the "balanced" semi-feudal constitution of George III and IV, civil society was in fact restricted to the great families in their great houses. In the utilitarian England of the first half of the nineteenth century, the church, the aristocracy, and parliament would have to accept working with the new professional class on an agenda of national modernization. But the trio-of-the-traditional plus one (the representatives of the middle class) — not "the people" in civil society — would define the limits of that agenda.

Not that these views were accepted uncritically. Utilitarianism was widely condemned as fit only for beasts, as it made no room for any other impulse but the base stimulus of sensual pain and pleasure. Worse, it obliterated any concept of a social contract, despite James Mill's general comment that one role of government is to protect the weak from harm by the strong — a point of demarcation that, as political scientists Pierre Manent and Pierre Rosanvallon both underline, is an important divide in liberalism today between laissez-faire or "free-market" liberals and communitarian liberals who accept that governing includes an obligation to ensure that society is both fair and co-operative. Bentham was one of the most important political theorists to break with the pre-eighteenth-century orthodox view that society is a contractual relationship. In his view, reason alone was sufficient to generate a liberal civil order, so long as the laws were written to encourage rational virtue over irrational vice. In Bentham's view, society is no more and no less than the individuals, and perhaps the families, that compose it. Laws that encourage virtuous individual behaviour based on a rational calculation of pleasure and pain are sufficient to ensure good order and stability.[11]

James Mill's argument for middle class rule by a minimalist government underwent scathing critique from his nonutilitarian peers. Consider, for example, this salvo from Lord Macaulay against James Mill and his *Essay on Government*:

> We think that the theory of Mr Mill rests altogether on false principles and that even on those false principles he does not reason logically. Nevertheless, we do not think it strange that his speculations should have filled the Utilitarians with admiration. We have been for some time past inclined to suspect that these people, whom some regard as the lights of the world and others as incarnate demons, are in general ordinary men, with narrow understandings and little information. The contempt which they express for elegant literature is evidently the contempt of ignorance. We apprehend that many of them are persons who, having read little or nothing, are delighted

to be rescued from the sense of their own inferiority by some teacher who assures them that the studies which they have neglected are of no value, puts five or six phrases into their mouths, lends them an old number of the Westminster Review, and in a month transforms them into philosophers.[12]

The aristocratic put-down should not seem surprising. But it failed to address the real point, namely that in the face of a massive popular exodus from rural life to industrial centres little or no preparation was being made to receive the new arrivals. Available housing was poor to non-existent. Social services as a concept belonged to a later age, and local poor relief was overwhelmed by the migrants. Today, we would call the millions of migrants cut free from their estates after the end of the Napoleonic Wars a crisis of internally displaced people. Our contemporary liberal enthusiasts for market solutions to social problems often refer to spontaneous organization of firms and workers along the lines of Coase's Laws (that firms emerge as organizations to meet needs that existing firms fail to serve).[13] Somehow, the radicals felt the same certainty. In reality, the "spontaneous organization" of firms and workers in the early nineteenth century was made up of vastly uneven bargains between desperate workers offered daywork and mill owners who were themselves pressed by the competition of their rivals and landowners hungry for rents. Adam Smith's argument in *The Wealth of Nations* for a system of natural liberty foresaw competition led by consumer demand buoying up prices and increasing the demand for labour, and therefore raising wages. Instead, competition for wages pushed wages down, and demand remained inadequate to support all suppliers.[14]

Under these conditions, another of Smith's postulates went into reverse — the power of community sympathy to change the behaviour of the fortunate, the better to aid the unfortunate. Sympathy existed within the classes, but little of it passed between them. Utilitarianism and Malthusian strictures about excessive population placed the blame for horrible conditions not on the failure of liberal public policy, but rather on the allegedly prolific breeding of the poor.[15] The middle class, after being granted the franchise in the 1832 Reform Act, was content to abandon its erstwhile working class political allies, pushing instead to complete its agenda of free trade and an end to the Corn Laws — that is, the wartime protection from imports of wheat. As landlords switched from crops to livestock and to rents from industry, wheat imports grew. The effects of the Irish crop failure — the last major famine in Europe until the famines in the young Soviet Union — were intensified as the immediately available surplus food stocks fell while protection lessened. Ultimately, only massive Irish migration to the New World relieved the disaster. This is history, but the similar disasters of war, misgovernment, and over-farming by subsistence agriculture also lie behind the great migrations across the Mediterranean today. One could be forgiven for perhaps thinking that our "New World Order" in too many ways resembles the old, and for much the same reasons.

Nevertheless, one should not therefore seek to diminish the actual achievements of the classical economists — Ricardo, Jean-Baptiste Say, and John Stuart Mill — as well as, perhaps unexpectedly, Professor Malthus. Wilhelm Roscher, one of the best known of the nineteenth-century German historical school of economists, wrote that the abstract economics of the classics attained an important goal of the Enlightenment. But he also noted the astonishing absence of social factors in their economic reasoning. He mentioned that classical economics for the most part used abstract models that were fact-free and deductive, rather than inductive, and not based on observed behaviour and statistics, the approach favoured by the Germans.[16] Obviously, in the circumstances, something else was required — namely, a more comprehensive theory that would adjust itself to actual results.

Malthus, who is associated with his harsh theoretical proposition about population growth, unsupported by data, also produced a work of economics in which he suggested criticisms of Ricardo's abstractions, along with some remedies. In particular, in regard to the economic stagnation in Britain following the end of the Napoleonic Wars, he challenged the views of Ricardo and Say that such situations are best remedied by deepening investment. On the contrary, he correctly identified the lack of demand as the problem, in effect describing what Keynes made famous as a "liquidity trap." The solution he proposed was massive government spending on infrastructure so that wages could be raised and demand restored.[17]

More philosophically, Hegel, probably the greatest of the nineteenth-century German philosophers, also took notice of the disastrous consequences of the Industrial Revolution in England:

> When the masses begin to decline into poverty, (a) the burden of maintaining them at their ordinary standard of living might be directly laid on the wealthier classes, or they might receive the means of livelihood directly from other public sources of wealth (e.g. from the endowments of rich hospitals, monasteries, and other foundations)…. (b) As an alternative, they might be given work, i.e. the opportunity to work [and thereby produce] … but the evil consists precisely in an excess of production and in the lack of a proportionate number of consumers who are themselves also producers, and thus it is simply intensified by both of the methods (a) and (b) by which it is sought to alleviate it. It hence becomes apparent that despite an excess of wealth civil society is not rich enough, i.e. its own resources are insufficient to check excessive poverty and the creation of a penurious rabble.[18]

Very interesting is Hegel's reference to "civil society" — a term virtually unknown in England in the 1840s. Hegel also added the following, in the same place: In the charitable approach of option (a) "the needy would receive subsistence directly, not by means of their work, and this would violate the principle of civil society and the feeling of individual independence and self-respect in its individual members." This should not be read, in my opinion, as a condemnation of emergency relief, but rather a concern for the psychological condition of aid recipients, and the importance of solving the underlying problem not only so that the poor may quickly resume a productive life, but also so that the relief programs should not violate the self-respect of the recipients. Again, the reference to civil society and its principles takes the discussion beyond the confines of utilitarianism and parliamentary government.

Other critics, such as Matthew Arnold, came to a similar conclusion, albeit some twenty years later (1869):

> Now, having first saluted free trade and its doctors with all respect, let us see whether even here, too, our Liberal friends do not pursue their operations in a mechanical way, without reference to any firm intelligible law of things, to human life as a whole, and human happiness; and whether it is not more for our good, at this particular moment at any rate, if instead of worshipping free trade with them … as a kind of fetish and helping them to pursue it as an end in and for itself, we turn the free stream of our thought upon the treatment of it, and see how this is related to the intelligible law of human life, and to national well-being and happiness.[19]

There can be little doubt that Bentham's radical simplifications appealed to minds inflamed with "the modern" — experienced as desire for a kind of Euclidian scientific clarity and certainty in human affairs. Admirers of reason, imbued with the program of Enlightenment thinking and industrial enterprise, saw Bentham's ideas as a tool to clear away the musty mix of half-forgotten feudal privileges that still entangled England. Such were the philosophical radicals, led by James Mill, John Stuart Mill's father. John Stuart Mill is quite clear about this. In his autobiography, Mill explains that his early education, under the strong influence of his father, had been "a course of Benthamism." Indeed, Bentham and Ricardo were intimate family friends. He writes (in 1821 — Mill was just fifteen) that, when he first read Bentham's introduction to the *Principles of Morals and Legislation,* in which the greatest happiness principle is applied to legal reform,

> it burst upon me with all the force of novelty. What thus impressed me was the chapter in which Bentham passed judgment on the common modes of reasoning in morals and legislation, deduced from phrases like "law of nature," "right reason," "the moral sense," "natural rectitude," and

the like, and characterized them as dogmatism in disguise imposing its sentiments upon others under cover of sounding expressions which convey no reason for the sentiment, but set up sentiment as its own reason.... The feeling rushed upon me, that all previous moralists were superseded, and that there was the commencement of a new era in thought. This impression was strengthened by the manner in which Bentham put into scientific form the application of the happiness principle to the morality of actions, by analyzing the various classes and orders of their consequences.[20]

Mill goes on to write:

The principle of utility understood as Bentham understood it, and applied in the manner in which he applied it … fell exactly into place as the keystone which held together the detached and fragmentary component parts of my knowledge and beliefs. It gave unity to my conception of things. I now had opinions, a creed, a doctrine, a philosophy; in one among the best senses of the word, a religion; the inculcation and diffusion of which could be made the principle outward purpose of a life.[21]

Inspired by some of the principles of the American Revolution and Hume's "discovery" of the greatest happiness principle, Bentham set himself the task of modernizing political science and in particular the system of British law; as he put it himself, his aim was to rationalize the laws. Politics in England was dominated by two great "houses," the Whigs and the Tories, whose rivalry led to calamitous consequences (such as gaining and losing most of North America within thirty years); they represented a squirearchy whose parochial and corrupt system of government matched neither the country's world role nor the challenge of its industrializing domestic economy. In the words of his executor, John Bowring, "But for one circumstance, the Bill of Rights [of 1689] would have transformed the fiction [of a social contract] into a reality. That circumstance was that the Revolution of 1688 transferred the excess of power from the king, not to the people, but to the aristocracy … split into two hereditary parties which assumed the names of Whigs and Tories…."[22]

Bentham's utility-based system of law reform, as Alan Ryan reminds us, omits the customary guarantees of property.[23] It is worth underlining, I think, the importance of the liberal promise: political freedom, democratic governance, and an advancing material life, together with the ability of these ideas to capture the imagination. Yet it wasn't long before Mill noticed that something was missing. Scarcely five years after his first encounter with Benthamism, Mill had his (as he called it) "mental breakdown." Today, we would probably term it "burnout." As he later wrote, he found himself emptied out, quoting lines from Coleridge's "Dejection":

> A grief without a pang, void, dark and drear
> A drowsy, stifled, unimpassioned grief,
> Which finds no natural outlet or relief
> In word or sigh or tear.[24]

Alternative Scenarios and Extraparliamentary Opposition

One strand of anti-utilitarian and anti-individualist criticism is particularly worth noting — the argument for co-operation rather than the ruthless competition that was the order of the day. Not only was its intrinsic logic eventually adopted by John Stuart Mill, but it remains valid as a critique that offers working people an alternative to the capitalism associated with the myth of laissez-faire, and is nevertheless entirely compatible with liberal principles.

I am of course speaking of leading social reformers like Robert Owen — whose name was synonymous with socialism at this time. He stepped forward to propose new co-operative forms of industrial organization to ensure that workers could share in the profits earned from their labour. These included factory-centred communities organized to meet the needs of families and their children. He backed up his demands with personal investment in a model community, New Lanark, and a scathing report on manufacturing and its social consequences.[25] While his system is still discussed even today, his blistering critique of Manchesterism is rarely reviewed. Here is a sample:

> The general diffusion of manufactures throughout a country generates a new character in its inhabitants; and as this character is formed upon a principle quite unfavourable to individual or general happiness, it will produce the most lamentable and permanent evils, unless its tendency be counteracted by legislative interference and direction.... The industry of the lower orders, from whose labour wealth is now drawn, has been carried by new competitors striving against those of longer standing to a point of real oppression, reducing them by successive changes, as the spirit of competition increased, and the ease of acquiring wealth diminished, to a state more wretched than can be imagined by those that have not attentively observed the changes as they have gradually occurred. In consequence, they are in a situation infinitely more degraded and miserable than they were before the introduction of these manufactories upon the success of which their bare subsistence now depends.[26]

In this publication, Owen called for regulation against child labour, an improvement of working conditions in factories, and a national system of public education for the children of the poor. In subsequent publications he went further, outlining the success of his co-operative factory project at New Lanark and drawing attention to other successful examples as well.

In the sixth and subsequent editions of his *Principles of Economics*, John Stuart Mill came to adopt Owen's views. He argued that under the laissez-faire system in which small government was considered a virtue, the establishment of workers' co-operatives would ensure working people higher incomes and fairer treatment than were available from proprietors who wished to keep the profits for themselves and their shareholders. What convinced him of its practicality was the French workers' revolution in 1848.

> The form of association … which if mankind continues to improve must be expected to predominate, is not that which can exist between a capitalist as chief and work-people without a voice in the management, but the association of the labourers themselves on terms of equality, collectively owning the capital with which they carry on their operations, and working under managers elected and removable by themselves.[27]

By 1840 civil society had, despite James Mill, discovered itself and begun to push back against the neglectful and occasionally repressive treatment of masses of the population at the hands of the state. The Chartists — whose Charter of 1839 was presented to parliament with 1,280,000 signatures and constituted the largest popular movement in favour of political and economic reform — demanded what we take for granted as "liberal" in our own day: equal representation among all districts in proportion to the population, universal suffrage, and the guarantee of a living wage for all who worked for a living.[28] (At least we did until the neoliberal accession to power returned precariousness of employment to labour markets.) Because of this pushback, the issue of the internally displaced and the later question of working class integration refused to go away. As early as the mid-1830s it had become the question on everyone's lips — the "condition of England" question.

Impressive as the Chartist mobilization was, yet another mass movement came into being following the rejection of Corn Law repeal in 1839. That was the mobilization of the Anti–Corn Law League under John Bright and Richard Cobden. Bright, one of the most gifted orators of his generation, sat in parliament from 1843 to 1869. Cobden kept his seat in parliament from 1841 almost continuously until his death in 1865. John Morley, a Liberal member of parliament and minister under Gladstone and after, provides a description of the reaction to an early defeat (1839) in his biography of Cobden, which draws extensively on Cobden's papers.

> [Cobden] recalled the delegates to the fact that in spite of the House over the way [Parliament] they represented three millions of the people. He compared the [anti–Corn

Law] alliance of the great towns of England to the League of Hanse Towns of Germany. That League had turned the castles which crowned the rocks along the Rhine, the Danube and the Elbe into dismantled memorials of the past, and the new [Anti–Corn Law] league would not fail in dismantling the legislative stronghold of the new feudal oppressors in England.[29]

The Anti–Corn Law League was able to obtain repeal of the Corn Laws in 1846. Of particular interest is that the anti–Corn Law agitation — one of the largest and most effective in British political history — was directed by MPs in defiance of the position of their party leadership. To be sure, it can be argued Bright and Cobden epitomized James Mill's ideal of middle class universalist representation. But it is also instructive that without the support they mustered from what today we would call civil society, they would have been unable to pass this historic measure, which in effect broke the parliamentary chokehold the landed interests maintained on British government during the Victorian era.

One further example must also be cited to underline the point that it is civil society that, even in the days of restricted franchise, held parliament to account. That is the growth of the trade union movement after the failure of Chartism and the revolutionary hopes of the 1820s. The gradual development of trade unions and the eventual formation of professionally managed trade union councils took forty years, aided by the long period of economic growth between 1848 and 1867. The franchise was extended to virtually every adult male voter by a second Reform Act in 1867. This in turn enabled work to begin on the creation of a workers' political party.[30] This involved significant legal assistance from sympathetic middle class professionals, the professionalization of union management, and the creation of a robust nationwide network of "friendly societies" to help workers through hard times and strikes, and even provide funds for emigration to the British dominions and the United States.

These gains were hard won: they were not in the gift of James Mill's middle class representative government's "virtual" concern for working class families who, it will be remembered, still lacked the right to vote. Nor were they strictly an expression of particular interests. Much of the political strength of these early labour organizations came from the solidarity generated by the inclusiveness of the insurance benefits they organized and managed for working class families. The trade unions became the vehicle for political organization against the ideology of "atomized" individuals whose only connection with others is a "cash nexus." Eventually, the trade union councils became the basis for a great socialist party fighting for a better system than the harsh capitalism of the classical liberal period. However, that stage of development did not quite constitute the full development of civil society. The unions succeeded in organizing industrial crafts, but they could do little for the unskilled labourers whom they not infrequently regarded as a threat to the higher wages unionized skilled artisans could command. Not until all social programs became available to all citizens was the status of civil society as a community of needs recognized. Additionally, the union challenge was largely depoliticized until the creation of a class-based Labour Party. A number of fundamental issues were only partly addressed by collective bargaining among private interests. These included such questions as how much control labour has over its own work process; how much control factory owners have over their workforce and the conditions under which workers are employed in the factory; and, by extension, whether there is a public interest in ensuring safe working conditions and high average productivity (and thus high average incomes) nationwide. As the next chapter shows, the issues would not fully be resolved until the example of German industrialization showed the way, guided by a system of economics and law that emphasized co-operation as well as competition and recognized the status of civil society as a system of needs that includes a public interest.

The Challenge of Mass Destitution

What the English examples show is that under liberal ideological governance, civil society can act as an important control mechanism against the capture by parliament of particular interests — whether feudal aristocrats or industrial sectors. An important gap remains, however, because if civil society has an important function, it still has no significant status in liberal concepts of governance. On the contrary, the sight of tens of thousands of responsible

protesters in the streets often becomes an occasion for a piece of street theatre in which the police act as the agents of order against the danger of chaos
represented by the "mob" — a historic dread of the propertied classes. One
consequence of this is that these large popular agitations are of limited effect.
They can help pass or reject specific policy measures with a clearly negative
impact. But complex, specialized instruments of policy — however brutal
and repressive — can often escape civil society's control if civil society has
only function and no status, such as civil rights provide. Under Benthamite
utilitarianism, "rights" were considered "nonsense on stilts."

An early example of this is the 1834 amendment to the Poor Law, the
"reasoned" attempt by the government of the day to deal with the problem
of claims for poor relief made by the displaced and destitute working populations flooding into ill-equipped new industrial towns and cities.

Alarmed by the rising number and cost of claims under the so-called
Speenhamland system of poor relief, Earl Grey's government established
in 1832 the first Royal Commission of Inquiry, directing it to inquire
into the administration and practical application of the Poor Laws.[31]
Essentially, the Speenhamland system was a locally administered system
of relief to the poor; it took various forms, depending on local conditions,
and comprised fifteen thousand administrative units. For those unable to
work, a simple payment was usually made, based on an assessment of their
situation. For those able to work, or working for low wages, the parish
would top up wages, again based on their situation. Effectively, then, it
was a system of keeping labour in place and subsidizing or compensating
for low-wage jobs.

However, as more and more workers were displaced by the enclosure
of land in the countryside or by machinery, the workers would take their
labour to more promising locations. Others would join better-off members
of their family where they then might apply for relief. In many smaller
towns and parishes, there was only one building capable of housing those
who needed indoor relief. These would hold the sick, the halt and the lame,
the old, the maimed, and the destitute who had nowhere else to go. There
were no fixed standards, common approved practices, or best practices, and
hardly any oversight at all — nothing but the parish vestry council whose
rulings could be appealed to the local magistrate.

Such was the casual nature of the system that many local poor relief operations had been captured by the local farming or building interests and the professional overseer of the poor relief recipients. By 1830, the system was eating up 20 percent of the national income — how much of it actually went to the intended recipients was unclear. Government sought an end to the rise in its cost and, if possible, a reduction in benefits — a policy that set off a fiery labourers' revolt that ringed London with burning hay ricks. It was put down with hangings and six hundred deportations.[32] After this, the most common position on poor relief was to question why it should exist at all. Both Malthus, the Cassandra of overpopulation, and Nassau Senior, a commissioner of the Poor Law inquiry, agreed on this point. The question found a solution in the person of Edwin Chadwick, a disciple and friend of Bentham whom Senior had engaged as an assistant commissioner. Chadwick had, as befitted a budding utilitarian technocrat, a more sophisticated view.

Chadwick quickly hypothesized that the problem was that the subsidy for low-wage work — known as the allowance system — was drawing workers from the labour market. The challenge for poor relief was to make the conditions of relief so unpleasant and degrading that few if any workers capable of working would be induced to leave the labour market and apply for relief. Thus, only the most abjectly distressed and vulnerable — those whose choices were between death or a life of despair — would even consider relief as an alternative. From this emerged the concept of the workhouse: the separation of family members to prevent them from having more children; the wearing of drab uniforms; a work regime that involved the dreariest repetitive labour, even treadmills; and a barely adequate and unappetizing diet. In effect, Chadwick's solution was to punish the worst off to discourage those however so slightly better off from claiming relief.

To the other members of the commission, it was a brilliant example of the power of utilitarian reasoning — maximizing pain to the vulnerable to underline the relative pleasure of being among those less distressed, thus encouraging them to seek alternatives to relief. Additionally, to put the scheme outside the reach of elected officials who might flinch at inflicting such suffering, the system of workhouses and relief would be administered by permanent paid "guardians" under a central agency with all necessary power. Bentham's own scheme, while similar, was to place the paupers in factories and finance them through joint-stock companies, which Chadwick rejected. Nevertheless, Bentham's concept of the panopticon prison model inspired Chadwick's choice of administrative mechanisms.

The amendment to the Poor Law of 1834 passed, and the release of information was timed to persuade an impatient public that the solution was the best available. There was as yet no civil society to stand up for the pauper and the low-wage worker. Indeed, the Poor Law system remained in place until the end of the nineteenth century, despite sporadic protests against its intensification in the 1870s, and remnants survived to be incorporated into the British welfare state in the 1960s. In this we can see what was invisible to the Victorians — a glimpse of the Gulags and concentration camps of the twentieth century, and the analytic computative approach as the essence of government, which Michel Foucault warns lies within the Benthamite system of liberalism.[33]

The Condition of England

A striking part of the development of English civil society in this period is the growth of English literary culture, in particular the harsh criticism of industrial conditions in a new form of writing, the "social novel."[34] In fact, however, the immediate response to reform was support for industrialization and its potential for national improvement. The accomplishment of political reform and the incorporation of the industrial towns into the system of parliamentary politics was generally welcomed. Indeed, thanks in part to the efforts of James Mill and Macaulay,[35] the nation felt fortunate to have taken action to avoid revolution, in contrast to the example of France in 1830. But the agitations of Luddites and Chartists, and the visible disaster of poverty and the condition of labour, weighed on society.

Popular writers worked at humanizing their working class subjects and bringing to middle class and other readers the condition of life with which the working class had to cope. These realist social novels emerged alongside other signs of deep concern with society, including a revival of religious issues in the Oxford Movement and the parallel "broad church" movement. Meanwhile, Darwin published his theory of evolution and the geologists demonstrated their growing understanding of Earth's timeless origins. Tennyson's poetic trilogy, "Princess," "In Memoriam," and "Maud," captured a zeitgeist in which brutal, commercial modernism cloaks a feeble, struggling humanism: ultimately, the narrator can only register his rage and disgust at his civilization, unable to effect any real change. "Maud" in particular provoked indignant objections from such contemporary figures as the essayist Leslie Stephen and even Liberal prime minister William Gladstone.[36] Sir Walter Scott's romantic Waverley novels and the striking historical and social reflections of Thomas Carlyle coexisted with the emerging materialistic social critique by pro-labour figures such as Thomas Hodgskin, whose *Labour Defended* (1825) is said to have influenced Marx[37] and the co-operative movement associated with Robert Owen.

The historical novels and religious revivals reminded England that there were other virtues and more permanent social values than Bentham's self-interested calculation. The social critiques underlined the weaknesses of Ricardian economic theory and the harsh reality that lay beneath the scientistic abstractions of his deductive analysis. In the 1830s and '40s England began to experience a deep crisis of spiritual and ethical values that lasted well into the 1860s. The social novels were one striking element of an emergent civil society that was experiencing the challenge of modernization. Edward Bulwer-Lytton's novel *Paul Clifford* exposed the horrors of a hardly reformed, still vicious penitentiary system. Dickens's *Hard Times* (among other novels) effectively satirized the constricted emotional and cultural life of utilitarianism, while exposing its cruelty. Elizabeth Gaskell's *North and South* effectively contrasted the harsh reality of Manchester and northern England with the still peacefully pastoral southern counties. Charles Kingsley's *Alton Locke* sympathetically shows the abuses in the textile and clothing industries, together with the hopes and frustrations of the Chartist movement as it struggled to advance the cause of political reform.[38]

The novel, says the Russian aesthetic theorist Mikhail Bakhtin, is the only literary form that can take all of reality into account, bringing the writer's consciousness into full contact with society. The Victorian social novel is a study of human beings undergoing varying degrees of economic and social oppression against which they struggle to maintain their dignity and self-respect. It is the drab, invincible mediocrity of their condition in tension with the characters' personal hopes and dreams that propels the stories forward. Perhaps inevitably, the goal of successfully humanizing the social conditions of liberal capitalism generated an aesthetic impulse, such as the sentiments captured in Matthew Arnold's conclusion to his *Culture and Anarchy*:

> We are sure that the endeavour to reach, through culture, the firm intelligible law of things, — we are sure that the detaching ourselves from our stock notions and habits, — that a more free play of consciousness, an increased desire for sweetness and light, and all the bent which we call Hellenising, is the master-impulse even now of the life of our nation and of humanity, — somewhat obscurely perhaps for this actual moment, but decisively and certainly for the immediate future; and that those who work for this are the sovereign educators.[39]

Suppose fictional engagement with social reality, after all, is primarily a question of individual psychology. How then can a middle class writer, whose own life is buoyed upward by the same conditions that consign others to poverty and the threat of the poorhouse, resolve the conflict between the need for social change and the desire to maintain his own situation? This is the dilemma George Eliot, perhaps the best English novelist of her generation, tried to face in her novel *Felix Holt, the Radical*. As one of Eliot's biographers wrote, explaining her rejection of Radical politics, "She sympathized too intensely with the old ways to understand the new."[40]

Yet there is an author's passion in *Felix Holt*, the passion of an idealist who believed in love and who challenged Victorian manners by accepting an unconventional marriage arrangement in its name. That idealism is evident in the letter Eliot wrote to the working people of England on the occasion of the second Reform Act in 1867. This bill extended the franchise to all men who paid ten shillings or more in rates (local property tax) per year — in effect, all the industrial craftsmen of England, a decision that Carlyle warned was a "leap in the dark," a potential menace to all that was noble in Victorian society. Eliot shared those concerns. In her "Letter from

Felix Holt, Radical," published in the *Westminster Review,* Eliot revived the character from her novel. Felix Holt had this to say, in effect underlining the importance of civil society and its importance for good government:

> A majority has the power of creating public opinion. We could groan and hiss before we had the franchise. If we had hissed and groaned in the right places, if we had discerned better between good and evil, if the multitude of us factory hands and miners, and labourers of all sorts, had been skilful, faithful, well-judging, industrious, sober — and I don't see how there can be wisdom and virtue anywhere without these qualities — we should have made an audience that would have shamed the other classes out of their share in the national vices. We should have had better members of Parliament.... Now the only safe way by which society can be steadily improved and our worst evils reduced, is not by any attempt to do away directly with the actually existing class distinctions and advantages, as if everybody could have the same sort of work, or lead the same sort of life (which none of my hearers are stupid enough to suppose), but by the turning of class interests into class functions or duties. What I mean is, that each class should be urged by the surrounding conditions to perform its particular work under the strong pressure of responsibility to the nation at large; that our public affairs should be got into a state in which there should be no impunity for foolish or faithless conduct. In this way the public judgment would sift out incapability and dishonesty from posts of high charge, and even personal ambition would necessarily become of a worthier sort....
>
> I say, let us watch carefully, lest we do anything to lessen this treasure which is held in the minds of men, while we exert ourselves, first of all, and to the very utmost, that we and our children may share in all its benefits. Yes; exert ourselves to the utmost, to break the yoke of ignorance. If

we demand more leisure, more ease in our lives, let us show that we don't deserve the reproach of wanting to shirk that industry which, in some form or other, every man, whether rich or poor, should feel himself as much bound to as he is bound to decency. Let us show that we want to have some time and strength left to us, that we may use it, not for brutal indulgence, but for the rational exercise of the faculties which make us men. Without this no political measures can benefit us. No political institution will alter the nature of Ignorance, or hinder it from producing vice and misery. Let Ignorance start how it will, it must run the same round of low appetites, poverty, slavery, and superstition.[41]

Eliot, like Arnold, feared most of all that mass democracy would spell the destruction of the "common estate of society," the "treasure held in the minds of men," the "treasure of knowledge, science, poetry, refinement of thought, feeling and manners, great memories and the interpretation of great records, which carried on from the minds of one generation to the minds of another." Austin Harrison, the son of Frederic Harrison, a parliamentarian and lawyer helpful to trades unions and a champion of labour, became a journalist with a wry view of the Victorian age as he experienced it. Remarking on the pivotal character of the 1850s for the period, he wrote: "Victorianism itself was a growth or attitude which had no psychology, indeed it can hardly be explained otherwise, and it was this quality, the quality of sanctimonious success, that gave to every branch of life its pomp and form. Dickens never wearied of squeezing fun out of this religion of self-sufficiency. Insularity became a cult and phlegm its outward sign of culture."[42]

A modern sociologist might conclude that at a certain point, the Victorian bourgeois simply decided to put a bracket or frame around the working class, forever after thinking of them as "the other," and ceasing to worry about their inclusion in or exclusion from civil society. Victorian "phlegm" and "insularity" were devices to avoid troublesome introspection and to reduce the duty of care to a tolerable minimum. Thus, a society of two complementary solitudes arose, one that worked in domestic service or the industrial machinery of production and the sharp end of sales, and another with rentier income that constituted society's "managers" — erecting a nearly impenetrable class barrier to the other's entry into that functional level. Instead, each class developed its own norms and mores, and managed to coexist in the same space but at a different level, an upstairs/downstairs world. Over time, however, this division persisted and came to characterize English society as a whole. Peter Gay, in his history of nineteenth-century middle class culture, remarks on a general trend among the European bourgeoisie in the middle of the nineteenth century to isolate themselves in particular neighbourhoods, to send their children to particular schools, to skirt the working class districts as much as possible en route to the office, and to cultivate distinctive styles of dress, speech, and behaviour. In England, these Victorian divisions were wired into the constitution. Harrison described the process in terms of "Constitution worship" — that is, the controlling system of government and the place carved in it for the upper middle class, the bourgeoisie.

> For the Constitution lived and depended upon "form," since its reality depended upon sanction. Out of it, as its secondary and legendary manifestation — there arose the English code — the "gentleman," the straight bat at cricket and all that we understand by "fair play," our solemn institutionalism, our prodigious snobbery, our religious sense of position as distinct from merit, our insular rectitude, our superb and challenging spirit of assumption which we playfully attribute to common sense.[43]

Ultimately, the election reform of 1867 was as far as the Victorians were going to go in the creation of a civil society of community need. The direction of the country changed after the midcentury mark, and a new leader emerged — one of the social novelists. Benjamin Disraeli would take newly industrialized England back onto the world stage after its brief moment of introspection between 1830 and 1867. A fuller development and a broader inclusion would have to wait another decade, and for women, longer, a wait that included the greatest war the world had hitherto seen.

The social process of "othering," as I call it, which was seen by each class at the time as "self-identifying," constituted a significant bifurcation in Britain's social and political development. What characterizes this English experience is that thereafter groups of any kind were rarely able to bridge the gulf created during this period of industrialization. Among other things, this helps explain why liberalism in the English-speaking world never developed a unified concept of civil society until the twentieth century. Even today, civil society is considered by liberals as comprising competitive needs that can be played off one against the other, rather than constituting an overarching community of needs that can be serviced by government provisions of public goods.

Eliot's "Letter from Felix Holt, Radical" is remarkable not only for its concern about the expansion of the franchise, but also for its rejection of the utilitarian calculating mind and economic incentives. For liberals, these are the embodiments of public reason in market forces. Eliot's arguments were about literary culture. She feared that the expansion of the franchise would also expand the reach of popular mores and thus undermine the elite cultural heritage that bourgeois England had built upon the ruins of feudalism. There was some merit to those fears. The England of *Middlemarch* was confronting a new reality. The industrial working class represented the forces of modern production, its science, its practicality, and its mechanical power. The arrival of the skilled working class to political power heralded the arrival of a new kind of civilization based not on philosophical critique and the wisdom of ancient Greece and Rome that led to the French Revolution, but rather on science and technology, and what was becoming known as "positive knowledge." The question is whether a general social culture or a general knowledge of science is enough to create a unified civic culture, or if it would simply produce a higher level of single-interest-group political behaviour.

In her comprehensive appreciation of the social ideals of Victorian writers, Vida Scudder, famous as a champion of the pro-labour Christian social gospel, summarizes them this way:

> During fifty years, the prose authors whom we have considered were more thoroughly awake to the gravity of the social situation than any other group of men in England. Politics went serenely on its accustomed path; philanthropy was a modest thing, reforming prisons or founding hospitals, but happily unaware of the widespread social

disease which neither strove nor cried, but endured in silence. The arts lamented the absence of great inspirations in modern life, and struggled to create their own inspiration from within and to become ends in themselves, an effort in which no human power has ever succeeded. Political Economy throve and grew fat in many volumes, doing much fine work, but building on a foundation far narrower than that actual humanity whose varying impulses are irreducible to obedience to the cleverest set of mechanical laws. Only the great prose authors felt the irregular pulses of the fevered social organism, and mourned, pleaded, and hoped, as we have seen.[44]

Then, she notes, in the 1880s, the flame passed from the poets to "the men of action." That was the English reaction to the German "swerve" toward a sociological orientation. Scudder's characterization of classical economics in the above citation is also noteworthy: its base, she says, is too narrow for humanity, whose impulses are "irreducible to obedience to … mechanical laws." That comment, seamlessly included in a homage to the "great prose authors," underlines a distinction in social thought that utilitarianism raised and that subsequently would grow in importance well into the twentieth century: the distinction between understanding and control, and then, the question of which one would become dominant in the new social sciences.

FRENCH POSITIVISM

If the "men of letters" could not reconcile the "two Englands," then what solutions were available? The twin processes of modernization and social division had also become the subject of movements in France that attracted the attention of John Stuart Mill — especially Auguste Comte's positivism. Historians often underestimate the contribution of this movement to our understanding of society's dynamics and history, and the impact of technology.

For not only was positivism a challenge to religion and metaphysical speculation, but it also opened the door to a new relativism of all values, presaging the devastating critiques of Nietzsche in its historicism, its theory of sociohistorical transformation. This struck at "eternal" values such as those the liberals claimed as the basis of their ideology. As we shall see, the German school of historical economists managed to strike a balance between "eternal" principles and the specific socioeconomic relations a historical situation required. But the implied bases for that balance were the neo-Kantian belief in transcendent reason and the Hegelian concept of progress as working toward universal comprehension of the Absolute Spirit. Both of these were attacked by positivists in the 1880s and '90s, as science continued its rapid advance, as the theories of Newtonian physics began to give way to the new physics of relativity, and as mathematics itself revealed its paradoxes and contradictions.

The Brazen Inspiration of Saint-Simon

While Britain grappled with its "dark, Satanic mills" and its "dismal" science of economics, in France a singular voice announced the law of progress made manifest by industrialization and the unification of social and empirical science under the law of positive knowledge. The voice was that of Count Henri de Saint-Simon, one of the most stimulating and influential public intellectuals of his generation. Saint-Simon's voice was extended and intensified after his death by his last amanuensis, Auguste Comte, who is credited with first coining the word "sociology" to encompass Saint-Simon's idea of society as a historical entity that emerges from the ideas dominant in any one historical period, and the material life that those ideas enable. For Saint-Simon and Comte, history can be resumed as society's search for an optimal organization that corresponds to the knowledge and technology it has mastered.[45]

The gist of Saint-Simon's doctrine is contained in the following story:[46] In 1819, Saint-Simon found himself on trial in Paris for having produced a brochure entitled *The Parable* that scandalized the officials of the Restoration, the government led by Louis XVIII, who had been installed by the Allies after the defeat of Napoleon. As an indication of the temper of the times, 1819 was the year of the so-called Peterloo massacre in England, in which ex-soldiers and other protesters against the harsh postwar economic conditions were struck down by the authorities who continued to fear the return of Jacobinism.

What would happen, Saint-Simon asked, if France suddenly lost its fifty top physicists, its fifty top painters, its fifty top bankers, its six hundred most productive farmers, and so forth, all its three thousand top scientists, artists, and tradespeople? And what would happen if, on the other hand, death were suddenly to strike the Duc d'Angoulême, the Duc de Berry, the high-ranking officers of the royal household, the cardinals, the archbishops, the ten thousand richest proprietors of the kingdom "from among those who live nobly," and all thirty thousand individuals who are said to be the most important figures in the country? In the second case, while the loss would certainly leave all of France grief-stricken, no real harm would be done to the body politic of the state. In the first case, on the contrary, France would find herself bereft of talents that are not easily replaced from one day to the next, and the nation would become a body without a soul. The conclusion: our society is at the current time an upside-down world in which those who are of positive use are consigned to serve princes. Saint-Simon was acquitted by a jury over the protests of the state prosecutors.

As a young aristocrat on the eve of the French Revolution (he was related to the Duc de Saint-Simon, author of salacious memoirs of the court of Louis XIV), Count Henri de Saint-Simon served with Lafayette in the American Revolutionary War against the British, where he was wounded. Upon his return to France, he renounced his nobility and threw himself into study, guided by young alumni he hired from the École Polytechnique, then Europe's most important hub for advanced scientific research — of whom a certain Auguste Comte proved the most brilliant. Comte provided coherence and expertise to Saint-Simon's inspirations, and substance to Saint-Simon's intuitive linking of the industrializing process to society's intellectual and scientific development. Civilization, Comte argued, advanced by stages related to command over scientific or positive knowledge. Superstition and unquestioning religiosity give way to metaphysics and reflection based on doubt, which generates critique. The French Revolution marked the end of a feudal society in which tradition could no longer withstand the power of rational critique. The modern age, however, incorporates critique into its daily operations, and especially into its search for knowledge through skeptical inquiry. These lead to scientific discoveries and the scientific age, which is ours.

In their original concept, these ideas were the brainchild of Henri de Saint-Simon. But it was Comte who built upon those insights to develop the ideas and ultimately write the book, the *Course of Positive Philosophy*, that explains the doctrine. So successful did Comte's *Course* become that it stirred to the core the whole of Europe and the Americas, and led to the creation of a new academic discipline that still carries the name Comte originally gave it: sociology.

Saint-Simon heralded a historic transformation of the nation's "power elite" from those learned in the law to those learned in the natural sciences, from "critique" to positive, factual knowledge, from metaphysical political debates about ends to knowledgeable decisions about technique. Saint-Simon became a target for classical liberals because of his planner's view of industrialism as an integrated system and his view on the national governance of industrial states, which was close to what we would today call "technocracy." Comte developed those views into a historical system in which society changes its character dramatically in response to new knowledge. Positivists forecast that industrialization would turn over control of the world to a small number of gifted engineers who would run the key machinery by which the rest of humanity lives, eats, works, and dies, unless governments took specific steps to preserve equality and justice from a new feudal tyranny based on property and inheritance.

Mill wrote of the positivists he met and their views in the 1830s:

> Their criticisms on the common doctrines of Liberalism seemed to me full of important truth, and it was partly by their writings that my eyes were opened to the very limited and temporary value of the old political economy, which assumes private property and inheritance as indefeasible facts, and freedom of production and exchange as the *dernier mot* of social improvement. The scheme gradually unfolded by the St. Simonians, under which the labour and capital of society would be managed for the general account of the community, every individual being required to take a share of labour, either as thinker, teacher, artist or producer, all being classed according to

their capacity and remunerated according to their works, appeared to me a far superior description of Socialism to Owen's. Their aim seemed to me desirable and rational, however their means might be inefficacious; and though I never believed in the practicability, nor in the beneficial operation of their social machinery, I felt the proclamation of such an ideal of human society could not but tend to give a beneficial direction to the efforts of others to bring society, as at present constituted, nearer to some ideal standard.[47]

This is not the text classical liberals usually cite when they call on Mill's writing as support for their views. Yet it is clear from this that through the course of his self-education and self-development, Mill arrived at a similar place to Hegel in his outlook for mankind. He also accepted the positivist ideas that science and technology were the shaping forces in the evolution of humanity, a view not uncongenial to his own *System of Logic,* nor to the broad thrust of utilitarianism as a description of the force driving humanity to satisfy its desires.

Also present in Mill, as in Kant and Hegel and the earlier thinkers of the eighteenth century, is the idea of the development of humanity as a moral project driven by reason and imagination, in contrast to desire. Mill rejected the political structure and the New Christianity of Saint-Simon, as he rejected Comte's Religion of Humanity. Nevertheless, his acceptance of the positivist social ideal and later his embrace of co-operative socialism signal an opening in the hold of the myth of laissez-faire upon the liberal mind and a movement toward a socio-anthropological perspective around the significance of status and function.[48] From there, however, the necessary climb is steep. What is missing from Mill is an explicit recognition of the danger warned of by Saint-Simon's critique of industrialism as a device for re-establishing a renewed and strengthened feudalism. Comte and Saint-Simon warn that industrialism is more than just a new way of producing things more economically; rather, it is also a system of social organization and control that operates through its own logic and without the explicit consent of anyone.

Saint-Simon and Auguste Comte

To liberals, especially classical ones, Saint-Simon seemed unacceptably authoritarian.[49] To Saint-Simon himself, he was simply logical. The power of science at that time was just starting to invade public consciousness, as new technologies, particularly railroads and the telegraph, were beginning to impose themselves. Paris at that time was the global capital of applied science and mathematics, centred on the École Polytechnique, the great French national engineering school created in 1794 after the French Revolution, when the challenge was to find the engineers and scientists France now needed. Later, its mission (after its militarization by Napoleon in 1804) became the creation of a national technocracy, a *"noblesse d'état."* Scientists at the time understood laws of nature as deterministic forces that, if known with sufficient precision, would replace liberty with positive knowledge. Pierre-Simon Laplace, the brilliant mathematician who extended Newton's work with a more rigorous mathematical treatment, is also famous for his articulation of scientific determinism:

> We may regard the present state of the universe as the effect of its past and the cause of its future. An intellect which at a certain moment would know all forces that set nature in motion, and all positions of all items of which nature is composed, if this intellect were also vast enough to submit these data to analysis, it would embrace in a single formula the movements of the greatest bodies of the universe and those of the tiniest atom; for such an intellect nothing would be uncertain and the future just like the past would be present before its eyes.[50]

From Laplace comes the dream of a computable universe, an intelligible order that once understood becomes entirely predictable. It is a persistent idea. In Saint-Simon's era, it was an intrinsic part of positivism's rising orthodoxy, the context within which his ideas of a new social pattern based on industrial organization took shape. Moreover, if Saint-Simon saw in science and technology a way forward for mankind, one should also remember that the political background to his writing was the turmoil of French affairs that comprised the fall of Napoleon, a failed restoration, and class pressures building toward revolution (which occurred in 1830 and then again in 1848). To Saint-Simon, the stakes were clear: positive scientific and engineering knowledge placed feudal Europe on the cusp of transformation into a state of "industrialism." This new state, if correctly organized, could ensure that all Europeans would be gainfully employed doing work of their choice, under what we would call today a technocratic administration.[51]

This technocratic administration would have the competence to assert a new public interest — namely, that the industrial system worked to the benefit of all. The requirement of a system of governance that is self-aware and capable of ensuring that it performs as generally intended is a precursor of the need for a political status for civil society, or a "fourth branch of government," as Rosanvallon recommends.[52] Such a concept is in stark contrast to either the feudal system or the form of industrialization that was developing in Great Britain under Manchesterism. To many observers, the Manchester formula for industrialization reduced civil society to the market exchange between individuals and thus entailed every other negative consequence, including harsh treatment of those dependent on the earnings of their labour, widening class differences, and growing political fragility.

Saint-Simon saw more clearly than most the power of technological innovation as a force for social improvement if the institutional and organizational changes it implied could be achieved. For the gains of industrialism to be fully realized and its immense civilizational possibilities to be captured, it was critical that certain institutional changes occur. Besides controlling capital investment, these included the abolition (or at least the weakening) of the custom of inheritance to control the allocation of significant property. Saint-Simon was a keen student of Adam Smith. He believed people wanted "least-cost" governance. He also understood the importance of the rational allocation of resources if individual welfare was to be maximized. He believed in the application of that logic to inheritance and indeed to all unearned income — which he regarded as a feudal hangover clearly visible in the palatial estates of the richest classes. He also understood that these reforms were unlikely to occur without a political program spearheaded by those who understood what the future implied.

For Saint-Simon, public policy should aim to keep industrialization from becoming grounds for a new, even more oppressive, feudalism in which a few gifted engineers enriched themselves while everyone else was forced to work long hours for barely enough to live on — that is, an extension of Manchesterism. The single change of eliminating inheritance as a means of allocating capital, argued Saint-Simon, was essential to eliminate the major inequalities of capitalism.[53] It would also ensure large amounts of capital could continually be reinvested in improving the general welfare rather than reinforcing division and class rule. For this he advocated a government-owned and controlled central bank that would anchor a network of sector-oriented subsidiary banks. These would have the knowledge and incentives necessary for the allocation of credit to the most effective entrepreneurs.[54]

On the question of inheritance, he argued the case against the legitimacy of passing on wealth through inheritance indirectly, from references to the warrior beginnings of feudal nobility through the aristocratic abuses of wealth under the Bourbons, with citations from Montesquieu, Rousseau, Mirabeau, and Say. His conclusion was that these modern authorities offered no justification for allowing wealth, and thus social status, to be acquired by heredity rather than by merit, by which he meant aptness for managing industrial firms. Considering, therefore, the harmful effects on society — especially in preserving an idle class of ultra-rich and a larger general population at various stages of poverty — these thinkers asked, why not use the wealth accumulated by the super-rich to provide education and instruction to the poor, and thereby generate a more just distribution?

In effect, this is a modern argument for redistribution by market mediation in the name of constructing a superior society, based on science, technology, and full employment. It takes the English craft union argument against owners' total control of the plant, wages, and working conditions to the next level: the impact of property on average incomes and opportunities. The continued relevance of the argument was demonstrated at the end of the nineteenth century, some sixty years after Saint-Simon's death, by Henry George (who instead proposed a progressive tax on land),[55] and more recently in the twenty-first century by Thomas Piketty.[56] At the beginning of the twentieth century, as the working class gained the franchise and formed the urban majority, governments began to respond to the new political pressures and to make adjustments. As to Saint-Simon's proposed financial structure, and his intuition about a networked industrial structure, these remain current coin in our own economic debates.[57]

How Knowledge and Technology Drive History

Saint-Simon's vision of technology as a historical force is described with even greater clarity in Durkheim's analysis. In Durkheim, the fact that the unit of analysis is society rather than individuals or aggregations of individuals in political parties is a major step forward toward a public "sociological imagination." It underlines an important development in Western consciousness and its deepening understanding of aggregate social forces propelled by technology beyond those of Smithian or physiocratic supply and demand:

1. Emergent societies undergo a slow bifurcation — a splitting leading to complete division — around competing principles. In emerging industrial societies in Europe, the bifurcation occurs around the military-theological principles of the feudal nobility against the capitalist-scientific-positivist principles of the emerging industrial order. Old status is challenged by new function.
2. The new industrial order transforms the role of property such that it is put to productive use under the guidance of science and engineering. This leaves the "idle" property owners faced with dispossession and even disappearance, as capital reaches out to acquire more assets to add to production. Ultimately, in industrial society, function determines status.
3. The mass of industrial society is made up of propertyless workers who offer only their labour. The stability of industrial society depends upon a rate of redistribution and public education sufficient to let this class become more closely integrated into industrial life. The working masses must achieve both function and status.
4. At the level of governance, industrial society contains a tension between the world of classical politics, controlled by lawyers and scholars and the industrial world of technology, whose order is understood by technocrats.

Saint-Simon laid down no timetable for achieving the changes he fore-saw. Rather, he underlined the point that industrialization marked a new stage in the history of mankind, a stage operating by its own laws rooted in engineering and technology. Comte added to the Saint-Simon schema a comprehensive overview of mankind's developing scientific consciousness — an alternative scheme to that of Hegel and an explicit rejection of Kant. Comte argued that as mankind moved from the age of theology through the age of metaphysics and critique, arriving at the present (1840s) age of positive science, metaphysics would now have no place and positive science would banish all "superstition" — by which Comte meant not only witches but all Kantian *noumena,* or innate ideas.

One of the stakes in the debate about positivism is society's quest for certainty in its political arguments. Since Comte, mankind would no long-er seek explanations of "why" but plunge into the investigation of "how" — a question that positive science could answer beyond dispute. Comte's *Course of Positive Philosophy* linked fields of knowledge in a hierarchy show-ing mankind's growing mastery over the physical world, and ending in mankind's exploration of mankind and a spiritual exploration of science as the new religion to succeed all others, including Christianity. In this he sin-gles out the dilemma of postmodernism and contemporary liberalism: In a world of incommensurable views of equal relative value, how can useful agreement be achieved and maintained? The reply of positivism must be the consequentialist credo: by their results shall one judge them.

Comte's *Course of Positive Philosophy* was a significant *succès d'estime,* although it brought him little money. Indeed, for a time Comte subsist-ed on contributions from England organized by Mill. Nevertheless, after 1840, Comte's ideas enjoyed enormous impact. In a world roiled by po-litical disputes over such *noumena* as social values, ethical values, theol-ogies, and philosophies, positive science seemed to point the way to the emergency exits, beyond which lay calm reason and experimental verifica-tion. Positive ideas indeed swept aside Hegel and even Kant, as positivism appeared to promise a world of triumphant human development by itself, without the cobwebs of inexplicable metaphysical or transcendent ideas to encumber mankind's material progress. Comte ignited a train of enthusi-asm for materialism in general and its application as a lens to a great many activities, reviving an Enlightenment tradition embodied by Condorcet, d'Alembert, and Hume. Comte was followed in publication in 1859 by Charles Darwin, whose *Origin of Species* offered a scientific, materialist explanation of human creation, and in 1885 by Herbert Spencer, whose *Principles of Sociology* built upon Darwin's work to develop an evolutionary view of mankind and its institutions, driving toward greater complexity and then splitting up to form new organizations and industries.

Émile Durkheim

Comte's greatest student was the sociologist Émile Durkheim (1858–1917). His pioneering sociological analyses of the division of labour and suicide underlined the complementarity of sociology and economics.[58]

With metaphysics and religion on the defensive and feudal status in decline, industrial society sought a new framework within which to organize the integration of status and function, and to understand civil society. Durkheim led the way in developing the concept of the nation as the next framework for this integration — one might say, Hegel with a twist. Individual human consciousness, he found, cannot be counted upon as always capable of self-integration into a society based on division of labour and uncertain wages. In confirmation of Hegel's belief that a society based solely on interest could not transcend a self-interested and individualist level of interaction, Durkheim's research showed that division of labour imposed on society — as a nation — the duty to combat individual alienation by promoting community solidarity. In this, Durkheim directly contradicted Herbert Spencer, whose views recapitulated Fichte's concept of mankind as united by contracts and markets under the control of *Naturrecht* alone.

Durkheim was more than a positivist: he was also a neo-Kantian. The concept of the human mind — and how it might react to forces generated by social organization — is the key to his concept of sociology. For Durkheim, alienation is the cause of maladjustment and social problems. It is also, in both Hegel and Marx, at the heart of the mental changes that promoted successive stages of human self-consciousness. For all three theorists, mankind's alienation leads to challenges to the established order, and it explains how humans can reorganize society at one point and yet be remade by society at another. Theories of alienation, however, have trouble accounting for the creation of a civil society integrated across classes and interests to form a community of needs, whose consciousness of itself transcends the self-interest of individuals and groups, so that the general interest can prevail over the interests of powerful parts of the society.[59]

The Influence of Positivism

The influence of positivism in the nineteenth century was both broad and deep. Virtually every movement both for and against socialism, however conceived (including the use of national organization to maximize industrial power, as conceived by Maurras[60]) could trace its ideas back to Saint-Simon. This is true of Marx in particular. His *Communist Manifesto* is full of worked-over Saint-Simonisms, from its opening praise of the economic potential of industrialization to the results achievable under control of the working class: "From each according to his abilities, to each according to his needs," reminiscent of positivism's "To each according to his wants, from each according to his work." In *Anti-Dühring,* Engels credits Saint-Simon with "the breadth of genius" whose ideas inspired all the elements of socialism that are "not strictly economic," including the submission of politics to economics.[61]

More recently, Saint-Simon was harshly criticized by Hayek as a precursor of Soviet central planning. Perhaps taking a leaf from Mill, many liberals regard the early positivists as proto-totalitarians, forgetting that as *Polytechniciens* they shared a theory of nature as being determined by its laws, that is to say, not by the will of a "maximum leader." At the same time, Saint-Simon, and subsequently Comte, also sketched a positivist religion, a "religion of humanity." Among twentieth-century commentators, only Raymond Aron seems to have taken seriously this aspect of positivism, seeing it as a sign of understanding the destructive consequences of applied science in the absence of strict ethical guidelines.[62] Saint-Simon was a harbinger, a canary in the mine of technological progress.

Considered in their broad outlines, most of the dilemmas that Saint-Simon signalled are those that trouble us today. For example, the power of private technocratic management has successfully challenged the authority of government, even if it has not yet acquired government's power of legitimate sovereignty. Technology remains a transformative force, especially since the start of the digital revolution.

Saint-Simon and Comte advance the concept of civil society by showing the importance of an integrating process in society. Utilitarianism and individualism combined with minimalist government and laissez-faire economic policy do not constitute that process. On the contrary, the early sociology discussed here shows in abstract what England (and most other countries since) experienced in the nineteenth century when governed according to the ideas of James Mill's single-class government — meaning that of "the middle class," supposedly the most representative of "the people" and the most likely to share the interests of the community as a whole (in contrast to both the aristocratic landholders and the labourers with negligible property).[63] The new technology and advancement of science threw up new challenges to tradition that imposed nearly unbridgeable social class divisions. The solutions that evolved, including the trade union movement, actually exploited these divisions. At the same time, those same forces of change also accelerated the social divisions that held back Britain's economic performance and, most important of all, political freedom.

LIBERALISM AND LAISSEZ-FAIRE

The foregoing is not the usual picture of the British nineteenth century. In that connection, it is interesting to compare two texts from J.M. Keynes, written after the Versailles peace settlement, which he vigorously questioned. The first shows pre-1914 England as it is often portrayed, in which the achievements of classical liberalism are the stuff of nostalgia and warm memories:

> Any man of capacity or character at all exceeding the average [could enter] into the middle and upper classes, for whom life offered, at a low cost and with the least trouble, conveniences, comforts, and amenities beyond the compass of the richest and most powerful monarchs of other ages. The inhabitant of London could order by telephone, sipping his morning tea in bed, the various products of the whole earth, in such quantity as he might see fit, and reasonably expect their early delivery upon his doorstep; he could at the same moment and by the same means

adventure his wealth in the natural resources and new enterprises of any quarter of the world, and share, without exertion or even trouble, in their prospective fruits and advantages; or he could decide to couple the security of his fortunes with the good faith of the townspeople of any substantial municipality in any continent that fancy or information might recommend. He could secure forthwith, if he wished it, cheap and comfortable means of transit to any country or climate without passport or other formality, could despatch his servant to the neighbouring office of a bank for such supply of the precious metals as might seem convenient, and could then proceed abroad to foreign quarters, without knowledge of their religion, language, or customs, bearing coined wealth upon his person, and would consider himself greatly aggrieved and much surprised at the least interference. But, most important of all, he regarded this state of affairs as normal, certain, and permanent, except in the direction of further improvement, and any deviation from it as aberrant, scandalous, and avoidable. [64]

This well-known passage from Keynes's *Economic Consequences of the Peace* (1919) rather eloquently summarizes the material achievements of nineteenth-century industrialization, which, broadly speaking, occurred within a liberal framework of free markets, expanding political freedom and, toward the end of the period, increasing social justice. It is particularly noteworthy for its description of what one might call "the economy of delight" that was one of the characteristics of nineteenth-century progress.

Liberals in particular like to imagine that the world Keynes described of well-functioning, globe-girdling, semi-automatic interconnected systems was the unforeseen and unforeseeable result of laissez-faire economics. In a later publication, *The End of Laissez-Faire* (1926), Keynes took pains to explode that myth. He points out that popular belief holds that economists endorse laissez-faire as the scientific formula that enables the practical person to reconcile the contradiction between egoism and socialism "which emerged from the philosophizing of the eighteenth century and the decline of revealed religion." But that belief is incorrect. "This is what the economists are supposed to have said. No such doctrine is really to be found in the writings of the greatest authorities. It is what the popularisers and the vulgarisers said. It is what the utilitarians, who admitted Hume's egoism and Bentham's egalitarianism at the same time, were driven to believe in, if they were to effect a synthesis."[65]

In the same pamphlet, quoting one of Frédéric Bastiat's[66] rhapsodies on the harmonies produced when people act as free agents, Keynes flatly states, "From the time of John Stuart Mill, economists of authority have been in strong reaction against all such ideas." Keynes also notes, "The language of the economists lent itself to the *laissez-faire* interpretation. But the popularity of the doctrine must be laid at the door of the political philosophers of the day, whom it happened to suit, rather than of the political economists."

Later, still in the same text, Keynes writes:

> The beauty and the simplicity of such a theory are so great that it is easy to forget that it follows not from the actual facts, but from an incomplete hypothesis introduced for the sake of simplicity. Apart from other objections to be mentioned later, the conclusion that individuals acting independently for their own advantage will produce the greatest aggregate of wealth, depends on a variety of unreal assumptions to the effect that the processes of production and consumption are in no way organic, that there exists a sufficient foreknowledge of conditions and requirements, and that there are adequate opportunities of obtaining this foreknowledge. For economists generally reserve for a later stage of their argument the complications which arise — (1) when the efficient units of production are large relatively to the units of consumption, (2) when overhead costs or joint costs are present, (3) when internal economies tend to the aggregation of production, (4) when the time required for adjustments is

long, (5) when ignorance prevails over knowledge and (6) when monopolies and combinations interfere with equality in bargaining — they reserve, that is to say, for a later stage their analysis of the actual facts. Moreover, many of those who recognise that the simplified hypothesis does not accurately correspond to fact conclude nevertheless that it does represent what is "natural" and therefore ideal. They regard the simplified hypothesis as health, and the further complications as disease.[67]

Keynes's arguments were published in the mid-1920s. Even now, so many years after the Great Depression, it is amazing that the historical picture is no clearer for many liberals. Magnificent as Victorian England was in many dimensions, its failure to generate a unified civil society was a serious handicap to the country's progress in the twentieth century. As the world discovered in 1929, small-government liberalism with small to zero attention to the structure and functioning of society is an accident waiting to happen. Ideological firmness does not make up for its weaknesses; it actually accelerates and deepens the social divisions this system causes. Yet the historical record also shows that social processes can be understood, and prosperity, a strong civil society, and political freedom can advance together as a mutually reinforcing trio. Indeed, shortly before the outbreak of the First World War, it was possible to believe that Britain and all of Europe were on the verge of overcoming their divisions and creating a civil society that encompassed all classes.

CHAPTER 2
The German Historical School

TO MANY CONTINENTAL OBSERVERS, England in the 1840s and '50s exemplified the problems to avoid under a "small state" as much as it also showed the strengths of industrialization. It was obvious that so-called Manchesterism, combined with the reigning British public philosophy of utilitarianism, free competition, and limited government, risked exposing a majority of the population to misery and even destitution. It was also obvious that beyond the 1832 Reform Act, nothing further could be expected in the way of significant changes to the system of upper and middle class rule. The 1834 amendments to the Poor Law showed that the shortcomings noted by, among others, Thomas Hodgskin, Robert Owen, William Thompson, and even Bentham and Ricardo, who both advocated universal male franchise,[1] would mostly be ignored.

FRANCE: THE SECOND EMPIRE AND THE POSITIVISTS

As early as 1828, the French economist Jean-Baptiste Say claimed that the English obsession with a handful of abstract principles "transformed political economy into a science of words and arguments which, claiming to extend it, they pushed into the void."[2] Yet if the anarchy of free-market production generated social problems it seemed only a stronger state could solve, was there an alternative to Manchesterism that was consistent with liberal values? Yes, but it remained to be invented. After about 1840, it is fair to say, finding a more successful formula for industrial society became a top priority for many European thinkers in France and, in particular, in Prussia, whose project for a customs union (*Zollverein*) of the German states had come into effect and was gathering strength.[3] However, it is essential to note that such thinkers were in a minority, struggling for recognition against a dominant utilitarian liberal paradigm. Not until the century passed its midpoint did that dominance begin to weaken.

Following the coup of Napoleon III in 1851, France turned to the positivist followers of Saint-Simon and the Crédit Mobilier, the bank organized by two brothers, Émile and Isaac Pereire, while operating an open bar of government-supported projects that enriched the friends of the regime. The regime governed by popular referendum, suppressing all political parties, especially those with socialistic views. The bank prospered by taking positions in the companies it financed. Eventually, following a crushing failure in 1867, the bank was swallowed by its rival, Rothschild's. Nevertheless, it represented a substantial banking innovation, and it mobilized considerable amounts of capital that created the foundations of modern France, including a large portion of Haussmann's modernization of Paris.[4] Yet the personal rule of Napoleon III and the crony capitalism of the Second Empire could not be sustained. A pro-business dictatorship ruling by referendum drove French modernization, perhaps. But it was not a solution to liberalism's problems.

PRUSSIA'S DIFFERENT COURSE

Prussia followed a different course. Prussia, to be sure, was a monarchy in which aristocrats filled the top ranks of the civil service and military, and only aristocrats could stand for election to public office. In other words, Prussia was not particularly committed to liberal political values. Yet to supplant Austria as the leader of the German Confederation, Prussia would have to accommodate itself to liberalism in Germany as a whole and also in a Europe whose major powers were beginning to embrace some form of liberal ideology, coupled with continued support for hereditary kingship in the British mode. How and to what extent Prussia was prepared for the challenge is the subtext to Bismarck's desperate political manoeuvres following German unification; these include notably the adoption of worker protection in a system of state socialism. Prussia's experience is a repeat of the drama in which a preindustrial society has to find a way to accommodate itself to the imperatives of industrial organization. In the British experience, the result was "Victorianism"; in late nineteenth-century Germany, it was the Wilhelmine Germany of Emperor Wilhelm II (from 1890, his dismissal of Bismarck, to 1918, his abdication). France, despite a brilliant cultural adaptation, never fully became an industrial society until the Fifth Republic.

For our purpose, a deeper understanding of liberalism, the most interesting element of Prussia's accommodation was the development of a Hegel-inspired concept of civil society and how it handled the new challenges posed for it by industrialization. This it did mainly by increasing the economic role of the government, within a framework of a constitutional state (*Rechtsstaat*). In France, prior to 1848, the positivists Saint-Simon and Comte opened a door on the possibility that a combination of social morality, history, and science would permit the design of a state whose functions would include the active creation and sustenance of an industrial civil society. They, too, consciously or not, adopted the idea of a Hegelian "community of needs," in that its economic transactions would satisfy its own material requirements by constantly increasing productivity. That increased productivity would ensure that the amount of capital available would be sufficient to sustain the whole population without destitution and extreme social division. The researchers of the German historical school came to a similar conclusion, although they tackled the question in an original way.

Achieving this would require (as Comte suggested) a comprehensive social science that included law, economics, and history, based not upon metaphysical abstraction (like Manchesterism) but rather upon scrupulously collected and analyzed empirical data. These ideas found particularly fertile ground in Prussia, where economists — most notably at the University of Berlin — began to undertake research along those lines. As Ferdinand

Tönnies pointed out in the Festschrift for Gustav Schmoller,[5] German intellectual life in the nineteenth century became dominated by three interacting and interdependent streams of inquiry: philosophy, history, and natural science.[6] The German experience was part of a wider European skepticism about eighteenth-century Enlightenment abstractions after Napoleon and an emerging embrace of more historical and juridical perspectives on freedom in society. These were influenced by the alternative Enlightenment perspectives of Vico and Montesquieu, and they further responded to the Romantic movement that underlined the historical nature of human experience.[7]

One of the outcomes of that interactivity was the body of work of what became the German historical school of economics (although its forte was actually what we would call sociology); its realization enabled Germany to claim world leadership in social science from roughly 1880 to the Great Depression. (After that, due mainly to the rise of Hitler and Nazi anti-Semitism, the centre of gravity shifted to London; Cambridge, Massachusetts; and the University of Chicago — the places of refuge for many of the intellectual elite of German universities.) In its wake, similar groups of researchers also formed in England, France, and the United States, but these never achieved the same significance or critical mass of the German social research seminars in the late nineteenth and early twentieth centuries.[8]

Indeed, the basic research question for German social and historical researchers was the arrival of the whole German "nation" to statehood. The basic question of meaning went along with the national concept of *Bildung,* or formative development. To a large extent, the great historians like Leopold von Ranke and Gustav Droysen linked German success to religious or spiritual destiny — with Hegel, they accepted an underlying spiritual force behind historical events, like Hegel's *Geist* (Spirit) that drives his philosophy of history, or from another angle, the belief in a force common to all animals that energizes evolution. At a cultural or aesthetic level, too, the standard plot line in German novels during this period was a coming-of-age story in which a character either lived out his destiny, or overcame what was thought to be his destiny, to become accepted or not into a select company of people who held the keys to the ultimate questions of life — the *Bildungsroman.* Looking beyond the novel, it forms the backbone of German letters in this period and after, from Goethe, Fichte, and Schiller to Hermann Hesse.[9]

The name "German historical school" suggests a cohesion that never existed, and actually refers explicitly to the *Verein für sozialforschung* (Association for Social Research) convened in 1870 and established officially in 1872 under the control of its most active promoter, Dr. Gustav Schmoller. It is generally accepted by today's economists that the approach adopted by this group, despite their many publications, amounted to a conceptual dead end both in its approach to history and, especially, in its approach to economics.[10] Where are the theoretical insights that match the analytical work of, say, the marginalist school of economics that was its intellectual rival at the University of Vienna? In its defence, it might be observed that the group shed considerable light on aspects of economic transformation, and showed by example that economic policy is itself historical, and when it is applied in the historically appropriate or optimal way it can accelerate economic and social development. The example of late nineteenth-century Germany speaks for itself. However, the achievement of German researchers goes beyond that: rather than content themselves with new theorems of market behaviour, they incorporated their own work and that of others, including the Austrian concept of subjective prices, into a broader, more comprehensive theory of social development that we would recognize today as sociology. Not content with economics as they found it, they broadened it into a whole new discipline that differed from the French concept of sociology on the issue of the historicity of social phenomena. That is what renders this approach of interest today. For all its advances in technique, economics is still only a branch of sociology. Its failure to understand that underlies its shortcomings in our own time.

The German historical school of economics comprised a number of different strands.[11] The names of many of those involved — and which were once renowned — have now been largely forgotten. Here is a partial list, beginning with precursors: the romantic nationalist Adam Müller (1779–1829), hostile to free-market ideas; Friedrich List (1789–1846), a "post-Ricardian" nationalist, who advocated trade protection and industrial policy; Friedrich Carl von Savigny (1779–1861), who pioneered the historical study of positive law as the basis for a whole-of-Germany legal code; Wilhelm Roscher (1817–94), whose *Grundriss zu Vorlesungen über die Staatswirtschaft nach geschichtlicher Methode* (1843)[12] set out a manifesto for combining historical and economic research; Bruno Hildebrand (1812–78), whose *Die National-ökonomie der Gegenwart und Zukunft* serves as a bridge to the second generation, led by Gustav von Schmoller (1838–1917), discussed later in this chapter, along with Karl Knies (1821–98), author of *Politische Ökonomie vom Standpunkte der geschichtlichen Methode* (1853). Perhaps the most influential scholar on methodology was Johann Heinrich von Thünen (1783–1850), whose *Der Isolierte Staat* (1826 and 1856) developed theories of spatial economics or location theory that still echo today.[13] Clearly, however, the most practical thinker in the early days of interest in the problems of German industrialization was Karl Rodbertus-Jagetzow (1805–1875) — the thinker and theoretician who most resembled the English classical economists, especially Ricardo.[14]

BISMARCK'S HIGH POLITICS AND GERMANY'S NATIONAL INTEREST

With all this intellectual capital as its basis, it fell to the second generation, under Schmoller's leadership, to establish the school officially in 1872 as the *Verein für Sozialforschung* and as an authoritative guide to social reforms during the Bismarckian period. Before then, economic policy was essentially a form of Manchesterism in which support for education was a major public policy component, under Prussian industry minister Rudolf von Delbrück. The consolidation of the German states following Bismarck's wars of unification, ending with the Franco-Prussian War, was the occasion for a new imperial constitution. It brought Bavaria and Württemberg officially into the German Empire, to which was added newly obtained Alsace-Lorraine. The constitution also confirmed universal male suffrage. These important national events took place under a liberal-minded economic administration, with relatively open markets and few social services. Over the same period, Bismarck manoeuvred to maintain Prussian and his own political leadership by combining with liberals against conservatives, and with conservatives against liberals, and then holding out the prospect of a political alliance with the working class socialist parties against the ultramontane Catholics.[15]

In considering the process of German unification, it should be remembered that its success was a stunning event that completely upset the Continental balance of power and created a revisionist interest of varying intensity among all of Germany's most powerful neighbours. This was shared especially by France over the loss of Alsace-Lorraine and the humiliation of forced reparations, and by Austria, which had previously dominated the German-speaking territories. Now Austria was reduced to a small German community claiming to rule over a Central European polyglot empire of Magyars, Slavs, and other nationalities, and facing a disintegrating Turkish Empire in the Balkans. If much of German economic development seemed to have a military purpose, as some contemporary observers pointed out,[16] it is not difficult to understand why.

In this lively political climate, it is noteworthy that it was at Eisenach, famous for its conference of radical socialists in 1869, that a preparatory conference for the *Verein für sozialforschung* — the official home for the historical economists — was held at Schmoller's urging. This meeting in 1870 set the foundations for the official launch of the *Verein* two years later. Those who attended were mainly German-speaking economists who disagreed with Manchesterism, the group thereafter to be known as the *Kathedersozialisten* — that is, armchair socialists or academic socialists — to distinguish them from actual militants belonging to a socialist party. Schmoller's speech at Eisenach set the tone for the *Verein*'s research program. The objective was to develop an approach to the problem of industrialization — the social question — that would command consensus support from academics and could also build public support; thus it would avoid the divisions between classes and interests whose conflict could upset the bright future awaiting the newly united Germany.[17] As it turned out, Schmoller may very well have read the political context correctly, especially since the following year, 1873, was the first year of what became the long recession of almost ten years.

The German political context was challenging. Bismarck wanted to secure for all time the political control of the new Germany by the Prussian landed aristocracy, the Junkers, leaders of Germany's largest state. He only partially succeeded. To achieve his end, he accepted a liberal legislature, but — to summarize the history — he managed to arrange matters so as to bypass its full control of the government by giving the state direct access to indirect taxes, and exempting national security and foreign affairs from full parliamentary scrutiny.[18] He also made political war on the main enemies of aristocratic power, the Social Democrats. In 1878, Bismarck banned them from holding any public discussion outside the legislature or displaying any physical signs of their party's existence — a ban that lasted until 1890, the year of his departure from public life. Perhaps not so paradoxically, the result of the ban was that Social Democratic Party membership grew faster than that of any of the other parties, and it became a kind of state within a state, making full use of its only legitimate outlet — the state and imperial legislatures.

In that political context, therefore, the *Verein* not surprisingly became a champion of state socialism, carefully steered by Schmoller and his influential friends high in the Prussian public service. The best guarantee of social peace and steady economic development would come from the expansion of a *Rechtsstaat* with a highly capable civil service as the motor of Germany's socioeconomic transformation to an industrial society. Although its standard of work declined in the prewar years, the influence of the *Verein* persisted into the 1920s, owing to the prominence of such international academic stars as Max Weber and his brother Alfred (who supervised the thesis of Talcott Parsons), and Werner Sombart. Hitler closed it down in 1935.

BISMARCK'S STATE SOCIALISM

In the world of events, practical politics continued to impose its imperatives. The year 1873 was a year of political scandals that combined with national tensions around the inclusion of Alsace-Lorraine in the empire. Almost immediately Bismarck's government moved to increase its authoritarian actions, appointing General Manteuffel to control the new province and attempting to gag the press with a new press law. Following two botched assassination attempts on the emperor, Bismarck realized he had to act to soothe the mounting social tensions. He decided to try to take control of the socialist program. For the means, he turned to the University of Berlin and to Schmoller and the historical economics researchers. The concrete result, after intensive research, was a comprehensive workers' insurance program that became a European gold standard for combating the causes of poverty in industrial society. It began to roll out in 1883, surviving Bismarck's departure (1890) and continuing to 1903. The program covered worker disability, unemployment insurance, and measures against worker abuse.[19] These measures were accompanied by renationalization of railways and communications and the institution of trade restrictions designed to accelerate the growth of the nation's industrial capacity.[20]

German state socialism attracted European attention to the work of the historical economists, and inspired the Fabians and American Progressives: by the mid-1880s, enlightened opinion believed the world was becoming more humane and working toward a constructive democratic socialism and world peace. Finished was the Gilded Age scandal of conspicuous consumption in the midst of appalling poverty … or so many thoughtful people believed.

To get a sense of how the *Verein* approached the problems of national economics, let us explore some of the main ideas of four of its principal exponents: Friedrich List and Karl Rodbertus, who served as a first generation of German historical economists; Wilhelm Roscher, one of its most prolific exponents; and Gustav Schmoller, who was the main organizer of the *Verein*. Taken together, their views constitute an objection to some of liberalism's main postulates, refining them by situating them in historical stages and by closing some gaps in thinking that were revealed by the actual experience of the Manchester school in contrast to its theory.

ECONOMICS AS A HUMAN SCIENCE
Friedrich List: Associative Power

The two most prominent thinkers whose ideas set the initial general direction of the *Verein*'s research were Friedrich List and Karl Rodbertus-Jagetzow. Both List and Rodbertus agreed that the main determinants of economic well-being for a country are its economic and technical production capacity, and the legal structure that determines allocation and distribution. Surprisingly, perhaps, the inspiration for List came from the American debates on the state's role in development launched by Alexander Hamilton. It was Americans who first developed an effective alternative to Manchesterism.[21]

Alexander Hamilton advocated what we would today call a national industrial policy and a national bank. These would, he argued, accelerate U.S. industrialization and lead to the rapid abolition of slavery. Bad timing, however: Hamilton's ideas encountered powerful opposition and were quickly shot down under the presidency of Andrew Jackson. Later, however, they were partially adopted through a tariff reform advocated by Senator Henry Clay of Kentucky (1777–1852), famous for proposing the Missouri Compromise of 1820, which set a northern limit to slavery in the former French Louisiana territory recently acquired by the United States. Clay's tariff reform created what was subsequently known as the American System: protective tariffs for northern industry that soaked up the earnings from southern exports of slave-produced cotton. The effect of deepening southern specialization in slavery retarded that region's economic development while encouraging the development of anti-slavery interests in the North, as well as the manufacturing infrastructure that eventually crushed the South when the differences over slavery became too heavy to bear, resulting in the Civil War.

Friedrich List took up Hamilton's ideas. He had been a university professor and a senior bureaucrat and then deputy in Württemberg, but was imprisoned for his advocacy of reforms. He escaped and found refuge in France in 1825. However, he returned to finish his sentence, from which he was released on agreeing to immigrate to the United States.[22] There he studied Hamilton's ideas and the effects of tariffs on industrialization, and returned to Germany, briefly holding the position of U.S. consul. Already a supporter of a German customs union (although he imagined it centred on Austria rather than Prussia), List developed Hamilton's ideas further. The key to national prosperity, he wrote, was the development of a country's "associative powers" to offset the high cost of Manchesterism's savage individual competition. Initially, he believed, this required a level of protection, especially for what J.S. Mill came to call "infant" industries.

Mill, it will be recalled, saw infant industries as a special case, an exception to the general Ricardian argument for free trade. For List, trade protection was more than that. List believed that Adam Smith misunderstood the distinction between private and public, and national and cosmopolitan market economies. In the world of the mid-nineteenth century, List believed, national economies competed with each other and were not yet ready for comprehensive free trade agreements. In that context, protection was a strategic tool for countries with world-leading potential to assemble national production platforms involving many complementary private industries. Instead of dividing the components of economics, land, labour, and capital into separate categories competing wastefully for dominance, List drew attention to the associative powers they share and argued for protective tariffs behind which countries can develop and "educate" those powers to form the necessary institutions and capacities to prepare them to take on the international competitors. Avoiding "suppressive" foreign competition would allow nations to develop industrial capacities by establishing large-scale industry that can become competitive and help integrate the nation rather than divide it.[23]

Karl Rodbertus-Jagetzow: Productivity

In a different court was Karl Rodbertus-Jagetzow. An original economic thinker with a deep knowledge of classical history, he developed a critique of Ricardo's theory of rent containing ideas that lay behind the political program that he worked out partly in correspondence with the socialist leader Ferdinand Lassalle following 1842.[24] Rodbertus was motivated to show that a national economy could be organized so as to eliminate poverty through productivity growth. He argued that landholders and holders of capital received a derived rent, which for landholders was due to the capital value of the land itself above its yield as cropland, and which permitted landholders to raise ground rents. This derived rent ultimately came from an additional charge on labour. For Rodbertus, this explained why agricultural output value was falling in relation to land value, imposing unnecessary poverty on the workers whose wages were reduced because of it.[25] He claimed that this was the result of the state's delegating its responsibility for ensuring the just economic organization of the economy to private interests concerned only with maximizing their own returns. In the absence of state protection, he believed, working class poverty would never be overcome.

Over ten years of historical study Rodbertus developed his views of how capital formed and circulated in ancient Rome, and he brought those insights to his analysis of modern European capitalism. He opposed Marx's analysis of capital and thought Marx failed to recognize that society needed classes of proprietors, entrepreneurs, and workers. In turn, Marx later wrote a ringing critique of the 1875 Gotha Program of the new Socialist Workers' Party of Germany, which had picked up many of Lassalle's ideas, especially the ideas of universal suffrage and state socialism instead of class struggle. The concept of state socialism that Lassalle and Rodbertus developed influenced the later growth of social democratic ideas; in particular, it included a theory of civil society as a community of needs, and an economic focus on rising productivity and the social sharing of the resulting gains to meet those needs.[26] In contrast to Manchester liberals, the historical school that Rodbertus drew upon considered society as an ordered entity produced by history, and within which its norms and market forces would interact dialectically.

The distribution problem that impoverished the working class, Rodbertus believed (like J.-C.-L. Simonde de Sismondi [1773–1842], an early critic of Manchesterism), was fundamentally a problem of laws and legal structures rather than economics. In this connection, he noted the critical link between salaries or wages and productivity. (Contemporary Germany understands the connection, but many jurisdictions still do not.) Conventional economics, even today, believes that wages rise automatically with productivity. But experience shows that the reverse is more likely true; that is, rising wages push companies to increase productivity. Otherwise, wages may not rise with productivity unless labour can ensure that this linkage is stipulated in the wages agreement, which management — especially in low-profit-margin companies — is often unwilling to grant. Rodbertus advocated that public policy must ensure that wages advance at least at the same rate as productivity increases. He wrote that the state could collect statistics on performance at the appropriate stage of the industrial process — primary extraction or harvest, basic processing, advanced processing, and associated services — to measure the productivity gains at each level and ensure that wage gains at least matched the smallest marginal productivity increase at each stage. To arrive at this conclusion, Rodbertus was implicitly relying on competition to force companies toward higher productivity; he also retained the classical economists' reliance on the labour theory of value, although his argument does not require it.[27] Wrote Rodbertus:

> My theory starts with the principle put forward by the English economists that the social product [*revenu*] taken as a whole is nothing but the fruit of social labour past and present and that, other things being equal, if one nation is richer than another, the cause lies uniquely in the superior productivity of labour in one over the other. Zachariae [presumably the jurist Karl Salamo Zachariae von Lingenthal (1769–1843)] has already said about ground rent that it is an advance taking of the salary that would return to the worker in its entirety if the land belonged to no one. I generalize this principle and I say capitalist rent is the same and would come back to the worker if the capital belonged to no one. It is the ownership of capital and land, it is the disposition by law in virtue of which the ownership of the product of labour is attributed to the owners of land and capital and in virtue of which the worker is forced to make do with a reduced amount of his work product.... I conclude that the rents on capital and on land exist not as a consequence of adding value to the product but because the workers' salary is reduced to a part of the total product value. It would only do to return to the workers that portion of their work product that was subtracted for the two rents.[28]

There then follows in the text a discussion of the effects of productivity improvements: first a reduction of labour time required to produce a given product, and next a productivity increase across the board, a universal increase. In the first case, Rodbertus argues, provided the product sold at the same price, the owner could pocket a higher rent owing to the lower salary outlay. But what is the effect of a universal productivity increase? He continues:

> At this point, incidentally, it confirms the point that one should search for rent not in its value, but in the productivity

[of its production process]. The highest value can still generate no rent: that is what happens when the productivity
is so weak that the product just covers the sustenance of its
workers. Inversely, a product value as small as you like can
still furnish a high rent if the labour productivity is such
that just a small amount of the product is enough to cover
the needs of the labour [required to produce it].[29]

He therefore concludes that generalizing across the whole of a
free-exchange economy, one must conclude that it is productivity that covers all the rents, both of land and capital, as well as the workers' salary, and
that while the two rents may differ as to proportionality in the production
process, they are both essentially the same. Like Marx and even Ricardo,
Rodbertus believed that the Manchester system was self-destructive. Marx
criticized Rodbertus's remedy of a guaranteed salary, pointing out that
while it might cover one deficit, such as that arising from the sales lost to
insufficient demand, it would still leave uncovered another deficit, such as
the factory owner's finance deficit.[30] Rodbertus, however, anticipates that
objection. He sees that absent other solutions, government would be called
upon over time to absorb property and to intervene economically to provide order to the anarchy of free-market production. Thus, inevitably, the
state would become the guarantor of conditions leading to steadily increasing productivity and thus living standards.[31]

Orthodox liberalism avoids this problem either by (1) closing the enterprise and laying off the workers — thus passing the misery onto the
workers, while protecting the financial assets of capital and its owners, or
by (2) paying the workers less than the productivity gain and using the income difference to pay down the whole debt. Over time, under this option,
as productivity rises industry is forced to reduce production to that which
the labour force can absorb through its purchases. As this process spreads,
the result is similar to the first — growing layoffs and unemployment, and,
ultimately the working class destitution known throughout the industrial
societies of the nineteenth century as "the social question."[32] Taking society
as a whole and including the costs of wasted human potential through
destitution and workhouse employment, the "socialism" of Rodbertus is a

better outcome for society and the vulnerable individuals concerned than the narrowly considered "efficiency" of orthodox liberalism — even if it is a less than fully satisfactory solution. Moreover, it can be improved by active government intervention to raise productivity still higher and to improve the capacity of the workforce to undertake higher value employment — a constructive use of public finance that can close the loop of the double circuit. In this way, Schmoller's objective of development solutions that avoid accentuating social division can be achieved.

Wilhelm Roscher: Basic Economic Ideas

Of all the scholars that comprised the German school, perhaps Roscher is a name that is still remembered by some elder economists in the English-speaking world. Roscher's concept of political economics extended well beyond that of a science of money-making to embrace the philosophical, cultural, and constitutional underpinnings of national economic activity — that is, the traffic, trade, or circulation of ideas, people, goods, and services, and the institutions that monitor and control these.

> National economics is not just a chrematistic, the art of getting rich; rather, it is a political science out of which men are respected and judged. Our objective is to represent what people hold in economic respect, what they desire and are sensitive to, what they strive for and attain, and why they do so. Such a representation is only possible in the closest connection with other sciences of everyday life, especially histories of law, the state, and culture.... One sees that this method will achieve for the national economy something similar to that which the Savigny-Eichhorn method accomplished for jurisprudence.[33]

Roscher is arguing that economic history can light the path to a kind of economic constitutional structure for a national economy that accords with the social and cultural norms of society, and which can also help it prepare for such innovations as are necessary for its further progress. British economic historian Keith Tribe is right to think this is outside the scope of economics as we think of economics today. But it is more or less what the West aimed to achieve with the welfare state, albeit with somewhat different tools than were available in the mid-nineteenth century. Certainly it is not far from the concept of German ordoliberalism developed by the group around Walter Eucken during the last years of the Second World War, and which formed a crucial basis for the subsequent social market economy — as I discuss further on.

Roscher's research methods combined history and geography with economics in order to widen our understanding of the forces that shape the course of national economic and political development. His concept of history was more like the Annales school of Fernand Braudel and his colleagues[34] than the strong narrative histories of Lord Acton or Henry Thomas Buckle, both leading British historians in the Ranke mode with its basis in diligent archival research.[35] Oddly, Joseph Schumpeter's treatment of Roscher in his history of economic analysis, while respectful, fails to underline his very effective contribution to economic science — namely, putting it at the historic centre of mankind's climb through various levels of civilization along with other, equally important, non-economic forces. However, in an appreciative review, Schmoller credited Roscher with putting abstract economic thinking on a firm historical footing and joining cameralist theory with English natural rights theory in historical perspective.[36]

Like the modern-day work of the Annales circle, Roscher's comprehensive principles of economics explain the workings of climate and average temperatures on crops, their yields and where they grow, and the importance of ocean currents and how they facilitated the rise of Europe and North America (rather than Asia). He treats in detail the geographic factors that explain the rise to power of Britain and the United States. He deploys statistics and economic data on geography, technology, agriculture — on all human engagements with nature and other humans — to identify and explain the routes taken in national economic construction.

Gustav Schmoller: Mercantilism

A particularly strong example of how historical perspective enriches the discussions of economic alternatives is Schmoller's defence of mercantilism against its liberal critics. Schmoller was no ardent protectionist. Indeed, he inclined toward trade liberalization when a Franco-German free trade agreement was under discussion in 1861. But, as the following excerpt illustrates, he was very alive to the importance of historical context. It will be remembered with what skill Adam Smith dismantled the case for mercantilism in *The Wealth of Nations,* using an argument that the ardent French liberal Frédéric Bastiat repeated in support of the English Anti–Corn Law League of Richard Cobden and John Bright during the first half of the nineteenth century. Schmoller's text constitutes an instructive reply.

Schmoller's paper defending mercantilism was published in 1884 and republished in English in 1895 in an economic classics series edited by the British historical economist William Ashley. It went through four successive reprints by Macmillan, the last in 1914. Schmoller argues that protection is a natural stage of national economic development and that the classical economists did not understand correctly the stages through which local economies pass on their way to national integration, and in particular the role protection played at each step.

> It was always the same conception that was involved: the resources of the land were thought of as a whole, which ought, first of all, to serve the needs of the country; they ought not to enrich a few individuals, but serve the home producer and the home consumer at a fair price. [As previously described,] the regulations hitherto employed to this end by the towns were now transferred to the territories. As hitherto the town had laid an embargo, so now the territory. As the town had, at times, prohibited the import of foreign beer and wine and manufactured articles, so now the territory. As the town had hitherto maintained an elaborate system of differential tolls, so now the districts and territories set out upon a similar course. Berne threatened its *oberland* [subject territories] with an embargo on corn and salt, if it did not bring all its butter to Berne. As Nuremberg forced to its territory all the cattle that came within a circuit of ten miles; as Ulm did not allow a single head of cattle fed

on the common pasture to leave its territory. So Florence secured for itself all the cattle sold from its subject districts without permitting their return, and exacted sureties from the owners of the great flocks driven to the Maremme that they would bring them back within the state boundaries a third larger. In the Duchy of Milan, an official permission was required for the transport of grain from place to place, so that the country might remain sure of its food.[37]

The idea that the territorial trade, its industry, and its market formed a united whole became even more powerful when one turns to the introduction of territorial currencies in circulation between the thirteenth and the seventeenth century. Although the earliest local currencies were introduced by the local prince, it was the commercial towns that took them over and made them reliable local monetary instruments. But the expansion of commerce and the rivalries involved undermined those currencies, without, however, creating the conditions within which a single regional currency could emerge. This led to attempts at creating reliable currencies within larger regions. Rulers of these larger regions who were able to coin their own currencies in sufficient volume to replace the local currencies, while forbidding export of the coins beyond their borders, succeeded in the attempt. As great princes emerged with an interest in the economic advancement of their territories, so also emerged a system of centralized taxation, legitimized by assemblies of the estates in the territories.[38]

However, Schmoller continues, this process of expanding states' territory combined with broadening territorial economic integration was interrupted by the disastrous series of interregional conflicts that made up the Thirty Years War (1618–48). When it was over, the states surrounding the German territories had matured. Economic and political interests, after centuries of mutual opposition, were now beginning to move hand in hand to form real national entities, the great European powers, and these were engaging in transoceanic trade beyond the Mediterranean. Germany, however, had not reached the same stage of development, despite its brilliant start before the war.

[Its major handicap] was the lack of politico-economic organization, the lack of consolidation of its forces.... Questions of political power were at issue, which were, at the same time, questions of political organization. What was at stake was the creation of real political economies as unified organisms, the centre of which should be, not merely a state policy reaching out in all directions, but rather the united heartbeat of a united sentiment. Only he who thus conceives of mercantilism will understand it; in its innermost kernel, it is no more than state-making and national economy-making at the same time; state-making in the modern sense which creates out of the political community an economic community, and so gives it a heightened meaning. The essence of the system lies not in some doctrine of money or the balance of trade; not in tariff barriers, protective duties or navigation laws; but in something far greater — namely, the total transformation of society and its organization, as well as of the state and its institutions, in the replacing of a local and territorial economic policy by a national state.[39]

Now, it is not a distortion of this idea to see within Schmoller's national state the central idea of a civil society that meets its own needs on its own terms and is no longer at serious risk of harm or destitution from the conditions of its everyday life. As Schmoller notes further on in the case of France under the Bourbons, the issue is essentially one of achieving transformation and union at home even more than of erecting barriers against the outside world.[40] After a comprehensive resumé of the history of Europe's commercial wars under its seventeenth- and eighteenth-century mercantilist systems, he turns to praise the system of reciprocal free trade that emerged between 1860 and 1875, as well as the system of international law that seemed to be emerging together with the treaty systems that characterized European diplomacy in the thirty years before the First World War.[41] Schmoller also reminds us:

The struggle of social bodies with one another, which is at times military, at other times merely economic, has a tendency, with the progress of civilization, to assume a higher character and to abandon its coarsest and most brutal weapons. The instinct becomes stronger of a certain solidarity of interests, of beneficent interaction, of an exchange of goods from which both rivals gain.[42]

He concludes by reminding his audience that "to our own time has been given to survey both periods from a higher standpoint; to give their due value to their theories and ideals, the real psychical motives and the practical results of both ages [Schmoller's own and the mercantilist age]; and so to understand them."[43]

Schmoller illustrates the power of adding a historical and sociopolitical dimension to the liberal analysis of mercantilism as an antithesis of trade liberalization that generates inferior results. Instead, Schmoller's analysis reveals "free trade" to be a successor strategy for which mercantilism prepares a nation. His analysis shares with liberalism an appreciation of the coordinating power of markets and prices, but underlines the importance these forces have in relation to other forces of social solidarity: political identity and political authority. Additionally, Schmoller underlines the importance of policy for creating a civil society that is confident and cohesive enough to undertake further liberalization successfully. There is thus more to the trade debate than simply the protective apparatus of trade barriers.[44] Unfortunately, even these elements have disappeared from the public discussion of trade liberalization. Reducing the issue to two dimensions (the open-or-closed binary) has trivialized reasonable public debate and enabled it to descend into a shouting match. Working through the Schmoller paper is as good a technique as any to begin to infuse this discussion once again with some of the nuance and historical perspective it deserves.

Friedrich von Wieser: Social Economics

Friedrich von Wieser (1851–1926) was not a member of the Schmoller group. On the contrary, he was a student of Carl Menger and one of Friedrich von Hayek's doctoral supervisors at the University of Vienna. Yet he, too, is interesting because of his direct application of economics to sociological processes. Taken together, these researchers further illustrate the achievement and further potential of a social science that brings together history, economics, and sociological understanding to human collective existence.[45]

Wieser's insight was that society is built upon an "acquisitive community" composed of the workforce and the firms and organizations that employ it. As competition promotes a continuous division and redivision of labour, including the deployment of new technologies, the same process also stimulates organizational changes that can threaten, reduce, or eliminate the individual freedoms of the members of the acquisitive community.

Wieser also echoed Thorstein Veblen's insight into the consumption behaviour — that is, conspicuous consumption of luxury goods — of the more affluent who buy goods because their value is in their exorbitant price tag as a display of wealth. Wieser observes that the price system can stratify, such that Veblen's conspicuous consumption can drive demand for luxuries and prestige goods, constituting another way in which social divisions are cemented by market operations.

Wieser argues that it is the duty of the government to prevent abuses that arise from new forms of authority and the actions of the economically powerful, just as government is also necessary to ensure that citizens have available the education and other services needed to make their way in the world. Unlike the German researchers in Berlin, Wieser, working in Vienna, called for placing social controls on market excess rather than paying new attention to designing more constructive transactional processes.

Often, Austrian economics is portrayed as focusing on individual choice, in opposition to the Berlin-based *Verein*. This is true. But it should be noted that it sees individual choices as a force that shapes society. Thus, it is also true to say that despite the famous *Methodenstreit,* or "methodological argument," between Menger and Schmoller, the German school and the Austrian school of economics arrived in the end in forms of social liberalism that agreed on a number of important points. Both conceived economics as a human science rather than a natural science. Both recognized a strong ethical dimension with respect to the protection of the vulnerable and the defence of individual freedom within society, and that this required a strong state.

In this discussion we have taken the long way around to conclude that, far from being on opposite sides, the researchers in Vienna and Berlin were running on parallel tracks toward the same destination: understanding how human society operates, understanding the forces shaping human actions, and discovering the determinants of the outcomes of those actions. However, they differed in their research perspective and in the role of theory — Vienna very much in the classical mode of general propositions, and Berlin concerned more with empirical problems and specific solutions to them, using statistical data as much as possible.

THE *METHODENSTREIT* BETWEEN VIENNA AND BERLIN

The *Verein für sozialforschung* produced over 130 major studies between 1872 and 1914, and was the flagship for an expansion of social science that put German universities in the front rank of a new discipline that had hitherto been led by France: sociology. This discipline was first developed by Comte, and its practicality first demonstrated by Émile Durkheim, a student of Comte who became the leading exponent of French sociological positivism in the nineteenth century. It was the wide-ranging graduate seminars of the German universities, which brought around the seminar table a multidisciplinary approach to problems of high social seriousness, that drew German sociology into its frontline position. Thus, Roscher's multivolume works on German industry became the gold standard for histories of economic development. Knies's introductory text on the historical method of economics and his work on the telegraph illustrated the importance of economics throughout the whole of social development. His emphasis on the need for a science of statistics, separate from the data collected, was an important contribution to the establishment of independent statistical agencies.[46] Wilhelm Dilthey's work on the distinction between social science and natural science underlined the importance of interpretation and the careful search for meaning in human action.[47] Ferdinand Tönnies's work on the transition from traditional communities to industrial societies became a classic of industrialization sociology.[48] These are just a few of the names that could be cited.

Ultimately, the work of those socioeconomic seminars underlined the fact that humans are social animals whose consciousness of their own mortality gives meaning to their lives and whose actions mark the evolution of human collectivities through the generations. These German thinkers took a view of economics as a human goal-directed activity organized around solving the problems of sustenance and settlement — including the beliefs and rituals that underpin social order and enable collective, as well as individual, action. As a general rule, if these thinkers recommended solutions, they were state-centred solutions; in effect, new legislation and/or government programs. This point of view was contrasted sharply with the project of classical economics and the research program around human decision and choice undertaken in Vienna under the direction of Carl Menger (1840–1921), which evolved into what is known as Austrian economics. The Berlin program built up a body of knowledge around specific situations and problems; the Vienna project aimed at discovering ahistorical, permanent relationships governing human goal-directed action. The Berlin project was humanistic; the Vienna project was scientistic in that it aimed at making its findings as close to natural science as possible. Its investigations sought solutions to problems that took the form of individual choices within a market framework. Menger did not use much mathematics in his economics, but he formulated his propositions so that they could easily be stated mathematically. Did that make his work as dogmatic and axiomatic as Ricardo's? Menger was inspired by the classical economists, but his work had none of the narrowness of today's neoliberalism, which denies the negative human impact that markets may impose.[49] Some discussion of Menger's economics is useful for an understanding of the development of liberal Europe's social consciousness before the First World War.

Austrian Economics and the Conflict with the German Historical School

So-called Austrian economics is based on a particular understanding of an economy, and in particular of the power of prices to constitute market structures. That view forms one side of the *Methodenstreit* in economics at the end of the nineteenth century.

Menger, its leading light, was a gifted, broadly cultured, extremely creative Central European intellectual. Perhaps coincidentally, Menger was in some aspects similar to Heidegger in that he was an Aristotelian and his economics was grounded in ontology — man's *Dasein* (a Heideggerian expression Menger never actually employed) and the choices that this imposed.

Menger was also a rational idealist in that he believed in a strict separation between pure theory and practical applications: political economic policy must solve the problems of political economy, not theory. Theory was based on observation and reflection in order to discover the essential relationships that explain economic phenomena.[50] His singular contribution was to show that subjective price formation constituted the basis of economic order in a free-market economy — a position that historical economists such as Roscher and Schmoller regarded as an excessively narrow and abstract view of empirical reality.

Menger's view was this: human beings are social animals whose needs exceed their means. They therefore need to trade, an activity facilitated by money but that can also be accomplished directly through barter. The aim of each is to satisfy the maximum need within the constraints of the individual's budget. They therefore value (subjectively) their prospective purchases on the basis of how much of their ability to satisfy other needs must be sacrificed for the needs they actually do satisfy. The less sacrifice, the better, of course, so a low price means that more additional needs can be satisfied. Each additional subjective need is weighed against the others; at the margin, therefore, each price is paid according to a strict hierarchy of needs as ranked by the individual.

Extending or multiplying the individual example to other like-minded individuals throughout society will also reverberate up the supply chain to production decisions as well as horizontally across the full spectrum of economic output. Over many repetitions, market exchange will lead to equilibrium of supply and demand at the margin: all the possible exchanges will have occurred. Menger (along with simultaneous and similar insight from Stanley Jevons and Léon Walras) thus resolved the relationship between subjective value and selling/buying price, thereby — he believed — putting an end to the strong claims for the existence of labour exploitation based on the labour theory of value espoused by Smith, Ricardo, and ultimately Marx.

Menger was just thirty-one when his book explaining his marginalist price theory appeared.[51] It launched his academic career at the University of

Vienna, where a generation later his work caught the enthusiastic attention of Friedrich von Hayek, the developer in chief (along with Ludwig von Mises) of the intellectual core of neoliberalism many years later, mainly in the United States.

The marginalist revolution dominated the classical economic thought of the 1870s and appeared to breathe new life into economic liberalism. (By that time it had nearly been given up for dead, slain by persistent criticism of the gap between results and performance, and by the example of Germany, for which the German historical school received a great deal of the credit.[52]) The economic historians eschewed theory for practical insight supported by statistics and an understanding of the evolution of economic problems. Today, they might share fellow feelings with the proponents of big data. Schmoller had little sympathy for the theorists' project of finding abstract expressions and unified theories of cause and effect. Instead, he urged that data be collected and scrutinized for the essential elements that pointed the way to the solution of the problem under attack.[53]

The twentieth-century Keynesian and post-Keynesian shift of economics away from its historical base in humanist reflection to its current obsession with mathematics and functional interdependence has meant that the question of the origin of value — to which Menger's solution (along with Locke's reflection on money) provides some clues — has been dropped. Nevertheless, if we follow Menger's lead and we accept that the value of a product is a function of subjective individual need, and its price a function of opportunity cost in relation to the total array of possible purchases, then we have in effect defined the outlines of a theory of individual material culture.

When Menger claims his theory of price is "constitutive," he is arguing that subjectively determined prices are sufficient to create the economic order of capitalism. In saying this, however, he is conscious of making an economic rather than a sociological point. He expressly states that he is discussing prices as signals about the economic use of economic goods under conditions of scarcity and rational decision-making in the presence of adequate information.[54] In reality, as became apparent some decades later, Vienna and Berlin were complements of one another.[55]

Today, Menger's German counterpart Schmoller is largely forgotten and, if remembered, he is recalled with disdain by mainstream economists.

Alfred Marshall, however, who was to early twentieth-century economics what Paul Samuelson became in the second half of the century, effusively recognized the contribution of the leaders of the German historical school. He wrote in the second edition of his *Principles of Economics*, in 1891:

> It would be difficult to overrate the value of the work which they and their fellow workers in other countries have done in tracing and explaining the history of economic habits and institutions. It is one of the great achievements of our age; and an important addition to the real wealth of the world. It has done more than almost anything else to broaden our ideas, to increase our knowledge of ourselves, and to help us to understand the central plan, as it were, of the Divine government of the world.[56]

Similarly, it is worth recalling that when Harvard professor of economic history W.J. Ashley[57] completed his *Surveys, Historic and Economic* in 1900, he dedicated it to Schmoller with the following brief letter, which forms a frontispiece to the main work.

> TO
>
> GUSTAV SCHMOLLER
> PROFESSOR OF POLITICAL ECONOMY
> IN THE UNIVERSITY OF BERLIN,
> HISTORIOGRAPHER OF BRANDENBURG
>
> DEAR PROFESSOR SCHMOLLER,
>
> To you I want to give myself the pleasure of dedicating this handful of essays and reviews. I have not always found it possible to agree with your opinions: with whose opinions would that be possible? And in reading some of your recent utterances about English policy in the eighteenth century, and indeed in times nearer our own, I must confess to a desire to criticise an epithet here and there. Yet

I feel that for a dozen years I have received more stimulus and encouragement from your writings than from those of any other; encouragement in the effort, which academic and popular opinion renders so difficult, to be an economist without ceasing to be an historian. You have shown me by your example how to carry the historical spirit into the work of the economist, and the economic interest into the work of the historian.

The rivalries of Germany, Great Britain, and the United States are likely to be altogether economic in the century which is about to open, and economists are in evident danger of becoming the mouthpieces of national sentiment. We may be confident, notwithstanding, that scholars who have caught your spirit will never altogether lose the scientific temper, and also never quite forget that even powerful nationalities are but steps towards something better for humanity in the future.

Believe me sincerely yours,
W.J. ASHLEY.[58]

Ashley's last paragraph reflects enlightened liberal optimism at the very beginnings of the last century. As we know, peaceful economic rivalry was the road not taken. By the end of the Second World War, Schmoller and the German historical view were no longer on the leading edge of economic or historical thinking. Hutchison's *Review of Economic Doctrines 1870–1929* treated Schmoller mainly as a participant in the *Methodenstreit* with Menger, commenting that the Austrian school represented the completion of the German historical school's program, with Menger at its head. Indeed, Menger merited a chapter to himself in Hutchison's review, as one of the three founders of the marginalist school of analysis and the centre of Austrian economic thinking up to and just after the First World War.

From our point of view of the importance of civil society, the nineteenth century ended by granting civil society a status as an entity upon whose wholeness and integrity the fate of nations rested. This interval may not have lasted, but the time of the *Methodenstreit* was a moment of increasing awareness of what must be done to alleviate poverty and integrate the working class into a capitalist and bourgeois liberal society.

As we know, the First World War and its aftermath — the mismade Versailles Treaty system, the creation of the Soviet Union and its export of revolution that continued to roil Europe well into the 1920s, and finally the forces leading to the Great Depression — all changed the global conversation. Liberalism wilted in Central and Eastern Europe as fascism and Nazism took the stage, and Soviet Communism consolidated itself in post-Revolutionary Russia. After more millions of dead and the civilizational legacies of the Holocaust and nuclear weapons, the post–Second World War period reset the European system back on the road to social democracy. Somewhat unexpectedly from the wreckage of the war — the second great European war for which Germany was to blame — arose, as a kind of memorial to the historical school, a non-Keynesian form of liberalism that actually does provide democratic governance, social and economic equilibrium, and a gradual improvement in living standards for all members of society. That is the German social market economy, with its origins in the concept of ordoliberalism. This economic form works along lines that Roscher, Schmoller, and Menger would surely have approved, as it contains a synthesis of their views.

GERMAN ORDOLIBERALISM

Throughout most of the 1950s and '60s, a form of the liberal state emerged that performed quite well until powerful interests subsumed it within a Keynesian government. This is the ordoliberal formula and the early realization of the social market economy of Germany under Ludwig Erhard, both as finance minister and chancellor.

This experience has not been particularly well reported in English-language sources, yet it showed that it was possible to generate a liberal economy that encouraged both the values of economic efficiency and the full development of the human being by state intervention to ensure a well-functioning social structure. Part of the ordoliberal formula — *Ordo,* the name of the journal in which these ideas were initially explored, underlines the concept of the economy as a deliberately constructed order — included strong support of small business and industrial crafts, through a different instance of the Hegelian *Rechtsstaat.*

In contrast to the Keynesian transfer state, Walter Eucken (1891–1950) and the Freiburg school (including Franz Böhm, Wilhelm Röpke, Alexander Rüstow, and Alfred Müller-Armack) developed and promoted a new concept of liberal government — at once capable of guaranteeing the preservation and strengthening of competition within a limited economic space; spreading around the productivity gains from competition by encouraging trade unions and professional associations, and other organizations; generating generally available welfare and solidarity programs to get unemployed people back to work quickly and under the care they need if unable to work; and providing worker retraining, excellent educational institutions, and other resources. At a theoretical level, they believed that they had a formula that would permit both a juridical and an economic constitution based on government as a reliable supplier of Pareto-efficient public goods.

These are *not* zero-sum redistribution programs: they are complementary parts of an economic landscape of growth, like highways and automobiles. Indeed, ordoliberalism offers a way liberalism can cope with social justice and yet remain liberal without burdening the national transfer system. Note that this system addresses every ill in the Weimar Republic: the Great Inflation of 1918–23, the cartelization and protectionism of the 1930s, the weakening and ultimate destruction of trade unions, and mass unemployment. Eucken pushes back against the List/Schmoller emphasis on associative relationships by emphasizing the fundamental importance in a liberal society of market competition. But he also advocates a reinforcement of the social measures necessary to enable competition to renew itself, rather than ending in higher market concentrations and more powerful networks able to crush or absorb rivals, starve the public sector, and eventually put an end to effective democracy.[59]

There are many strands to this story, and they include a synthesis of history and economics, as well as a solution to the dilemma of rules versus results.

Competition as a Socioeconomic Norm

The idea of competition as Eucken presents it is at once an ethical as well as a social and economic norm. Unusual in today's world of clear specializations in disciplines, Eucken the economist had a close relationship with Edmund Husserl, then the leading exponent of phenomenology, and a friend of his father, Rudolf Eucken, a professor of philosophy at Jena and the winner of the Nobel Prize for literature in 1908.

Another particularly important aspect of Eucken's ideas is his fusion of the claims of the German historical school of economics with its alleged opposite, Austrian free-market analysis, a conflict he called the Great Antinomy. Eucken argues that competitive markets are *not* natural but are artifacts of human design, made possible by particular laws and powers. (This point, incidentally, is also made in Lippmann's *The Good Society*, the pro–New Deal text discussed in Paris in 1938 as a possible starting point for a new European liberalism.[60] See the discussion of the Lippmann colloquium in the following chapter.) Eucken draws on German legal and cameralist ideas[61] to embed these functions in the national constitution. This is perhaps equivalent to adopting American economist James Buchanan's project for a second constitutional agreement to govern economic matters, but with an important twist. Whereas Buchanan rejected consequentialist arguments and based his constitutional concept on the Lockean model of a compact between individuals and the government for the preservation of liberty, and that alone, the economic constitution in ordoliberalism is embedded in the concept of a deliberate order designed to preserve and promote the public good in ways that are objectively verifiable.[62] Eucken embeds the necessary structure to accomplish his functionality in the state constitution, again in the spirit of a German *Rechtsstaat*. By so doing, Eucken ensures that the economy will be under state control at both micro and macro levels.[63]

Also of great importance for liberal political theory is that Eucken makes enhancing and preserving economic competition the central role of government, arguing that it is competition that safeguards individual liberty. Franklin D. Roosevelt, in his last State of the Union address,[64] similarly urged a guarantee against monopoly in his postwar welfare state plans. Both of these examples underline how twentieth-century liberalism was moving away from identifying government as the sole enemy of freedom and looking instead at markets as a potential source of economic oppression as well as individual freedom. Like Roosevelt, Eucken and, in particular, Böhm and Müller-Armack saw the defence of individual liberty in the constitution's protection against arbitrary government and promotion of human rights, but also sought to stabilize society and reduce the risk of political capture by powerful interests through the government's strengthening of economic competition.[65]

Taking on the Great Antinomy: History versus Economics

In reflecting on these points, one must not lose sight of the fact that Eucken's text[66] was first and foremost an economic treatise. It therefore reflected the technical economics of its time, some of which includes aspects of the monetary policy that Keynes called "the treasury view," and which Keynesian economics attacks vigorously. This includes a view of the money supply as exogenous to the economy and thus capable of regulating — indeed, stabilizing — price changes owing to inflation. It also includes a central bank independent and separate from government and thus exogenous to political decision-making.[67]

This concept of money as an economic regulator, which began making a comeback in the 1990s, still divides economists, as it seems to unite neoliberals. It is essentially the classical quantity theory of money restated, and as such is just as imprecise now as it was in the 1930s.[68] Ordoliberalism relies on the stabilizing force of its social safety nets to restrain deflationary reaction in a credit crisis and on central bank independence to intervene against inflation. Price stability, not full employment, is the policy objective under ordoliberalism, in the belief that with price stability competition will result in the optimal arrangement of productive resources. Free trade is advocated, but the clear assumption is that the dominant economic order is national, with trade competition as an additional economic regulator. It should be noted in this regard that Eucken's world included neither the modern multinational corporation nor the concept of a regional economy that transcends national borders. The translation of his monetary ideas to the regional level in the European Union, a monetary union (with a common currency) that has rejected a common debt, has proven to be a major policy error that has already — with Brexit — threatened the integrity of the European project.

The technical shortcomings should not obscure the philosophical strengths of Eucken's liberalism. Indeed, Eucken's concept of a liberalism that promotes economic competition as its central function, balanced by the social institutions necessary to keep competition from deteriorating into ruthlessness and destabilizing society, deserves further exploration.

As a principle, it underlines competition as a dominant social process that generates other processes, such as division of labour, technological innovation, scientific advancement, enhanced productivity, and cultural richness. But it also holds that competitive markets are neither natural nor spontaneous. They need careful legal structures, close attention, and diligent enforcement against anticompetitive practices and the emergence of large entities capable of abusive market power. There is an echo here of Saint-Simon's concept of administration of things rather than people. Above all, under competition, no industry would be "too big to fail."

Eucken's concept also encourages individual entrepreneurial plans over central planning and even large corporate planning, and enables the structures to form to finance middle class entrepreneurship based on highly skilled specialization, including the funding of applied research for commercializing scientific discovery. It thus generates a robust, highly differentiated, highly participative civil society for which liberal democracy is necessary for its proper functioning, and vice versa. This sense of civic participation deserves emphasis. Redistribution is minimized, but generally available government programs provide for loss, sickness, and other misfortunes, as well as providing the services that the population needs to participate fully, such as first-rate education. This approach, together with competition, helps minimize rent-seeking by special interests.

The emphasis on regulating and supporting competition also provides the common interest that retains the commitment of all political factions. In particular, public debt and taxation would have to be fair, owing to the need to maintain competition. Investment would more likely be allocated according to earned market success — profitability — in contrast to rising asset values that result from financial speculation.

Ordoliberalism is very German in its synthesis of both history and economics. In that sense, the independence of civil society from government, which is a starting point for the liberalism of the English-speaking countries, is less clear in the German tradition of a *Rechtsstaat*. Rather, a state constituted as a fair system of cooperation must operate economic and social policy as complementarities so that below average incomes are no barrier either to future advancement or to full participation as a citizen in the public life of the polity. The State is the tool by which civil society reconciles fairness and productivity.

The centrality of competition to ordoliberalism necessitates a review of economic competition and political action in the context of a *Rechtsstaat*. In particular, there is a need for a clear understanding of its forms, and there is the challenge of its careful regulation in a non-political context that emphasizes the general welfare. The perspective required goes somewhat beyond antitrust or competition policy, which aims solely at ensuring consumer protection from the abuse of market power. It is more like the search for a regulating structure in which an industry can be organized into competitive clusters with constituent partners such as financing banks, employees, and leading customers. The familiar industrial models are the industries located along the Rhine (Michel Albert's *modèle rhénan*) or the alliances of the Japanese corporate model.[69] The underlying unifying approach is the combination of history and sociology to provide context for an economic theory that is an alternative to the theory of traditional "context-free" liberal economics.[70]

Perhaps the greatest of ordoliberalism's political advantages is the legacy of Röpke's and Müller-Armack's commitment to a robust social justice that depends upon market and political freedom. Moreover, its Husserlian foundations — mutual respect between spenders and savers, borrowers and creditors as integral parts of a functioning system — enable the re-establishment of *logos*, reasoned political speech, as the basis for reconstruction of the liberal centre.[71] Certainly, the involvement of civil society in allocation decisions at numerous levels offers greater prospects for reintegrating public citizenship with private economic and industrial participants: credit unions, postal banks, and other methods for safeguarding community assets from speculation and offering wider access to necessary credit within a framework of safeguards for all parties.

As a general concept open to flexible adaptation to particular situations, ordoliberalism would appear to offer a cohesive and integral formula to all stakeholders in liberal societies — industry, labour, entrepreneurs, consumers, families, and investors — to better manage the dissipative and destructive internal power struggles that ultimately broke Keynesian strategies of industrial and regional (or sectional) fiscal transfers. It requires a consensus around competition, along with the recognition that competition can chip away at social coherence, as it did in Europe before 1848 and in the industrial laissez-faire period in the United States. In this way ordoliberalism detaches market competition from laissez-faire.[72] The regulation of competition and its enforcement is thus high on the political agenda of this system, along with maintaining the scope of democratic participation through unions, stakeholder representation on supervisory boards, and works councils in factories and large service industries. If the failure of the welfare state has any lessons to teach, one of them certainly must be that economic atomization gives rise to a politics that can become fatal to individual liberty.

ORDOLIBERALISM'S GLOBAL CHALLENGE

Perhaps the greatest problem ordoliberalism faces is how to operate in a globalizing world of increasingly porous borders. In a somewhat closed state in which producers and customers are drawn from the same population pool, wages can keep pace with productivity growth. But in a world trading state it becomes more difficult, if only because some multinational companies optimize their production across all markets so that productivity growth is captured and monetized at the centre. The multinational enterprise's business model does not always anticipate sharing those gains across all employees in all countries: minimum wages might not be raised in response to local legislation; production could simply shift to other countries.

All countries now face this problem. Ordoliberalism can only minimize the footprint of such companies in Germany, not the European Union as a whole. Thus, if liberal capitalism is to be "ordoliberalized" under free societies rather than state capitalist authoritarian states, additional legal measures will have to be developed; these are not yet found in international economic arrangements.

Again, where investment is concerned, ordoliberalism, a product of a particular set of historical circumstances, ideas, and beliefs, may not be generalizable across countries, especially in view of its rigid adherence to monetarism as a technique for achieving price stability. There is more than a soupçon of *ständisch* (class) stability as opposed to individual social progress in ordoliberalism. Indeed, the world has seen what hardship ordoliberalism can cause when imposed upon a country that does not accept its precepts, in the form of the Greek bailout crisis of this century.

There is an obvious reason why strict monetary principles are difficult to enforce from a central body of any kind, especially without broad social consent. Monetarism — especially control of bank credit through the reserve mechanism — is not effective if banks have access to additional sources of lending capital through securitization and derivative products. They will "financialize" themselves to circumvent regulations that confine them and count on the political support of those who benefit most from capitalizing their individual revenue flows: the top 20 percent.

Some noted ordoliberals have proposed a more flexible structure for Europe, in which countries and regions can form clubs that accept some rules but not others.[73] There may be scope for a workable arrangement based on ordoliberal principles. But ordoliberalism seems to demand a level of social consensus and cohesion difficult to imagine across the borders of states at different stages of economic development, or even with competing economic strategies and thus different ideas of competition.

ORDOLIBERALISM AS COMPREHENSIVE LIBERAL FRAMEWORK

Nevertheless, taken as a whole, the ordoliberal approach offers a comprehensive framework for modelling the management of the liberal state. In its original form, it offers few specific tools for balancing fiscal and monetary policy, or rebalancing these in a wider economic and political community. There is no getting around the fact that in any economic union, the weakest states must be compensated by the strongest: geography and history are usually more persistent influences than short-term restructuring strategies. Ultimately, a favourable entrepreneurial climate is a strong card in both the short and the long term, and ordoliberalism is well equipped to play it. Germany has developed a robust system of regional transfers internally, but these are based on shared historical and cultural characteristics — which help define the extent of the public goods available in different countries.[74] This is the arena of maximum friction between social contract liberal solutions and market-only solutions. Eucken offers a way to square the circle by using competition as one among many social processes, rather than relying on any one technique, such as fiscal transfers or deficit management, to address a variety of socioeconomic issues. The level of social learning and relearning involved is rather high for a greatly diversified multiparty polity.

Ordoliberalism is a system designed to reinforce its endogenous moral order of free individuals in a voluntary collective association for mutual prosperity, based on competition as a set of experiments. It is a social learning experience aiming for superior solutions, whose outputs are public goods as well as private goods. In the case of Germany, this means that ordoliberalism offers an increasingly high-performance economic base developing alongside a deepening and expanding national culture.

In anticipation of the discussion of postmodernism in the next chapter, one might remark that Freiburg school ordoliberalism is an interesting and encouraging contrast to the twentieth-century experience of relatively untrammelled state power supporting the mass pursuit of indefinable and unlimited consumer gratification — a result that sounds like economics, but is very far from the discipline's roots in reasonable household management. Ordoliberalism is a constitutionalization of the economy so that it runs according to the social norms of the state — the civil society consensus. It suited well the psychology of Germany as it recovered from wartime devastation and needed to reconstruct a moral framework and a sense of national community in which public confidence could be justified by performance. Unfortunately, perhaps, it seems in retrospect a period piece, well suited for an industrial economy, but rather heavy for the "lightness of being" sought by the post–Cold War West and its popular quest for authenticity. Yet its emphasis on individual freedom is consistent not only with liberalism but also with Heidegger's view of mankind's *Dasein* or ontological condition.

Ordoliberalism has suffered an unwarranted obscurity perhaps because it moved forward by minimizing mathematization and disparaging axiomatic proofs of the kind preferred by economists in the English-speaking countries.[75] More encouraging, however, is that theories of economic development have begun to follow similar lines to those of the Freiburg school, and they do so with an exposition that addresses itself to mathematically inclined economists.[76]

CHAPTER 3
The Rise and Fall
of the Welfare State

THE WELFARE STATE

FROM THE END OF the Second World War to the end of the 1970s, Western governments operated as welfare states. These states offered another version of the German *Rechtsstaat*, one more easily conformable to Anglo-Saxon models of government. They were intended to be the incarnation of the Four Freedoms upon which were based the Allied war aims and for which people mobilized to fight: freedom from fear, from hunger, of religion, and from want. The success was remarkable, compared to the problems of the state under classical liberalism: persistent full employment and financial stability; stunning expansion of popular education, embracing primary to post-secondary; improvements in public health, including state-sponsored medical insurance, generally for the entire population; growing economic prosperity — until, sometime around the mid-1970s, the system stopped behaving as it had and instead stagnated, and puzzlingly generated inflation rather than growth. What happened?

As everyone knows, there is a plethora of explanations, almost all of them economic, that overlook any cultural or sociological changes that may have had a bearing on the issue. One of the arguments of this book is that cultural accommodation to material and philosophical changes can itself dramatically affect the success or failure of adaptation to industrialization. As we have seen in the case of England's early industrialization, even though utilitarianism was difficult to accept culturally, it proved difficult to do without once the idea had been widely adopted. Accordingly, the failure to do more for the working classes between, say, 1850 and 1870 can be traced to beliefs that (1) the adjustments already in place were sufficient and the destitute were protected to the extent affordable by the state, and (2) Malthus was right to have put the finger on population growth rather than policy as the main cause of widespread squalor and destitution. Ultimately, as we saw in Thomas Carlyle and George Eliot, middle class fear of cultural dilution was an important barrier to greater social inclusiveness. Then, by the 1880s, the middle class was sufficiently confident and the German example sufficiently encouraging that more progress could be made.

As for Germany, as we also saw, the advancement in economic and social thinking, developed in part from a desire to avoid the social costs of laissez-faire, led to a deeper understanding of the relationship between society, those who composed it, and the importance of productivity and the role of law in solving the so-called distribution problem. Rethinking the national economy in a national socioeconomic strategy enabled Germany to move from laissez-faire liberalism to a national industrial strategy that included working class accommodation.

The welfare state — a dramatic extension of the role of the state in meeting the needs of civil society — began in the United States with the New Deal following the October 1929 stock market crash, and the election of the Democratic Party's candidate Franklin D. Roosevelt. It would be consistent — and, I suggest, illuminating — to back up a bit to examine the rise of a privileged oligarchy in the post–Civil War United States and the roots of the Progressive movement that mobilized American reforms after 1880, and then to discuss the intellectual changes between the wars that challenged some of the country's optimism.

I will then look at the thinking behind the welfare state and the challenges it faced from some of the ideas that arose in the interwar years, and then I will examine the political pathologies it developed in the course of its thirty-year dominance.

When we pull these strands together, we will find the following: (1) the fluidity of civil society and its decline from a collective agreement on a society of liberty and justice to a battleground of self-seeking interests, (2) impatience with structure and a desire that society be a theatre of individual authenticity, (3) a gradual reassertion of the control of politics by insiders, and (4) a major failure in conception that ensured the Keynesian formula would destabilize. I will make little to no mention of the Cold War or the existence of the USSR. That is because I believe the forces that undermined and destroyed the welfare state were almost entirely endogenous, as intrinsic to liberalism as the tension between the collectivity and the individual.

WESTERN CULTURAL TRANSFORMATIONS AT THE END OF THE NINETEENTH CENTURY

Cultural Change in the West: "Management" as a Progressive Solution

The transformation of Germany from the relatively loose, free-market North German Confederation to the centralized and state socialist German Empire also marked a sea change in the rest of Europe, and by extension the rest of the West as well. Not only was Germany preoccupied with finding a new political equilibrium, which eluded it until the years after Bismarck's retirement in 1890, but as a society it was also experiencing a leap forward from what was in many cases persistent feudalism to a modern, scientific system, organized not around obligation, but rather around money and finance. For many this was a jarring change. Not only do the financial needs of an industrial economy significantly exceed the capacity of private savings, but the complexity of contracts also exceeds the legal competence of a single practitioner. Thus, the first years of empire saw a dramatic expansion of private banks, most of which, after a series of banking crises, were absorbed by the German central bank, the Reichsbank. Indeed, the expansion of banking is a characteristic of late nineteenth-century finance, and its consolidation a prelude to the large capital exports that characterized the new Imperial Age and the late nineteenth-century scramble for control of overseas sources of raw materials.[1]

The sociological features of these changes caught the attention of German social thinkers, whose work contributed mightily to the way we think of modernism today. Schopenhauer, Nietzsche, and, later, Freud sounded warnings of modernism's culturally cataclysmic effects. Moisey Ostrogorsky and Robert Michels provided skeptical portraits of political parties.[2] Social researchers from Schmoller's *Verein,* among others, such as Tönnies, Dilthey, Simmel, and Weber offered the new modernism only ambivalent approval — an elaboration on the positions of Saint-Simon, the later Comte, and Mill. The new Germany had perhaps solved the problem of reconciling economic efficiency with social justice, and its model, to be sure, stimulated the integration of the working classes elsewhere into the normal party political process, especially in England and North America. But the new, money-based, utilitarian society was a far cry from Kant's moral structure based on the imperatives of reason, and Adam Smith's natural liberty constructed around human sympathy.

Instead of the communitarian solidarity of shared values and traditions characteristic of preindustrial generations, the new society ran on calculations of price and personal advantage, a "disenchanted" world of positive science applied to machines of mass production, mass labour, and economies of scale. Just as English society's first reaction to utilitarian government was a flight to the romantic histories of Carlyle and the novels of Scott, so Germany took refuge in the operatic sagas and thunderous musical themes of Wagner.[3]

Ultimately, the German example of state socialism inspired the contemporary advocates of the welfare state in the West. The Fabians took their place in the political arena. At the same time as the so-called British Hegelians, philosophical idealists such as Edward Caird, David Ritchie, and T.H. Green, they created an enriched version of liberalism in which positive freedom supported by the state would mitigate the material differences that underlay social divisions so as to promote democracy and strengthen market stability. To be sure, this Hegelianization of liberalism was contested by political philosophers such as J.T. Hobhouse and J.A. Hobson. But its spirit infused a transformation to New Liberalism, moving from a philosophy of lending a helping hand to a philosophy of gradually constructing a new state that championed the collective interest over individual desire.[4]

Writing in 1910 in the *Cambridge Modern History* series begun by Lord Acton, the distinguished labour historian Sidney Webb explained how European minds gradually changed over the course of the nineteenth century. Technology by itself did not improve working conditions of labour, he noted. Rather, as noted earlier, it was

> a certain subtle revolution in the ideas of men; a certain advance in our acquaintance with those social laws which, to use Montesquieu's pregnant phrase, "are the necessary relations derived from the nature of things"; and, therewith, a certain increase of power to influence social phenomena. This power to influence social phenomena has taken shape in specific social movements associated with such appellations as municipal action and cooperation, factory legislation and trade unionism, sanitation and education, the Poor Law and the collective provision for orphans, the sick, and the aged, and all that vaguely defined social force commonly designated socialism.[5]

The American view was different: one of exciting change rather than comfortable continuity. President Wilson described the New Liberalism as follows in his book *The New Freedom,* published in 1913:

> We are in the presence of a new organization of society. Our life has broken away from the past. The life of America is not the life that it was twenty years ago; it is not the life that it was ten years ago. We have changed our economic conditions, absolutely, from top to bottom; and, with our economic society, the organization of our life.... We have come upon a very different age from any that preceded us. We have come upon an age when we do not do business in the way in which we used to do business — when we do not carry on any of the operations of manufacture, sale, transportation,

or communication as men used to carry them on. There is a sense in which in our day the individual has been submerged.[6]

Wilson's "new freedom" was an attempt to find political consensus in a rapidly changing United States. By the 1880s, liberalism in the United States had begun to spin off a new, Progressive version. Stimulated by the ideas of Herbert Croly, whose *The Promise of American Life* became a Progressive manifesto, Progressives advocated a larger, more interventionist, and more expert federal government to take on the trusts and political machines.

American Progressivism

It was "that damned cowboy" Theodore Roosevelt who first seized upon these ideas after becoming the youngest president in U.S. history following the assassination of William McKinley in 1901. His Square Deal was the first step in an assault by the executive branch on the strongholds of local power in Congress that lasted through the Woodrow Wilson presidency. Beneath the political history lies a powerful and unique intellectual current that strongly marked American liberalism until the 1980s.

So who was this Herbert Croly, an almost forgotten writer and founding editor of the *New Republic,* the man behind this so-called Progressivism?

Croly's intellectual biography passed from a rejection of his father's Comtean positivism in favour of the philosophy he encountered at Harvard: Josiah Royce's version of Hegelian idealism, which he seems to have maintained in tension with William James's pragmatism. The fullest expression of Croly's political ideas evolved into an advocacy of the Progressives' version of industrial democracy.[7]

Croly's intellectual path was not unusual for Progressives who sought a middle way between classical liberalism, by this time clearly passé, and the rising appeal of Marx-inspired socialism. His influential book, *The Promise of American Life,*[8] is a plain-language, comprehensive analysis of how a laissez-faire society with a democratic constitution evolved so that its biggest, most advanced enterprises and those who run them came to control nearly every level of democratic political institutions. If ever there was an accessible argument against the liberal myth of a benign social order of Big Men — as we find in Ayn Rand, for example — Croly's book offers it.

His argument goes like this: Typical Americans, including recent immigrants, are essentially optimistic. They understand very well the promise and capacity of the United States to offer its citizens a prosperous life while accomplishing great things for the world. In general, they are preoccupied with the challenges of raising a family and working for or running a business. The gradual changes that occurred in American life after 1870 were largely unanticipated. The determining event was the building of the intercontinental railroads. That brought all Americans much closer together economically as well as geographically. Thereafter it became much easier and more economical to move product all over the country and to trade with the rest of the world.

However, these changes also changed the demands for labour. Once the rail lines were built, there were far fewer opportunities for unskilled men. Even farming changed as the scope and scale of competition expanded. Finding employment required skills. After 1870, the expert became a familiar class of employee in American industry.

> The dominant note … of the pioneer period was unformed national consistency, reached by means of a national community of feeling and a general similarity of occupation and well-being. On the other hand, the dominant note … from 1870 to the present day has been the gradual disintegration of this early national consistency, brought about by economic forces making for specialization and organization in all practical affairs, for social classification, and finally for greater individual distinction. Moreover the tendency towards specialization first began to undermine the very corner-stone of the pioneer democratic edifice.[9]

Instead of the identity of private and common interest in which the politician and the pioneer shared the same practical knowledge and view of the world, specialization began to drive "the man of industry, the politician and the lawyer off on separate tacks." Business demanded all a person's time and energy; successful lawyers after the U.S. Civil War found lucrative practice in aiding industry to develop, leaving public affairs largely to the unsuccessful lawyers. Politics also became a specialized activity that "made very exacting demands upon a man's time and upon his conscience.... Along with the leadership of statesmen and generals, the American people began to recognize that of financiers, 'captains of industry,' corporation lawyers, political and labor 'bosses,' and these gentlemen assumed extremely important parts in the direction of American affairs."[10]

A number of contemporary observers made similar observations. One of these was Sir James Bryce, whose *The American Commonwealth*, a two-volume study of American government in the 1880s, is a kind of complement and update to Tocqueville's dissection of America in the 1840s.[11] Bryce devotes over half of part 3 to a discussion of the political machine and how it works, and the reasons for its existence. As did Croly, Bryce saw politics at virtually every level as under the thumb of unelected party bosses who controlled the primary election process for candidates in gerrymandered districts, where a primary win was a guarantee of office. Behind the bosses were the interests of big money, the largest, most prosperous companies in the country, including the railroads, whose networks linked every big city and every tiny town and hamlet — atop of which sat the money trust.[12]

One of the most distinguished thinkers who explored the same themes was Walter Lippmann. Croly and Lippmann met in the editorial rooms of the *New Republic* magazine, which provided a regular outlet for progressive views. Lippmann's book *Drift and Mastery* came out in 1914. Lippmann, widely considered the brightest Harvard graduate of his class, whose intellect led him to friendships with William James, Karl Jaspers, George Santayana, and British socialist intellectual Graham Wallas, also became perhaps the most authoritative columnist of his generation. At this time of his life, Lippmann was a democratic socialist, advocating industrial democracy in which trade unions and management collectively decided on the work and working conditions; he was skeptical of state socialism on the German model, which he saw as a precursor of Belloc's "servile state."[13]

Lippmann hoped instead for an energetic central government that used its power to tackle specific social as well as economic problems — in fact, a New Deal on the scale of Franklin D. Roosevelt in the wake of the Great Depression two decades later. As we discuss later on in this chapter, this seemed to him the direction liberalism needed to go in if it was to remain relevant to the contemporary world. Wilson's New Liberalism seemed to Lippmann merely a new gloss on an old story. Wilson, he believed, was torn by an internal contradiction. "He knows there is a new world demanding new methods, but he dreams of an older world" — the world of small businesses and small farms. Lippmann was thinking of the world of giant corporations and scientific management. "Nowhere in his speeches will you find any sense that it may be possible to organize the fundamental industries on some deliberate plan for national service."[14] A generation later, this indeed became a major theme in writings on the new industrial state that emerged in the United States by the early 1960s. Lippmann's position was restated by J.K. Galbraith at that time, during the heyday of the welfare state.[15]

It is noteworthy, and in retrospect only too obvious, that this kind of progressivism was in effect a democratic view of Saint-Simon's agenda of political control of industrialization. Underpinning it, therefore, was a strong reliance on positive science in the service of mankind — norms rooted in evidential proof and demonstrable material gains, which assumed a utilitarian scale of values that were generally shared by the population at large. If the population was divided, it was divided by economic position — rich versus poor — more than any other consideration.

A uniquely American quality in this version of state-led liberalism is the combination of idealism, which emphasizes human consciousness as the key to political progress, and the pragmatism of William James, which opened a door to the interpretation of experience as a tool for advancing toward one's life goals. The Jamesian elements of this line of thinking had radical implications. They potentially swept away all established ideas, such as the ideas underlying the U.S. constitution, and permitted the reconceptualization of the world according to the personal use value of ideas. Ultimately, practice, not authority, determines which interpretations turn out to be beneficial. Ultimately, only democracy combines the rigorous critique of ideas and projects that enable society to advance along lines akin to those of science — but of course with no guarantee that it actually will.[16]

THE WORLD WARS AND THEIR AFTERMATH: TIME RUNS OUT ON THE ENLIGHTENMENT

In retrospect, the First World War was a first step in the "decentring" of Europe as the global intellectual and economic hub, confidently radiating its cultural brilliance to the rest of the world. Not that Europe would go quietly. Instead, much of it turned from liberal humanism to extreme forms of political expression that placed supreme value on power, cruelty, and expansionism. From Bolshevism to fascism, the violence preached and practised re-enacted and reconfigured the terms of conflict as if struggling to grasp the enormity of Europe's spiritual and physical agony amidst the ruins of the war.

By 1919, when an unstable and unworkable peace had finally been concluded, it was clear at least to Europe's intelligentsia that every underpinning of the European bourgeois liberal world had failed. For most countries apart from the Soviet Union and, soon, fascist Italy, the only course that could be agreed upon was a return to "normalcy," which meant a return to the now exploded faith in the myths of prewar liberalism, including laissez-faire. Now, however, it was laissez-faire with a more human face, in the form of an augmented supply of public services, including some care for the wounded survivors.

In the final analysis, the Treaty of Versailles satisfied practically nobody. Distinguished French commentators claimed that its terms would enable Germany to recover faster than France;[17] Keynes famously predicted the collapse of the reparations–war debt regime.[18] The United States, after rejecting membership in the League of Nations, nevertheless insisted that its allies Britain and France repay the financial obligations they incurred during the war.

NEW PHILOSOPHIES

The realm of philosophical ideas was not unaffected by these same forces. As the 1920s drew to a close, it seemed clear that time had run out on the Enlightenment world view. The attempts to prolong it at the end of the nineteenth century, by such means as the shift to neo-Kantianism and the reanimation of the Hegelian belief in History, especially the connection between

137

History and Absolute Reason, had reached the end of the road. American pragmatism was standing by to replace Europe's grand narratives.[19] The early years of the twentieth century were also the sunset for many of the intellectual certainties of the nineteenth. Einstein's theory of relativity extended Newtonian physics; and Russell and Whitehead's attempt in the years before the war, and in a second edition of their treatise in 1927, to justify mathematics through a series of logical propositions ran headlong into Gödel's incompleteness theorem in 1931. That same year the Great Depression hit the newly created countries of Central Europe hard, with the collapse of Austria's Credit-Anstalt.

A few years later, Edmund Husserl (1859–1938), one of Europe's leading philosophers and the founder of phenomenology,[20] declared what others had been thinking for some time: the modern idea of a universal philosophy constructed upon a scientific base that culminated in a comprehensive metaphysics of reason had been fractured by positivism and the multiplication of scientific specialties. A new, comprehensive methodology was required to bring together the sciences and provide guidance on the great questions facing mankind.[21] For Husserl, phenomenology was the answer to that challenge. Although it was not often remarked, Gödel's theorem, the Great Depression, and Husserl's diagnosis left very little if anything intact of the Cartesian framework that underpinned the economics of the time. It, too, remained to be reinvented, as it was to an extent, by Keynes.

PHILOSOPHICAL ENCOUNTERS: POSTMODERNISM AND LIBERALISM BETWEEN THE WARS

Two separate meetings of very different intellectuals during the period between the wars marked the establishment of the initial conditions for what later became the construction and subsequent decline of the post–Second World War welfare state — although that was not apparent to the participants. The first of these took place at Davos in 1929, between a prominent neo-Kantian philosopher from the University of Hamburg, Ernst Cassirer, and a younger philosopher from Marburg University, Martin Heidegger, seen by many as a rising philosophical star who could respond to the challenges facing German philosophy. Heidegger, like Husserl, had studied with Franz Brentano. He later became an assistant and friend of Husserl, to whom he dedicated his important new book, *Being and Time*; it was received as a revolutionary attack on the foundations of modern idealism. Heidegger at this point was gaining increasing recognition, and the work was published in 1927 simultaneously as a book and in the *Jahrbuch für Phänomenologie und phänomenologische Forschung* (Yearbook for phenomenology and phenomenological research), a journal edited by Husserl.

The second meeting took place in Paris, in the summer of 1938, the so-called Lippmann colloquium. At this meeting, organized around the French translation of Lippmann's new book, *The Good Society*, were gathered many of the most important liberal thinkers and political leaders still left in Europe, including the Austrians Friedrich von Hayek and Ludwig von Mises. Absent, because he was unable to obtain an exit visa from Germany, was Walter Eucken, who, as discussed in the previous chapter, later became known as a major theorist of the postwar German social economy.

The Davos meeting, which occurred in the midst of the intellectual turbulence of the Weimar Republic, marked the decisive collapse of representational philosophy as developed since Plato, and in particular the annihilation of modern philosophy rooted in Descartes, Hume, and Kant. Modern philosophy's champion, Ernst Cassirer, pursued a unified version of empirical science allied with reflection. Heidegger proposed a different approach to understanding the modern world — a return to the ancient Greek philosophy of Being that was prior to a metaphysics rooted in consciousness (and thus was also a pre-political condition, like Hobbes's view of man in a state of nature).

It will be recalled that Kant's concept of the human mind was the Enlightenment basis for the possibility of social organization based on collective freedom. It intended to supersede contentious and unprovable metaphysical propositions, such as religious dogmas. Kant's philosophy allowed that such propositions could be rational and deeply felt. But they could never be confirmed by experience, as were the propositions of natural science. Values, in other words, remained discussable if unprovable, whereas scientific propositions could be proven by experiment. Freedom, Kant argued, arose in this space: mankind could imagine freedom, even if it did not exist in nature. Reason could reveal to mankind how freedom could be lived — namely, the moral law in which all valid propositions could be universalized (a rule for one only if it could apply to all). Elsewhere he argued that representative government was a rational way to select those who would determine the laws. Even after the First World War, Kant's ideas were the basis of whatever remained of European liberalism.

HEIDEGGER AND CASSIRER AT DAVOS (1929)

At Davos, Heidegger attacked the duality that lay behind Kant's liberal freedom. Kant pictured humanity as an association of semi-sociable individual beings whose reason and imagination guaranteed individual freedom within a universal moral structure based upon mankind's growing powers of understanding. To Heidegger, that picture made no sense: mankind exists and must itself discover the meaning of its own existence. Cassirer, drawing on the heritage of Kantian critique, claimed on the contrary that learning to transcend our limits and capacities to understand marks the only pathway to human emancipation.[22]

That was all conceit, countered Heidegger. Prior to any of that is the absolute fact of existence, or as he sometimes defined it, *Dasein,* specific "being-there," in a place, in a moment. Mankind is a being that can contemplate its own Being, but for whom thinking begins and ends with the facticity of its own *Dasein* — that is, the specifics of its own finite existence. Heidegger argued that philosophy since Plato (the philosophy of "objectivism," of the "God's eye view"[23]) was little more than academic rule-making to enhance the power of rules — grammar — over experience. Philosophy sought to make thinking a tool, to reduce thinking to technique and obscure real thinking, as expressed in language about existence. The basis of all thought for Heidegger was of necessity man's finite existence.

Later, Jean-Paul Sartre, a student of Heidegger before the war, would claim (in a 1946 essay) that existentialism was a humanism: that humans, as lonely and rather bewildered individuals thrown into an indifferent world in which they must make their way based on their own perceptions, without reliable guides from human nature, can define themselves only through action and authentic engagement. Heidegger shot down Sartre, as well, in his *Letter on Humanism* (originally published in 1947), which underlined his rejection of idealist notions.[24]

Surrendering the problem of existence to humanism, Heidegger argues, meant surrendering the power of authentic language to grammarians, to the thirst for power to decide truth and error on the basis of cate-chism and grammar, to "objectivism." Sartre later renounced his work *Existentialism Is a Humanism*,[25] moving leftward to embrace Marxism.

Ernst Cassirer, Heidegger's opposing debater at Davos, was a very different kind of philosopher from Heidegger. His research opened up a pathway in what was called in those days "philosophical anthropology," the analysis of mankind's use of symbols of all kinds to make sense of the world — an extension and development of Kant's concept of the human mind. From this research, Cassirer reached the disturbing conclusion that reason does not replace myth; it encourages it as an alternative. Thus the more science advances, the more anti-science mythology will emerge.

A further factor intensifying this pattern is the desacralization of the world, or what sociologist Max Weber called the "dis-enchantment" of the world, under the pressures of positivism and the growth of the natural sciences. As established religions, which moderate the gap between myth and science, decline, so the fundamentalist myths intensify their hold. Thus, for Cassirer, the Kantian model is at risk not from its conception of freedom, but from its conception of reason and imagination as allies, when in fact they are becoming enemies.[26]

Heidegger's philosophy blocked any attempt to take this debate very far. But the debate is worth taking seriously for an understanding of what happened later in Germany, as a kind of tribal or *völkisch* imagination drove out Enlightenment ideals and created a climate in which National Socialism could flourish unchecked. Kant's concept of freedom counted on imagination to conceive that which did not exist in nature, and on reason as the mode of thinking to build the institutions that enable it. Only Reason, he argued, could have the logical force necessary to meet the criteria of universal applicability that the categorical imperative required. But if imagination instead starts with an individual existence that links only through a vague notion of care and the sharing of common tools to "the other" and wraps all that in self-affirming myth, then what emerges is more likely to be tribal than universal — or in the context of German politics in the early twentieth century, *völkisch* — in which people and nations vie with each other for supremacy.[27]

Heidegger's arguments at Davos emphasize his opposition to Kantian theory, but also his rejection of Comte's concepts of intellectual progress toward positivism and of positivism itself. As mentioned, his own contribution to the world of ideas was elaborated shortly before the Davos debates in the work for which he is still best known, *Being and Time*, considered now as a work of epochal philosophical importance.

Being and Time

There are a number of ways of reading Heidegger's book. If read as a scientific report on the problem of existence as an objective phenomenon, *Being and Time* may seem as much an act of destructive creation as of creative destruction. This is especially true if one learns that after Heidegger, prewar Western culture lay in ruins — some fifteen years before the Holocaust made the term "Western civilization" an oxymoron. Regarded by an "objective" outside observer, Heidegger's account of Being is much less than what it used to be — that is to say, splendid, sensual, and glorious ("What a piece of work is Man!" leavened with "Man is the measure of all things"). Instead, it seems drab, ambitionless, and uninspiring.

In this kind of reading, Heidegger's picture of human existence is ontologically the reverse of Kant's. Kant was awed by Newton. Kant's human beings are intelligent enough that their mind can contain the secrets of the universe; they are imaginative enough to summon inspiring and beautiful works of art from the *noumenal* world, and thus transform thoughts into the elements of a living culture. Kant's human beings are also responsible social creatures who, while seeing to their own interests, are able to see clearly their integral role in supporting the moral growth of the community.

For this kind of reader, Heidegger's picture of humanity is much less encouraging. Heidegger's human being is simply thrown into existence. Each of us arrives into a world of other similarly "thrown" people, other objects, and other identifiable substances. There is no loving family nor associations in Heidegger's picture: only possibilities based on one's own capacities and the relationships one forms.[28] For the Jacobean poet John Donne, "no man is an island." For Heidegger, every man is a castaway. Ultimately, every person's choice is to lead an authentic life on his or her own terms, or an inauthentic one as the instrument of others' goals and desires.

This is the kind of reading that an "objective" liberal or Kantian scientific approach provides. Yet in all probability this is not the reading Heidegger intended for his work. There is an alternative reading.

If one takes a different approach and reads the work in the spirit of an unfolding phenomenological investigation in which the structure and properties of Being slowly reveal themselves to an inquiring mind, then the work is a masterpiece. In the light of this reading, Heidegger corrects the philosophical errors of centuries and takes the reader into new conceptual territory — a first-person description of existence out of which the meaning of that existence gradually discloses itself. It is thus an example of the investigator and the investigated together pursuing a truthful understanding, a growing understanding of a situation shared by every living organism — Being and its finality.

The key to this approach is an understanding of the individual human's condition as a Being within a context, not only *Sein* but *Dasein* (*Da-Sein*),[29] "being-there" and able to reflect on his or her situation. Heidegger's treatment of Being is thus a treatment of the individual's existential condition as a Being capable of reflecting on that condition. Heidegger's phenomenological method is to lay bare the ground upon which human beings encounter their own being and construct its meaning, upon which they build out a wider meaning for their existence. In so doing, Heidegger reverses the direction of philosophy since Plato in which Reason seeks to describe a universal condition from on high. He also collapses Kant's divide between metaphysics and science by placing his starting point for consciousness at the *Dasein* of the individual human being rather than in abstract categories and phenomena. *Dasein* is the core of human existential consciousness. It is mankind's primordial approach to reflection upon life, and it is marked by the inevitable terminality of human life. Camus reacted to Heidegger's discussion of human finality:

> Heidegger coolly considers the human condition and announces that our existence is humiliated. He writes without trembling and in the most abstract language imaginable "that the finite and limited character of human existence is more primordial than man himself." ... For

him it is no longer necessary to doze, indeed he must remain wakeful into the very consummation. He persists in this absurd world; he stresses its perishability. He gropes his way among the ruins.[30]

In a subsequent work,[31] Heidegger elaborated on his arguments at Davos, attempting to reset Kant's *Critique of Pure Reason* from his existential and hermeneutic perspective of *Dasein*. Effectively, Heidegger's demolition of the representative structure of Western philosophy overlapped surprisingly well with the similar demolition job emanating from the United States as modern pragmatism, in the work of William James and John Dewey. Indeed, Dewey's *Reconstruction in Philosophy* predated *Being and Time* by seven years.[32] The points of alignment are striking. Where Dewey stressed empiricism, Heidegger emphasized "facticity." Where Dewey advocated that science orient itself to stewardship rather than mastery, Heidegger warned of technology's power to impose on human *Dasein*. Where Heidegger underlined plurality and multiplicity or variety in *Dasein*, Dewey advocated rejection of monism. Where Heidegger denied "truth" in favour of "truths," Dewey advocated "truth" as an adverb, rather than a thing.

Heidegger loved the poetry of Hölderlin and the *gemütlichkeit* of small German villages. He favoured the arts over philosophy as a fuller, more complete human response to the mystery of existence. The reception of his arguments has been coloured by the fact that, like many young Germans between the wars, he joined the Nazi Party and as a party member became rector of Freiburg University. (However, he resigned his membership before the war.[33]) His take on history was that of a Greek tragedian — one cannot know what one's life means until it is completed. He was a man of his time and place, grappling with issues as he encountered them. He was no liberal and no particular friend of the Western project of modernity. His philosophy stands as a warning to liberalism about the dangers of distortions and traps hidden in self-serving rules and principles, and in particular, their capacity to obscure fundamental realities that define the human condition.

The Front Generation

Post–First World War Germany was ideal terrain for the reception of messages about the bleakness of the human condition. The recent experiences of the horrors of trench warfare at the front and of defeat dissolved the credibility of a Kantian moral structure for perhaps most of the German "front generation" and others as well. Dismay at the outcome of the Versailles Conference in which Germany was charged as the sole guilty party responsible for the war also tainted the idealism behind Woodrow Wilson's New Liberalism. The pessimistic turn in Germany was underlined by the immense popular success of Oswald Spengler's *Decline of the West.* Its historical and anthropological sections have been condemned as pretentious nonsense and "refuted" many times over since its publication in 1918 and 1922. Yet many of its arguments would be familiar to contemporary readers of today's "decline-ist" literature. The chapters on politics exemplify many reasons for its popular uptake: its breezy dismissal of political theory and of any notion that "real" politics is about improving the human condition; its reduction of interests to money and power; its "Wake up, little man!" tone; and its warning that the rule of money produces Caesarism, which rides in on democracy and completes itself in tyranny. Spengler's politics of realism ultimately rides into a dead zone within which civilization becomes irrelevant. He did not say that the name of that zone was the Weimar Republic. But many perhaps already believed it.

In contrast to this mood of despair, the Bolshevik overthrow of the Tsar and the spread of communism westward in a series of Red revolutions, including the failed Spartacist revolt in Germany, offered hope to those who adopted a Marxist frame of reference, in particular its left-wing Hegelian idealism. An important work published at this time, George Lukacs's *History and Class Consciousness* — which appeared in 1923, just a few years before Heidegger's book was published — argued for the rise of the working class and joined Spengler in the view that history was hammering nails into the coffin of the bourgeois era. To any bourgeois readers, Lukacs's arguments would appear to confirm those of Spengler.

Heidegger's ontological analysis of the human condition — that is, mankind's everyday or "ontic" world — was not friendly to Marxism.

For Marxists, purposeful action among a self-conscious and energized working class can achieve both political and moral victories, advancing the "history of reason" and social justice. For Heidegger, existence occurs in a resistant environment in which the availability of tools suggests that there may be or may have been other toolmakers, and that they may be able to use the objects that Heidegger's individual human can make for them by using the tools. By so doing, individuals form connections with other individuals, based on care or solicitude. When death comes, it is the one inalienable property, the ultimate individual ownership: one's own death is unique to each of us. There is little prospect of history-changing collective action, no public purpose to be pursued. As noted earlier, existence is a "pre-political" condition.

Heidegger's unusual use of language to make his arguments is singular: by emphasizing the fluid and malleable properties of modern German, he seeks to communicate the figurative properties of ancient Greek, finding words that conceal and reveal simultaneously. Like Ezra Pound's attempts to make English convey the lyricism of Provençal, or Milton's forcing English to adopt the gravitas of Latin, Heidegger seeks to revive with German the texture of ancient Greek as well as the concepts of the ancients around the ideas of existence, of the Being of beings. The most beguiling and bewitching philosophers, such as Plato and Nietzsche, have been poets and innovators with language. Heidegger is no exception.

Nevertheless, his image of human existence is as bleak and as rich in implications as a Becket play or Eliot's *Waste Land*. *Being and Time* "solves" a number of long-standing philosophical problems at the ontological level: the subject-object divide is closed; "philosophical man" is certainly now "free" from history and social theory; there is a "structure" to Being. Yet a certain controversy clouds Heidegger's use of Husserl's phenomenological methods to "force Being to disclose itself." Social relations are "ek-static" — meaning that they can be viewed objectively and from the outside by the individuals involved — but what is the ontic level? It remains profoundly empty and finite. Eventually, individual lives come to an end. But the non-saga repeats with each new person "thrown" into existence. What is gained? Heidegger's *Being and Time* can be seen as a kind of philosophical expressionism, like Munch's *The Scream*.

For liberal idealists, by seeking to move forward Heidegger actually takes us backwards, to the incompleteness of the pre-Socratics. His failure to tackle the human being's social nature leads him astray. George Steiner asks us to compare Aristotle's picture of man. He is a social and political animal. He needs other people or he will die. He built a *polis* and participates in its public life, seeking glory in political action. He is expected to have a wife and children and enjoy the pleasures of family life as a child and a parent. Heidegger's picture, in contrast, is without music or art (despite his love of both). There are no passionate human relationships.[34] Liberty (of a kind) is a feature of the *polis* that is protected by political community. As presented in *Being and Time,* nobody protects anything in Heidegger's ontic world, and his ontological world lacks the most elementary but necessary aspect of all: love. Indeed, controversy still swirls about Heidegger's turn later in his career and his later focus on resuscitating a Western philosophy of Being. Yet *Being and Time* caught the bleak postwar Weimar wave, and the underlying chords seem to vibrate still.

Heidegger's Implications for Liberalism

For Liberal idealists, the convergence of Heidegger and pragmatism amounts to an arrival at much the same place by different routes. The philosophical basis for classical liberalism vanishes. In the place of a godlike perspective on human affairs and a mathematical modelling of all human activity, there remain only the possibility of individual consent and a variety of choices. Is this the same as Mill's version of liberalism, in which experience is interpreted without Kantian "categories" — that is, in which experience replaces consciousness? Heidegger reduces life to ontic experience, it is true. Heidegger and Dewey both agree that choices should be made on the basis of usefulness — individual personal utility. But Mill discovered that humans also have feelings, a point admitted in Heidegger's "research design" and hermeneutic approach to meaning — but not in fact applied with much attention in *Being and Time.* Yet because of those things there is "sympathy," as Adam Smith described it; there is value in association, as List pointed out; and there is collective action, as history shows.

Effectively, then, one might say that on the balance, Heidegger and Dewey cleared out a lot of intellectual baggage accumulated over the centuries and left the way clear for a liberal society based on social justice and economic efficiency, oriented to the individual and the individual's *Dasein*. The problem they seek to solve is, in effect, sociology, according to which society is more (sometimes less) than the sum of its choices. Unfortunately, they say, the general theory that underpinned sociology — the tension between subject and object, between particular and general, between particular will and general obligation — is dead. In its place there is just the individual *Dasein*.

Liberalism is a political theory that thrives on a balance of tensions: between security and liberty, between the individual's authenticity and the general will, between civil society and government, between duty and responsibility, between function and status. It therefore cannot easily dispense with Kant's division of subject and object, and the rest. "Heideggerism" and pragmatism — whether on their own or when elevated to postmodernism — have no tensions, only possibilities. For postmoderns, there is no culture, only pretended expertise. Professional jargon crowds out thought, dogma replaces argument, opinion prevails over evidence. There is no balance, only gratification or frustration: gratification defines the Good, frustration defines the Bad. To be sure, some communication can occur. But the only shared vocabulary concerns transactions.

Hence a space opens within which economism replaces political discourse, monetization replaces learning, and the power of commercial interest groups replaces the sovereign power of the people — a concept with little remaining validity. Instead, there are "target demographics." In such a sociopolitical context, the legal formalities of liberal government continue to exist, but they hardly matter. Elections are for sale, as there is no valid public opinion, legislation is at auction, because only the interests of the single issue groups are at stake. There is no longer any public interest. Spengler's fantastic reductionist realism becomes a reality, now grounded in mankind's quest for individual authenticity. Essentially, the political construction of public space becomes deconstructed into a combat among private interests for state control.

It is attributing quite a lot to philosophy to say that a work like *Being and Time* could have caused such devastating changes. More plausibly,

Heidegger signalled what was happening in the world of thought and managed to give it a profound and logical framework — as much to warn as to promote. The work is obviously incomplete: Heidegger never got around to finishing it. His later work, however, builds on some of his initial themes of the destructiveness of positivism and technology for the human prospect.

Eleven years after the Davos meeting, another pivotal gathering, this time of liberal intellectuals, occurred in Paris. It was the summer of 1938. This meeting offered a more hopeful perspective, while failing utterly to recognize or discuss the changes that had recently occurred in the "civilizational philosophy" that supported liberalism and the quest for a free society with justice. For the time being, that didn't matter.

THE LIPPMANN COLLOQUIUM (1938)[35]

In August 1938 an event took place in Paris that allows us to see the actual state of liberalism at that time, with Europe on the brink of the Second World War. Nazi Germany was already on the march, having re-entered the Rhineland in 1936, announced its rearmament the same year, and absorbed Austria in March of 1938 — with little beyond murmurs from the Versailles powers. The Czechoslovak crisis was just weeks away, in which the four powers would meet in Munich and consent to the breakup of an ally, Czechoslovakia, a lynchpin of the French post-Versailles security arrangements.

The event was a colloquium held between August 26 and 29 at the *Musée social* around the newly released French translation of the latest book by New York–based columnist Walter Lippmann — *The Good Society.* The colloquium was organized by Louis Rougier, at the time a philosophy professor at the University of Besançon. Dr. Louis Marlio, a *Polytechnicien* and director of the Mercier Group of hydroelectric companies and of the aluminium cartel (and whose own book, *Le Sort du Capitalisme,* also appeared that year), served as a co-organizer. Around the table were twenty-four of the brightest liberal-inclined intellectuals of Europe, including Austrian school thinkers Friedrich von Hayek and Ludwig von Mises, and a number of German economists. Walter Eucken of Freiburg University was invited but, as we have seen, was refused an exit visa; other scholars in his circle, including Wilhelm Röpke and Alexander Rüstow, were able to attend and later joined him in forming the ordoliberal school of economists that helped generate the postwar German "economic miracle." Other attendees who later achieved international distinction included Raymond Aron, Jacques Rueff, and Michael Polanyi.

The question before the meeting was this: What ought to be the steps forward for liberalism, faced with advancing totalitarianism and a general lack of public confidence in free markets and free-market institutions?

The first part of Lippmann's argument — that liberalism needed reinvention — gathered more support than the second — that Roosevelt's New Deal offered a sustainable answer. The monetarists present distrusted fiat currency and believed a return to the gold standard would offer the only realistic barrier to inflation by democratic governments. Those we might call market universalists (or fetishists) believed that free markets remained the most effective instrument for reconciling individual choice and efficiency, even if they were prepared to recognize that industrial societies, in contrast to agricultural ones, needed a reliable system of government-supplied social services. They warned, however, that there were limits to the usefulness of those services.

THE MONT PELERIN SOCIETY

The members of the colloquium agreed to establish a permanent centre for the promotion of liberalism. After the war this became the Mont Pelerin Society, headquartered in the small Swiss village of Mont Pèlerin. The society never accepted Keynesian economics. Instead, members spent the next thirty years after the war trying to rehabilitate an updated version of classical liberalism, succeeding eventually in the 1970s, first in the United Kingdom with the victory of Conservative Party leader Margaret Thatcher in 1979, and second in the United States with the victory of Republican Party leader Ronald Reagan in 1980.[36]

Gradually, the humanist New Deal/Lippmann perspective on the problem was overtaken by the more rigorous (in all senses of the term) scientistic approach of the Chicago school. The society's presidents were increasingly drawn from the University of Chicago's Faculty of Economics, as the ascendancy of the Chicago school continued apace. Some of the society's members were prominent contributors to the literature on public and social choice that sought to export the ideas of classical economics into political science.

THE POST–SECOND WORLD WAR PICTURE

The end of the Second World War in Europe revealed the profound depth to which Germany, perhaps the most advanced European country in the nineteenth and twentieth centuries, had sunk in its embrace of Nazi barbarity. The revelations combined with the collapse of classical liberal economics and democracies in the Great Depression as a sign that something had gone wrong with the Enlightenment program. The atomic bombing of Japan — justified at the time by the prospect of even greater casualties arising from an invasion of the Japanese homeland, and occasionally since by the demonstration effect it must have had on Stalin as he was beginning to tighten his grip on Eastern Europe — underlined the destructive capacity of technological innovation, which had been the positivist hope for the future.

Improbably, the Western spirit did not give way to despair. Instead, the moral courage that enabled the resistance to Nazi totalitarianism and the optimism that its total destruction encouraged fuelled the determination to reconstruct civilization on a more secure foundation of respect for the human condition. This not only meant establishing institutions to uphold the Four Freedoms of the Atlantic Charter, such as the U.N. family of multilateral agencies; it also meant reinventing and repurposing the state as a socioeconomic system in which the potential of mankind for constructive achievement would be encouraged by public programs. In Western Europe, this came about as a continuation of the wartime agreement between the Resistance factions of the socialist and communist left, on the one hand, and the nationalist right (Gaullist, in France), on the other. In Britain, the Beveridge plan added economic and social rights to the status of citizen — making full employment and universal health care the pillars of postwar governance. In North America, the experience of war moved society leftward to accept a larger role for government and social programs for average families. Notably, in the United States the GI Bill for returning soldiers opened the doors to university education for anyone who could qualify — a social revolution in itself.

As a practical matter, the welfare state lasted for about thirty years, from 1945 to a little after 1975. Its successes were substantial when measured in the aggregate terms of its stated goals: massive increases in national prosperity; important expansion of the middle classes; and income gains across the board, from the working class upwards. Steady employment and career advancement replaced the joblessness and employment precariousness of the interwar years, and even bettered the conditions of the *belle époque* before the First World War. Universities in particular flourished, trading in their role as finishing schools for social elites to become the educators of millions who would never have experienced higher education otherwise, in part through measures like the GI Bill in the United States. By the mid-1960s, the combination of government, industry, science, and material advancement that the welfare state encouraged was deemed by some observers as the "new industrial state." Those employed by it formed a national "technostructure" of interdependence.[37] It looked as though liberalism's optimistic vision of economically free and democratic societies could be made to work, and that it had established mankind permanently on the road to sustained prosperity. It barely lasted another twenty years. What happened?

WELFARE STATE FAILURES

So traumatic was the end of this era that a comprehensive account has yet to appear. Neoliberalism has emerged in the guise of its more efficient successor and thus thrown the focus on the welfare state's alleged economic shortcomings, in the form of a party line about the "bloated costs," "excessive debt," and "ruinous regulation" of free markets — to which its free-market answer is increased social division; higher risk from technological, environmental, and financial disasters; and shrunken economic growth rates. The result of neoliberal economic doctrine, which amounts to a return to the prewar "treasury view" of economics, is that ordinary people are worse off, the rich have a lot more money, and the global economy is — or has been — approaching hysteresis, despite the almost permanent state of war on the periphery of Western economic control and the continued growth in Asian countries. On the balance, neoliberalism from the 1980s on recapitulated the world of the 1880s. Until 2015 it resisted any meaningful response either to climate change or to the need to strengthen global institutions to cope with the geopolitical realignments stimulated by the rise of China and the shift away from hydrocarbons as a source of energy.

Unfortunately, at the current level of public philosophical imagination, many people find it difficult to envisage a plausible alternative. A good starting place for repairing that shortcoming and thinking about moving forward is to analyze the welfare state and its demise a little more closely.

The priority right after the Second World War was avoiding a return to recession. The policy emphasis was on stimulating consumer demand, and avoiding a liquidity trap from oversaving. Later, the Keynesian welfare state continued to focus on sustaining aggregate demand in the economy by using public spending on public works and other government activities to ensure what it calls full employment, and by encouraging firms to spend more on marketing their goods, competing for consumer demand and in the process raising consumer demand as a whole so that rising incomes would never encounter "sufficiency." A factor that rendered this strategy even more powerful was the advent of private-broadcast TV whose business model relied upon corporate advertising support. The impact of TV on consumer habits was supplemented during the 1960s with the introduction of consumer credit cards controlled by a consortium of banks rather than by individual stores, so that they could be used by participating merchants everywhere.

Within a few years of victory in 1945, every home in the West was flooded with daytime soap operas and evening comedies generally featuring stories about individuals making their way in an imaginary world of consumption without class barriers, underwritten by an endless stream of commercials. As a totality, the system trumpeted consumer materialism as the gateway to the realization of one's dreams. The new state also redesigned the national financial system to protect consumer savings from investment banking speculation, and to keep investment focused more on company performance than on paper vehicles designed for speculation — with the result that for the first time, Western countries experienced no major financial panic and few major bank collapses over the thirty years of the operation of the Keynesian system.

THE TRANSVALUATION FROM PRODUCTION TO CONSUMPTION

The welfare state claimed it had resolved the problems of capitalism. But some specialists knew better. The welfare state had simply placed demand at the service of production.[38] Firms grew by generating wants that they could then satisfy. The shift to the demand side — to marketing and promotion and to a certain neglect of concern about manufacturing processes — was at the heart of the "transvaluation" promoted by the welfare state. Government, with its programs, helped by clearing out social and cultural obstacles to increasing consumer demand. Example: the War on Poverty, which U.S. president Lyndon Johnson, a passionate New Dealer, launched in the mid-1960s. Instead of resolving the contradictions of capitalism, the welfare state traded the labour-capital contradiction for a deeper one: the contradiction between production for exchange and production for use. At its deepest level, this contradiction is between meeting wants — material desires generated by private sector marketing teams — and trying, rather, to meet actual human needs, such as reaffirmation, companionship, and emotional comfort. To be fair, of course, corporate capital did manage to come up with chemical substitutes to combat the blues.[39]

As a new TV generation passed through the new colleges and universities, it became increasingly clear that for all its successes, the welfare state had become a simulacrum of its own incarnation. Designed as a noble arrangement to enable families to enjoy some economic security and good living standards at modest and acceptable levels of inequality, the welfare state had become a powerful production machine. Its most important product was demand — for consumer goods, whose acquisition generated and preserved middle class jobs, and for perpetual readiness for war that generated the strongest military the world had ever known. Effectively, the end of the welfare state was preceded by its transition to a post-needs economy.[40]

RAWLS'S CHALLENGE: *A THEORY OF JUSTICE*

An alternative type of state — one based on restoring civic involvement to a central place in political life, to make inclusiveness more viable and exciting as a civic duty — was proposed and debated in the 1970s, by John Rawls in particular.[41] Rawls's theory aimed to justify a role for the state in rectifying the injustices of birth, and in particular being born into poverty.

Rawls proposed a transfer of income designed such that as national productivity improved and wages rose, the amount of money transferred to bring families out of poverty would also rise, with the fastest increase going to the most disadvantaged. The echoes of Rodbertus in this idea of productivity-related assistance and the implication that law is a determinant of social outcomes do not appear to have been heard, nor did the economic argument take up the issue of consumer debt. Rawls's assumption that rising wages can significantly redress social and economic inequality reflected the unwillingness at the time to consider issues of private economic power, often remarked upon by Galbraith.

Rawls's arguments resonated throughout the liberal world while generating considerable condemnation from the far right, the political consensus underpinning what became the Reagan-Thatcher period less than a decade later.

The Great Society programs and the War on Poverty launched by U.S. president Lyndon Johnson in the 1960s aimed at eliminating poverty and achieving a greater measure of racial equality. The arguments also resonated outside the United States, with Canada's prime minister Pierre Trudeau putting forward social programs aimed at creating a "just society." Other, mainly social democratic, governments did the same. Ultimately, however, Rawls's ideas about social fairness were rejected, as was his proposed formula for lifelong assistance for the measurably disadvantaged. His brave exercise of public reason would be the last time a leading liberal political philosopher challenged directly the capitalist boast that prosperity under capitalism "raises all boats."

The Keynesian welfare state may have found a generalizable formula for national prosperity and social justice, but it couldn't solve the more fundamental problem of individual acquisitiveness and the pathologies of democratic politics in the absence of a shared commitment to an active civil society. Such a vision existed in the preindustrial world of Adam Smith and emerged again at the end of the nineteenth century and in the early years of the twentieth century. The shared effort of the Second World War, and in Europe the accord between the communist and non-communist resistance movements, led to a broad and deep social consensus around the Atlantic Charter's Four Freedoms, especially freedom from fear and freedom from want. Yet by the 1960s, as relatively peaceful prosperity and security returned, that consensus slowly dissolved, eaten away by the cultural acids of a moneyed society that was now blind to its vulnerability.

POLITICAL PATHOLOGIES AND THE PUBLIC CHOICE CRITIQUE
Pathologies of Liberal Politics

In the course of its thirty-year existence, the welfare state developed a number of important political pathologies from which it never recovered.[42] In the final analysis, they all have one thing in common: a public disengagement from active politics and a desire for government on the cheap, a kind of *"Have I got a deal for you!"* TV-pitchman politics. Two insights explain most of what happened without, however, going the extra step to underline the social dimension. The first is Hayek's theory of knowledge.[43] This theory is a market theory claiming that one thing that makes markets and market societies so convenient is that they minimize the amount of knowledge a person needs:

> What he [the economist] may claim is that his professional occupation with the prevailing conflicts of aims has made him more aware than others of the fact that no human mind can comprehend all the knowledge which guides the actions of society and of the consequent need for an impersonal mechanism, not dependent on individual human judgments, which will co-ordinate the individual efforts.[44]

Or again:

> While the growth of our knowledge of nature constantly discloses new realms of ignorance, the increasing complexity of the civilization which this knowledge enables us to build presents new obstacles to the intellectual comprehension of the world around us. The more men know, the smaller the share of all that knowledge becomes that

any one mind can absorb. The more civilized we become, the more relatively ignorant must each individual be of the facts on which the working of his civilization depends. The very division of knowledge increases the necessary ignorance of the individual of most of this knowledge.[45]

Consumerism stimulated tremendous advances in transforming simple, easily repaired appliances into new, complex products offering amazing convenience: cars with automatic transmission and air conditioning that could travel only on paved roads and highways; refrigerators with cold-water fountains and distinct compartments for meat, fruits, and vegetables. In a famous face-to-face encounter between a U.S. vice-president and a Soviet leader at a consumer fair in Moscow, the American could show a clear Western lead in technology — even though the Soviets had already launched the first Earth satellite, *Sputnik 1,* and would put the first human into space in *Vostok 1* a couple of years later. The Western point was that the level of consumer production was organized by a profit-seeking enterprise; it put together the necessary skills around a design-produce-distribute sequence that employed teams of specialists. Their work embedded the necessary knowledge in the machines that then produced the product; it also informed marketing and distribution teams that got the product into the stores and promoted it with advertising so it could be sold — all without the need for a centrally planned economy.

Thus the point was powerfully made that markets efficiently assemble and organize the knowledge of needs and of the skills required to make successful products.[46] Labour can then be divided into categories and coordinated to create the panoply of products that satisfy customer needs. Because of the specialization encouraged by the market, workers really need to know only one thing well enough to earn a regular paycheque, which in turn opens the door to the things money can buy. The Moscow debate underlined an important turning point: in the West, the concept of politics was no longer a common search for the public good; instead, it was to be the search for available consumer goods and private purchasing power.

Apply the same theory to democratic politics, however, and you get the so-called rational voter paradox. The paradox arises when people who are rational about their use of time nevertheless invest time and effort in following the issues and carefully choosing a candidate, and then actually voting — although they also know their vote may not decide the election and indeed may make no difference, and the time and effort sunk into the election will never be compensated. (However, we know that voter turnout depends a great deal on the race and the candidates. The link between the electoral system and voter participation is a fragile one.)

When Hayek's theory of knowledge and the rational voter paradox are combined in voter behaviour, then the concept of parliamentary democracy undergoes some subtle but important changes. Ultimately, the theory of political representation becomes altered and the possibility of representative accountability disappears. As in Croly's account of U.S. politics in the Gilded Age, people ultimately can be persuaded to prefer the low-cost solution of leaving politics to "the professionals." For most practical purposes, these professionals have a concept of legislative oversight of companies and legislative accountability to voters that is probably more rigorous than that of the average voter — but it is used to enforce the power of the professionals and to drive the politicians to do what the party funders want as much as possible. Gerrymandering districts and monetizing power, unfortunately, are natural to liberal democracies unless the electorate insists on politically neutral management of the electoral process by bureaucrats rather than political parties. But that departs from government on the cheap.

Political Representation and the Single-Issue Pressure Group

Once the professionals start to take over, then public confidence falls in the effectiveness of elections for holding politicians responsible. This leads to a change in voter behaviour. The rational choice and public choice economists explain it as a kind of Coase's law[47] in which "market failure" — in this case, the failure of effective representation — is remedied by associations that form at the national level around particular issues and amass enough resources to make politicians pay attention.

Typically, such groups form in favour of industry sectors or professions. As they become more competent through centralizing expertise on policy, they rival the professional bureaucrats as sources of reliable information. As they also are capable of mounting public information campaigns that specifically single out recalcitrant politicians and "control" the votes of their industry employees and other stakeholders, they are effective players at key legislative stages.

For citizens, single-issue groups seem a much better way to ensure that politicians get the message than casting one vote at election time. In some cases, the single-issue group actually becomes the de facto national policy developer and decider. The difference in representation concepts is dramatic. Before the emergence of single-issue groups, legislative representatives actually represented states or provincial ridings: actual territories and the people living there. Now, wherever they are elected, they must still consider the single-issue group whose power is the greatest on national issues. That means that the local issues the representative was sent to deal with get neglected, while the big national questions get the time (and enable the representative's party to collect its funding).[48]

Iron Triangles

Maintaining policy continuity is also important for the economic interests that have the government's ear. But how to secure continuity, even as parties change? "Iron triangles" is the name given to the three-way coalitions that often dominate the results when a legislature discusses a particular issue. The triangle is made up of the single-issue group lobbies, the oversight committee, and the regulatory agency or government department that is responsible for the file. The iron triangle is largely anonymous, and the vote-trading it generates to produce a result is invisible to the public. There is no public accountability unless it is in the interest of the single-issue group to manage the story.[49]

Key to the triangle is the committee chair. The chair controls the committee agenda and the pace at which a bill moves forward, the hearings that are held, and whether they will be open or closed. As the committee controls the relevant regulator and the chair controls the committee, the next question is: Who controls the chair? Clearly, the single-issue group must be a dominant influence for the triangle to work. This is what a system driven by specialists looks like. The players all share a detailed knowledge of the file and the voting behaviour of the key districts, which are themselves designed to deliver predictable support to one party most of the time.

The bottom line is that taken together these developments at the legislative level are complements of industry's market power. Just as they generate demand for the products they want to make, contemporary industries are capable of generating the political climate they need, as well. Parliaments hold elections and go through the motions. But Saint-Simon was right: in an industrial age, technical information is needed to draft effective legislation — and the industries themselves monopolize almost all the necessary information, plus the money and power they need to get their point of view taken seriously.

This system of single-issue groups and iron triangles more or less runs itself. The politicians respect their own political interests, and therefore an industry can influence its key legislative committees to respect it, too. No matter who is in power or what the ideology, the technical information is needed to draft legislation that will have the desired effect: that is where the iron triangles make their great contribution. In orthodox liberal and neoliberal theory, markets reconcile competing interests and government handles any spillovers into the political arena. Under modern democracy, the market rewards companies that successfully generate wants, while government iron triangles reconcile competing interests. The space available for public concerns becomes negligible.

"Rational Choice" as an Economizing System

Another attribute of this rational choice system is that it operates largely in silence and in the dark — like a component in a complex machine — as a normal part of political life. There is no "mind" that oversees it all. It is driven by the expected value of convenient business regulation. In other words, this legislative process is a kind of "game" in which the players respond to the incentives that make up the system. Oddly, perhaps, these ideas, taken together, exemplify or instantiate the phenomena of modern society.

So-called "rational choice" and "public choice" models suffer from the same exclusions that characterize their mother discipline: there is no consciousness, only relative advantage; there is no sense of broader relationships, such as institutional failures and transformations, patterns of adaptation and social learning; and there are no indications of broader ambitions and ultimate goals of the actors involved. Rational choice models describe a machine-like process driven by rational economizing of resources to obtain individual gain. The problem with such explanations is that they explain nothing very important, such as why one would want to short-circuit public debate of important issues, or force single priorities despite possible connections to broader issues or even to other files.

Public Choice Critique

Explanations of the welfare state's end customarily refer to the public choice critiques. These caricatured governments as chronically bloated and controlled by ambitious bureaucrats subverting the public interest for promotions and power. Public choice theory — the formal basis of those critiques — based itself on the hypothesis that government officials are rational maximizers just as much as their private sector counterparts are. The results, it argued, were not pretty, particularly for taxpayers who, it was said, were coerced through tax laws into paying for inefficient and wasteful programs, boondoggles designed to win votes rather than add to productivity.

The critique was designed to make a point: mainly, Hayek's point in *The Road to Serfdom* that economic planners constitute a new class of powerful officials who operate outside effective legislative control. Most people did not fully understand the unspoken assumptions underpinning the public choice critique. One can argue that applying microeconomic logic to government may very well suggest the existence of boondoggles, if only for the reasons that public goods — because they are automatically shared at zero marginal cost — are not subject to normal marginal pricing, and that nationally owned firms are natural monopolies. But one should also understand that this is why they operate under public rather than private authority.

One can also claim that such government programs are financed by taxes and therefore the money spent on them is wasted in comparison to the money private corporations spend. But in the Keynesian system, in which demand is managed by fiscal policy, that is not strictly true. Taxes and interest rates are levers by which the central government manages the economy to achieve near-full employment without (much) inflation. Programs are services supplied by government. Tax receipts may or may not cover the outlays on programs, depending on the employment level and the tax structure. But the central government does not use tax receipts to pay for programs: the statement that it does is only a shorthand for explaining what actually happens.

National governments (in contrast to state or provincial and local governments) pay for programs the way they pay for war: they print the money. If they choose to issue bonds, it is to take cash out of circulation so as to reduce inflationary pressures. If they raise taxes to "cover" programs, it is to prevent the economy from overheating.

To put the matter more plainly, governments are not separate from the economy. The "costs" of policy expenditure have to be balanced not only by the "benefits" to stakeholders, but also the "costs" imposed on society if the policies are not put in place. It is sociology that reveals these social costs, as economics lacks the tools. Full employment benefits not just those at the margin of employment who are helped by full-employment programs. It also benefits society, which does not have to adjust to the problems of unemployment, including its impact on crime rates, family structure, prison populations, insurance costs, and so on. Health-care benefits similarly reach beyond the recipients to maintain a level of social cohesion that the private health-care system's high costs to individuals ultimately destroys, either through the rise in personal bankruptcies or through higher rates of serious medical conditions that result as the public avoids preventive care in order to meet other economic needs.

Neoliberalism has a truncated idea of money as a social technology, believing it to be either a private possession or a government possession. It refuses to recognize that money also has a social power that enables society to function at different levels of collective well-being, and that maximizing that level is a fundamental task of liberal governance. One of the reasons for the failure of the welfare state is that liberal philosophy forgot its roots. It forgot about the public sentiment that operated in preindustrial society to enforce a common level of respect for social norms of behaviour, including those touching on the relations between different social classes — the subject of Adam Smith's "other book."

Moral Sentiments

Perhaps ironically, some reasons for the failure of the welfare state have more to do with the failure of modern liberal philosophy than with economics. Arguably, causes are to be found in Adam Smith's *Theory of Moral Sentiments*.[50] This vastly neglected and underrated book analyzes the economy of "sentiment" — that is, popular feeling that determines what generates public sympathy and what does not.

At one time, it was fashionable to pose the "Adam Smith problem" of how an advocate of market capitalism could write a book outlining public sympathy as a form of social control. Today, perhaps, people can more clearly understand the complementarity of Smith's two major works. For *Theory of Moral Sentiments* shows how people think about what behaviour is "proper" or "appropriate" and what is not.

The underlying question — an important one for the Scottish Enlightenment as a whole — is how civil society arrives at moral evaluations of individual actions. This includes competitive business activities and economic distribution. In real life, many actions can only be correctly evaluated by those with an intimate knowledge of the people involved in a situation and who will have to live together in the same community afterward.

David Hume and Adam Ferguson also commented extensively on this question, both under the influence of Francis Hutcheson, a distinguished professor of ethics at Glasgow University, where Hume and later Smith also taught. Hutcheson believed that human beings have an innate moral sense, a not uncommon view among eighteenth-century Europeans. What emerges distinctly from these investigations is the critical social role played by that sense, as opposed to the Kantian view of imperatives based on reason. The *Theory of Moral Sentiments* in particular argued that civil society holds together not with reason but with a fluctuating sensitivity to the events taking place within it, through a mixture of emotional and physical reactions that Smith called "sympathy."

Some situations — fortunate and unfortunate alike — in which individuals find themselves stimulate sympathetic understanding on the part of their neighbours, even distant ones in some cases. Other situations inspire reactions of indifference or disapproval. The main point is that sympathy is an organic reaction of society based on shared conceptions of propriety or appropriate behaviour; unfairness in the treatment of another is particularly apt to mobilize sentiments of disapproval.

What enables sympathy to work is that the observer and the actor can see in each other a mutual humanity that establishes a connection. Sympathy is not Hegel's alienation. It is rather opposition to actions that violate assumptions upon which the day-to-day operations of society depend: trust, co-operation, fair dealing, peaceful dispute settlement, liberality in the manners of the more fortunate, compassion for the vulnerable and unlucky, and so on. Smith's sympathy, then, is the militant arm of community values and community standards of moral behaviour.

Sympathy is a more operational concept than Montesquieu's mores that govern public conduct under particular types of government, which in effect amount to the operating principles of different regimes: honour for aristocracies, *virtù* for republics, fear for despotisms. Smith's concept leads to similar conclusions about the basis of society and politics being grounded in anthropology and sociology even before they are organized according to economics.

Smith's sympathy is also one of the missing ingredients in Bentham's utilitarianism, the "imagination" factor that allows people to become conscious of the minds of others and to achieve a certain level of solidarity beyond the strict limits of personal material interest.

Without contradicting Hegel's observation that social systems based exclusively on exchange cannot advance in understanding past the limits of individual interest, Smith's concept of sympathy shows that even an exchange society offers the opportunity to move beyond mere private considerations. The genuine political question is whether a state will act to encourage public sympathy and solidarity or rather act to divide its citizens, the better to rule.

Charity and the Private Right to Give

The liberal political culture of private property enjoyed as a reward for hard work limits public sympathy for state-imposed generosity, but not the impulse for private generosity. Thus, in a paradox of the welfare state, public programs are supplied alongside private programs financed by tax expenditure (that is, by favourable income tax treatment), and which — unlike public programs — single out target groups by faith or ethnicity. Result: little actual income redistribution takes place. Donations generate tax reductions for the middle class.[51] Social and economic advancement in the welfare state resulted from greater access to education, more openness in hiring, and the relatively long periods of growth and net job creation. Grand strategy programs like the U.S. War on Poverty (as opposed to equal opportunity) ran headlong into the middle and upper classes' determination to preserve their right to make private donations as an example of an individual's private priorities — the "two freedoms" problem defined by Isaiah Berlin,[52] or the right to one's own preferences, even more ardently defended by David Hume.[53]

"Sympathy" and "Consciousness"

Individual countries differed, of course, in the success of state-supported "wars" on poverty. Much depended on the history and scale of the problem and the diversity of the populations. An additional factor was the extent of what Galbraith called the "self-exploiting" small- and medium-sized business sector that felt disadvantaged by the large national and global enterprises that operated everywhere with various forms of government support.

The primacy of private property ensured that the expansion of the service state could only occur in ways that respected private judgment. In effect, private interests imposed strict limits on the scope of state claims to rebalance society in the pursuit of public justice. The social construction of "sympathy" that complemented an exchange economy thus set a ceiling on the Hegelian expansion of consciousness that followed alienation. Sympathy and its boundaries set limits to Hegel's corresponding development of a state concept in which the condition of all depends on the condition of each. For example, one may question whether Hegel's portrait of the servant's confrontation with his master, and in particular its mortal challenge, would pass muster as appropriate in the circumstances of Smith's theory — unless the master was an outrageous tyrant.[54] Sympathy is a conservative system for reconciling public order and at least a superficially acceptable natural justice in a society in which social rank comes with public expectations. But it is not particularly emancipatory: under certain circumstances, it will prefer private affluence and public squalor to any hint of a reversal of those terms.

Interestingly, if sympathy is not Hegelian, neither is it utilitarian. Smith's concept of utility is that of an aesthetic property that contributes to a sense of propriety — in the way that an iPhone is "cool" because of its intrinsic blend of style and function in an arrangement that to the observer seems perfect. In the same way, Smith argues, utility can combine in generous actions of humanity, justice, and public spirit. In this sense, Smith recommends the study of political theory, as it rouses men "to seek out the means of promoting the happiness of society." For Smith is not a behaviourist — rather, he is a moralist, interested in the design and operation of human systems, in particular systems based upon sympathy and systems based on exchange and "natural" economy. With Smith, we are still a generation away from Ricardo. Even Heidegger recognized the importance of sympathy in his concept of "care" — the mutual interest friends and families — and beyond these, communities — have in preserving peace and some general level of prosperity.

A rounded understanding of the welfare state's failure can emerge only from expanding our view of causation from the "efficient cause" of empirical analysis to a more comprehensive view. To be sure, the last years of the welfare state were marked by high levels of public debt, significant levels of inflation, and, surprisingly for some Keynesians, low levels of economic growth despite the high public deficits. An important consideration, however, is whether these developments were themselves causes or whether they were effects brought on by using economic techniques to resolve deeper, more serious non-economic problems within the welfare state itself. An alternative view could add the following considerations to the discussion:

- **Program design — focus on aggregates:** Looking for one cause of the welfare state's decline, we might examine its origins in the operational concepts of wartime planning, in particular its ideas of optimization around the goals of maximum aggregates achieved at minimum costs. This approach was a linear programming model originally designed to help military planners maximize the strategic value of their forces in overcoming a powerful enemy on multiple fronts. Applied to society, the problem became one of redistribution from one aggregate class, the way-above-average-income segment, to another aggregate class, the way-below-average-income segment. Under this approach, a multiplier effect was said to exist for every dollar transferred, as the marginal propensity to spend among low earners was higher than among high earners for every dollar received. Thus, aggregate demand could be managed so as to ensure "full" employment.

  Such an approach is not without its problems, as suggested in a popular critique at the time titled *Social Limits to Growth.*[55] For example, once a certain level of general prosperity was reached, the difference between marginal propensities to consume would narrow. Indeed, it might go into reverse if, say, low-income families had enough spare income to think of saving for their children to attend college or some other longer term goal, or simply chose to retire the debt they incurred through their consumption. Additionally, as consumption preferences converged through rising prosperity, status preferences might replace income preferences, such that advances in income by one sector provoked a knock-on demand for additional income from another in order to preserve social status. The concept of general welfare and how to achieve it (through centrally controlled redistribution) was locked into the DNA of the welfare state from its initial inception onward, and it could not be addressed in time to adjust to the sociological changes that its success created.

- **The culture of narcissism:** Also, the welfare state ran on material aggregates. It built structures around their maximization. Yet its justificatory claim was permanent scarcity, particularly among consumers. A governing system traumatized by the collapse of demand during the Depression, it equated good economic management with sustaining aggregate demand for "stuff." Driving demand beyond sufficiency provoked a number of important cultural changes, as commentators at the time underlined in such works as *The Culture of Narcissism*[56] and *The Cultural Contradictions of Capitalism*.[57] Effectively, businesses began to cultivate the consumer as they might a prince or princess, accentuating the styles and sensuous qualities of their products such that their visible use would provoke envy and admiration in the purchasers' circles. Whereas earlier works had criticized the emerging world of the consumer as a culture of conformity, the challenge of managing a capitalist economy at full employment now meant breaking down the sense of "We" and privileging "Me." This was a further intensification of the market fragmentation commented on a hundred years earlier by Wieser and Veblen.

It was also at about this time that public philosophy caught up with postwar liberalism. The emphasis on the material expression of individuality was matched by an intellectual turn away from the idealism that underpinned the welfare state and was left over from its roots in the New Liberalism of the late nineteenth and early twentieth centuries.

- **The year of student revolt — 1968:** The popular existentialism of Sartre stimulated by that of Heidegger (despite his disavowal of French existentialism as humanism[58]), and especially its search for "authenticity," was a theme no marketer could resist. The search for personal authenticity hit its limits in the everyday experience of factory, office, and school, in which standardized throughput was still the ultimate goal. Under pressure in collective bargaining, management responded by redesigning the workplace, in particular differentiating and more finely granulating the categories of work and the qualifications for performing it.[59] In North American schools and universities, pressure also mounted for more student input to courses, more seminars to replace magisterial lecture courses, greater participation in program design, and greater flexibility in courses. Ultimately, the pressure against all structure in favour of the subjective individual blew up, fuelled by resistance to external obligations that the state was imposing. The year of "revolt" was 1968.[60]

In Paris, students rioted against the Gaullist state and its Cartesian imposition of structure. Under the influence of their philosophy faculties, which had imbibed at the Althusserian[61] and Heideggerian wells, they went on to contest all representation that was not rooted in the *facticité* of the observer. In the United States, the persistent draft of students for the interminable war in Vietnam was a mobilizing force around a core that consisted of the promotion of a new "consciousness." Later that same year, a liberalization movement broke out in Czechoslovakia, one of the freest states at that time in the Soviet bloc of countries. For a month or so, the Prague Spring electrified the world in the hope that the Cold War might somehow come to an end. The euphoria lasted until the Soviet tanks rolled into the capital, as they had rolled into Budapest under similar circumstances twelve years earlier. By the time everything settled down, it was clear that a sea change had nevertheless occurred. That change is perhaps the most important clue to what came next.

AUTHENTICITY TAKES PRECEDENCE OVER *CIVITAS*

At the basis of the welfare state as liberals conceived it lay an explicit model of the development of human consciousness, namely, that advanced by Hegel. According to this model — repeated in Bosanquet's treatment of the modern state at the same time as Fabian socialism was gaining ground in Britain[62] — the human mind expands to embrace the other in a dialectical progression from self to other, from we to us, from us to all of us, until mankind develops a generally held self-consciousness about its interdependence and interconnectedness. At this stage the human consciousness will be able to organize the world for the creation of freedom and justice for all.[63] Hegel recognizes, however, that the real obstacle to this is vanity and selfishness, which can arise at particular moments along this trajectory.

At such points the dialectical process breaks down and instead of expanding, human interpersonal understanding stops, entranced narcissistically by its own self-image. When that occurs, political self-realization stops in that polity, and the owl of Minerva moves on as dusk settles over that community. Hegel's historical progress has hit a wall — namely, the corruption of the state, to use an old-fashioned term.

In the eighteenth- and early nineteenth-century meaning of the term, "corruption" is not about illicit conflicts of interest or bribes or payoffs. It is about spoilage, as if a basket of fruit has turned rotten or a pitcher of milk has soured. Corruption of the state is more about the pitcher than the milk, the basket rather than the fruit. It is a transformation of what Montesquieu called the operating rules of the state. The incentives for doing what should be done corrode and become inoperative.

Perhaps it could have been avoided if, around the end of the 1950s and the beginning of the '60s, Western society had accepted the fact that its affluence had reached sufficiency and the economic emphasis should shift from private gratification to the improvement of public spaces and the restoration of "public man."[64] Examples are shortening the working week and improving the situation of the volunteer sector. Suppose governments had at that point recognized the need to build greater scope for *civitas* — the Roman idea of civic spirit[65] — a key ingredient of public life missing from utilitarian hedonistic philosophy. But that was not to be, although it was a near miss.[66]

Under President John F. Kennedy America started its journey to the moon, an achievement that generated considerable national pride. The energy of the civil rights movement cried out to be channelled into building a state that offered more scope for public involvement. But the assassinations — of Kennedy, and then Martin Luther King and Robert Kennedy — changed that. Perhaps if Moscow had allowed the Prague Spring to succeed instead of crushing it and all hope of reform with it …

Still, despite these things, powerful forces continued to press for the social renovation of the West and greater social justice in the United States. The Great Society programs of Kennedy's successor, Lyndon Johnson, provided greater hope and opportunity for poor families in the wake of riots in the cities following the assassinations. But in the context of the Vietnam War and American domestic racial and ethnic rivalries and tensions,[67] these programs were seen by a significant minority as a dangerous giveaway to the undeserving rather than an overdue attempt to reconcile racial tensions and reopen opportunity for all Americans. In the end, private fears about loss of social status took control of the public space and shifted debate away from democratic political remedies to private economic alternatives.[68]

Thereafter in the larger Western economies, skepticism about the welfare state grew, fanning fears of the economic impact of pursuing both guns and butter (the Vietnam War and full employment). The supply shock from the Arab oil crises of the 1970s then generated price inflation. Under pressure of imperial overcommitment, a centre-right president, Richard M. Nixon, put a temporary end to the free market with wage and price controls, with Canada following close behind. Postmodern consumption had hit a wall, followed in the early 1980s by double-digit interest rates on household mortgages.

There were those who hoped the welfare state would reverse its swerve toward becoming a materialist brave new world of scientifically manufactured desires. There were those who urged instead that the state deepen its commitment to political and social equality and solidarity. A "new consciousness" arose in the United States in the late 1960s that fused opposition to the war, civil rights freedom riders and their supporters, and the beats and hippies into a movement seeking to establish an alternative culture opposed to the rectilinear industrialization and uniformity of mass consumer prosperity. Unconsciously, this new consciousness — dubbed Consciousness III by a Harvard law professor to follow premodern Consciousness I and scientific-industrial Consciousness II — substituted ontology — Being — for the utilitarian world of established thinking, a kind of Californianization or surfer version of Heidegger's existentialism. It was the New World's version of French postmodernism — an individualist thirst for authenticity, characterized by a youth culture of bell-bottoms, long hair, psychedelic T-shirts, and music to match.[69]

After a short period of adjustment, the new consciousness went in unanticipated directions, revolutionizing marketing, changing pop music, and launching a wave of entrepreneurship that eventually developed personal computers and commercialized the internet, a system of interconnected computers designed by the Pentagon to maintain control after a nuclear attack. It turned out that authenticity was great for business. It was just what the economy needed to promote a wave of technology-led growth — and a strong measure of social disruption by "letting information be free." But it did not restore the public solidarity needed to restore the welfare state. Indeed, the new prestige of entrepreneurship arising from the dot.com successes encouraged voters to double down on individualism over social programs of all kinds.

THE TWO-SPEED SPLIT-LEVEL ECONOMY AND CONSERVATISM

The individualist response to the welfare state's emphasis on material throughput and one-size-fits-all was to succumb to the narcissistic appeal to the "authentic" self and its material expression. This cultural swerve helped legitimize the rejection of community obligation and any development of social interest beyond personal pleasure.

Another underlying factor was coming into view at about this time. That is the distinction between wants — which are more or less general, such as food, clothing, and shelter — and the more deeply felt need for individual respect, appreciation, and some positive resonance from one's presence as a human being. Despite every good intent, the welfare state was unable to generate that feeling. Instead, as it intervened with bundles of "stuff," its recipients felt demeaned.

Among those who felt this way was a class of hard-working people whom Galbraith refers to as the "self-exploiting class" of small business owners, entrepreneurs, and employees. These are people who, unprotected by unions and contracts, work long hours, pay taxes, and yet somehow do not qualify for many of the benefits of the welfare state. Faced with rising costs, they had no means of raising their incomes in response. With little chance of avoiding a decline in their living standard they could only respond by working longer hours, postponing retirement, delaying needed renovation on their homes and places of business, and resigning from the local service organizations of which they were the backbone.[70]

Ultimately, their effort to create a legacy for fellow citizens and their own families by passing on a farm or business was crushed by the emergence of national chains and global companies that simply outclassed whatever offer they could put on the table. This was a source of anger throughout a broad element of society — mainly in small towns and rural areas, but also within many urban neighbourhoods. The anger fuelled the idea that the welfare state was an immoral fraud based on vote-buying giveaways of taxpayers' money by ambitious bureaucrats and politicians.

This class of local small business owners and employees formed the core of the growing opposition to the expansion of government, big business organizations, trade unions, and ultimately to the national bureaucracies that operated and controlled the welfare state. Relatively silent, they fuelled a new conservative movement that began to feel its power as early as the mid-1960s, with the U.S. presidential bid of Arizona senator Barry Goldwater.

This new conservative movement both encouraged and was encouraged by the direction of Western opinion away from the welfare state toward a neoliberal definition of freedom as liberation from organization and control, to be achieved through a "return" to free-market economics.

It is here that the neoliberal thinkers of the Lippmann colloquium, now re-established as the Mont Pelerin Society, began to find the echo chamber they needed to put an end to Keynesian economics. In this they were encouraged by industrial and financial organizations in particular, who felt that the welfare state was bad for business and harmful to shareholders and investment, and who foresaw the possibility of a global economy that was driven by markets instead of government and intergovernmental relations.

In a steady stream of analysis from think tanks debunking the welfare state — mainly under the rubric of "public choice economics" — self-styled "conservatives" successfully challenged the public interest claims of the welfare state and its supporters. These analyses struck home. Their appeal hit a mass audience with some brilliant television as well, such as the British *Yes, Minister* and *Yes, Prime Minister* satiric series about government operations. These programs found sympathy not only with those outside government but also from the large number of midlevel bureaucrats who saw every day the self-serving logic imposed on policy by those who controlled its development. Not surprisingly, from the 1980s onwards the instruments of the welfare state were melted in the fire of neoliberalism and with them also any considerations of the public business broader than whatever market alternatives could provide.

THE WRECK OF THE WELFARE STATE

Ironically, while almost all Western public attention was focused on the Vietnam War and the social problems of poverty, the wreck of the welfare state was propelled by the postmodern cult of the personal and its destruction of the public space as a worthwhile idea, a space worth defending. In this, the trend was mightily aided by corporate marketing, which exploited the sovereignty of the consumer to generate wants at the expense of needs and, ultimately, to devalue the sovereign realm. Such was the success of the welfare state's institutional arrangements that the needs were mainly linked to public spaces and places, from which energy might easily be diverted by the politics of envy. Nevertheless, the result has some paradoxical consequences. The modern dream of large, powerful commercial entities organized by markets and technology into vehicles carrying us to a future world of yet more technology and unimagined gadgets has revealed its dark side: climate change, environmental degradation, and universal electronic surveillance. Pursuit of the same course will cause major catastrophes and change the character of the Earth as we know it to something far less benign for its human occupants. At the same time, it may be possible to reconstruct a new politics that mobilizes people to do what needs to be done. We explore that possibility in the next and final chapter.

CHAPTER 4
Rebuilding Liberalism: Where Do We Go from Here?

CAN LIBERALISM LEARN FROM ITS PAST?

READERS OF THIS BOOK may have noticed that our examination of the history of liberal ideas and culture over the course of the nineteenth and twentieth centuries strongly suggests that there is a way to rebuild a responsible liberalism that supports freedom with social justice. This seems to be required, although it will not be easy to accomplish. It will require coming to terms with liberalism's past and its major limitations, such as the inability of classic liberalism to control its own effects, and protecting society against the most powerful interests by providing constitutional status to civil society as a community of needs whose general interest is served by a professional civil service, responsible to the government. Nor is that sufficient, for liberalism in terms of its approach to economics must be able to rise above its obsession with natural science, especially physics. This can be accomplished by embedding liberal economics in sociology, similar to the empirical economics of the nineteenth-century German historical economists. To move forward, liberalism must also include explicit readiness for technological disruption. If this seems novel — it is neither socialism nor classical liberalism — it offers at a minimum a practical response to neoliberals who believe there is no alternative to their own accident-prone, stripped-down stereotype of liberal ideas, devoid of historically anchored social science.

A first step toward accepting the challenge of rebuilding liberalism may well be to overcome liberalism's legend of the past — the long-standing interpretation of the nineteenth-century experience of industrialization as a liberal success story. Like a great many legends, there is some truth to the standard tale, as indeed nineteenth-century liberalism emancipated its host countries from the mystical routines of feudalism and divine right, and created the tools of modern production. However, as we have also seen, it did so at the price of significant social hardship — disaster even — for the majority who experienced the transformation to industrialization and the fragmentation of society into bourgeois and proletarian classes. What's more, liberals were unable to critique their policies and positions sufficiently to resolve that issue, despite many attempts to do so. To grapple with its limitations, liberalism required the critique developed by the revisionist forces of French sociology and German historical economics, which diffused across the North Atlantic region from the 1880s onward. Put another way, liberal "Cartesian" — rational and deductive — economics had to open up to historically based empirical analyses of society, its institutions, and its economic development. These critiques also showed that industrial nations could manage their own needs if all classes of the population were provided even minimal social assistance and security, including adequate education. Unhappily, they had too little time to develop their conclusion.

Had that insight been exploited sooner, then the scramble for empire that characterized international relations in the thirty years or so before the First World War might have been less intense. The increasing stress that underlay the relations between the great powers in 1914 might have been mitigated, and the First World War and its consequences avoided. As I explain in more detail below, the reforms made in Western Europe and North America during the decades before the war enabled those countries to resist successfully the appeal of a working class, Soviet-style revolution and the westward spread of the Russian Revolution. It is important for liberals to understand this, if only because acceptance of the concept of "society" and the ramifications of a macro-level organization affecting the micro-organizations that compose it are essential ideas for understanding the impact of technological change.

Is liberalism's history a guide to its future?

According to numerous technology experts, the world of production stands on the edge of yet another transformational innovation: the application of artificial intelligence (AI) to every aspect of the company value chain, from demand analysis to running the production machines to loading and shipping the product, as well as operating the order/help desks and driving the delivery trucks. What's more, the products will remain in constant contact with after-sales service as well as with other machines. Ubiquitous computing in the workplace, and universal data storage combined with neural networks, are a recipe for capitalizing labour and eliminating most of the human workforce as a production factor: in effect, technology is providing us with a production/consumption system that reports on its own activities, provides the data access and tools to compute its likely future directions, and provides the capacity to evolve in the most profitable directions, with a minimum of human input.

Additionally, the potential for combining computer science and biology is also emerging into view. The long-term outcome from this is "enhanced" humans with new and expanded abilities owing to cybernetic implants.

Many people seem prepared to welcome this future as an inevitable extension of our own world, dominated by ubiquitous screens, apps, and the spectacular convenience offered by intelligent phones and the internet. To liberals concerned with the impact of these things on individual human freedom, the accountability of the state to the voter, and the civilizational progress that enhances mankind's ability to behave as moral agents rather than just economic ciphers, this future also has a distinctly dystopic edge.

Already, global business has escaped the obligation to pay taxes of which it disapproves, owing to its ability to circulate money electronically from tax haven to tax haven — effectively to place money anywhere in the world. The fiscal crisis of the nation-state is apparent now. Whether acknowledged or not, the state is therefore reduced to its early nineteenth-century condition of inability to employ or provide for the portion of the population excluded from private employment, for whatever reason. True, some basic medical, educational, and social services are on offer for those who cannot afford the privately supplied and superior services. But that is a far cry from citizens' equality of access to the services necessary to ensure every citizen can participate fully in society — the goal of the welfare state as a defence of human dignity. We seem to be on a downward slope toward the complete devaluation of citizenship except as a category for classification and surveillance.

There seems to be no alternative, and there probably is none, to our current neoliberalism of automatic behaviour guided by competitive prices and the disappearance of the middle class — unless we accept that the problem is not one of technological and other change per se, but rather the way we think about change and as a consequence evaluate it. Specifically, this result comes from looking at society through the lens of utilitarianism, and at economics through the lens of Newtonian physics. These are the cardinal errors. We need to take a leaf from the historical/institutional economist-sociologists and tackle the problem from a different angle, one that may permit a solution by which we are able to maintain a liberal society in which individual freedom remains a sacred value.

One of the main arguments in this book is that the swerve in late nineteenth-century economics toward social science created a genuinely useful tool for reinventing liberal society, an alternative to the grinding social divisions of Manchesterism. The influence of this development was such that it pushed the major European powers and the United States to reverse the hands-off state doctrines of classical liberalism in favour of activism that culminated in the welfare state — without a revolution like that of Russia in 1917.

Well before 1914, the major European powers had integrated most of the male working class into a democratic parliamentary system that allowed workers to use the machinery of government to address their most pressing concerns. By the outbreak of war, workers showed that they preferred to express working class solidarity as part of a nationally based order rather than a class-based order. This was directly linked to the reforms achieved through successful state socialism in Germany, which was based not on classical, market-focused economics, but rather on a comprehensive, historical treatment of the society and economy that included culture and institutions.

In contrast to the destitution and harsh "two nations" class conflict that marked the early to middle Victorian years of industrialization in Britain and elsewhere, Germany achieved a working arrangement with its Social Democratic Party that, despite the rhetoric of its leadership, effectively integrated the working class into the parliamentary system. At the same time, Germany's coordinated industrial strategy enabled it to achieve great power status within thirty years of its unification in 1871.

By 1945, with the failure of renewed laissez-faire in the Great Depression and the subsequent Allied victory in the Second World War, marked by government direction of the "total war" effort, it seemed only natural to continue with a big state to ensure a successful postwar transition to peace. This became known as the welfare state, based on the adoption of a coherent sociological approach to economic development. In Britain this approach represented the enlarged concept of citizenship of the sociologist T.H. Marshall.[1] The welfare state enabled a transition from liberalism to social democracy in virtually every Western country after the Second World War.

The useful takeaway for liberals today who face the challenge thrown up by a nihilist, technocratic future is that it will force them to rethink some supposedly firm assumptions about the state and society. Liberals in the nineteenth and twentieth centuries learned to accept that when economics focuses uniquely on market forces in opposition to all others, it becomes too narrow a field to support the political ideals of industrial liberalism. To be fully effective in offering the understanding and policy direction contemporary conditions require, economics needs to be considered as part of a broader discipline of sociology. Otherwise, the social forces that economics ignores, shown in the rage of the majority at their vulnerable and desperate condition, will overwhelm and undermine the "rational" market with the aggregate force of a community intent on self-preservation. This enraged mass may elect populist politicians, engage in civil unrest, and even form clandestine "armies" and engage in acts of terrorism. Or it may just target merchants for boycott. All this and more can happen, and indeed these things regularly feature in our newscasts.

Nevertheless, many liberals have now convinced themselves that "market-based alternatives," meaning less regulation and tax relief for business and the wealthy, would outperform the social democracies inspired by

Keynesian economics allied with sociology. That promise has delivered in terms of technological progress. But it has also proved to be missing in action on almost every front related to social well-being unless confronted by a strong — generally undemocratic — state. Instead, the neoliberalism of Hayek and the "Washington Consensus" have revived in the democracies the question raised in the late 1970s by the British political philosopher John Dunn: Do liberal ideas work?[2]

Dunn's commentary, written a generation before the fateful events of the early twenty-first century, reflected social preoccupations: Why were legislatures unable to stop the growing gap between middle class and wealthy incomes? This was to ask effectively the same question as much of the French and American electorates did in the presidential elections of 2016: Why had conventional democratic politics not done more to stop the erosion of middle class living standards, despite the dramatic increase in wealth among the top 1 percent of society?

Established societies are not philosophy seminars. They have limits to learning and adaptation, imposed by history and class. The experience of Victorian England showed that there were limits to the middle class's and the aristocracy's willingness to engage fully with the human misery in their midst — and by no means were they willing to eliminate the problem. The scale of the human problems brought on by industrialization seemed to oblige the utilitarian mind to require that the victims accept most of the blame for their own condition. Only over the course of some fifty years were improvements made, as the representatives of the working class were gradually accepted into the political community; still, very little was done to offset the horrifying and persistent abject poverty that became rampant in large cities such as London and New York. Only the increasing public prodding by social scientists, including the publication of graphic photographs, eventually motivated the state to begin to take seriously the humanitarian disaster unfolding at the heart of the capitalist system.

To turn more particularly to the United States, governance in the laissez-faire period was characterized by the gradual assumption of political control by the "professionals": the political machines controlled by powerful industrial interests and, finally, by the "money trust." Such was the appetite and were the apparent prospects for individual economic gain that ablest men and women in the United States put their faith in private enterprise and left others to handle the public purpose, until the social costs of its neglect rose to the point of urgency.

The challenge to contemporary liberalism is similar to the challenge then: how to create a society that combines political freedom with social generosity and care for those who need it. Already, it is obvious that treating individuals as utilitarian atoms controlled by market forces alone is not enough to create and sustain healthy communities in a fully livable society. The populist rebellions are proof that popular patience is not infinite. Yet, in the near future, it seems, liberal society will have to deal with an economy in which labour is not really much of a production factor any longer. True, AI may not eliminate all jobs right away. But AI will be carried on the books as a capital investment, thus reducing even more the importance of labour in the value of the enterprise.

Our challenge is therefore much like the historical challenge that faced the German-speaking peoples between 1848 and 1866 — finding a course of national development that would enable the pursuit of the good life under conditions that enable each person's uniqueness to express itself. Liberal societies today — faced with technological trends that threaten not only individual freedom, but also human primacy — have to reconsider many of their treasured ideas and repurpose some of them so as to be able to ensure a liberal future. Are liberals up to the challenge? It is especially difficult, because there are few if any positive examples to draw from and the terrain upon which we will soon be treading is unknown country.

Friedrich List re-examined Adam Smith's *Wealth of Nations* and asked why factors of production had to be exploited separately. By arguing that they could be assembled based on desired goals, he opened the door to planned economic relationships between the makers of components and subcomponents, and between producers and consumers. From this starting point, and adding the financial capacity of the state as financier of early resort, List created the intellectual basis for an economy that could be organized by planning, and protected in its infant stage by protective trade policy. Government coordination of the construction of common infrastructure also helped reduce waste and inefficiencies in the early development phases of industrialization. By reducing the anarchy of coordinating uniquely through market forces, he also reduced the time necessary to ramp up a national industrial economy, whose efficiencies could then be "tuned" by gradually opening it to competition in the international market.

Taking a leaf from List's playbook, let us consider the source of wealth in a digital economy. Mainly, this kind of economy is driven by the raw material of data and the processing speed of the microchip. It runs on the internet. The choke points in this system are (1) the source of new knowledge, namely fundamental research; (2) the monetization of knowledge through the patent system; and (3) the decisional power of the financial system — more specifically, its privatizing public lending on big projects and controlling the price of public debt via its credit ratings. These three elements constitute the system that at the horizon of its activities harvests the profits of global enterprises free of tax, and achieves its enormous capital market valuations by virtue of oligopoly, owing to the strength of patent protection and fantastic market shares arising from its enterprises' position as internet hubs for which they pay no rent.

Oddly, the tools for reasserting public control over this system have been in the suggestion box for almost fifty years. They are (1) imposing a turnover tax on global commerce, to be shared proportionately by governments or paid to central U.N. agencies like the International Monetary Fund (IMF), World Trade Organization (WTO), or United Nations Conference on Trade and Development (UNCTAD); (2) reducing patent protection periods to increase competition through faster innovation; (3) exacting higher rents from corporations on the patents they use, based on the patents' importance within their system architecture; (4) having governments resume public financing for infrastructure so as to reduce its initial cost; and (5) completing the Bretton Woods program to balance trade flows by penalties on persistent surpluses and deficits.

These steps would go some way to rebalancing the relationship between governments and private corporations, especially the global companies, and would also ensure that governments benefited from new technologies whose development they helped to finance. However, it would require a determined and collected effort for governments to take these steps, and corporate lobbies could probably continue to hold them off for some time yet.

Moreover, one may be forgiven for doubting that such steps would be sufficient to save liberalism from the impact of technology and neoliberal economic policy. Thus, liberals perhaps would make more progress in addressing the future by considering the following, as well:

1. **The separation of liberalism and capitalism:** Capitalism is now embarked on fulfilling its ultimate destiny: freeing humanity from the necessity of working for a living. This is as fundamental as it gets. Since the Garden of Eden, mankind has been obliged to live by the sweat of its brow. Since then, labour — mainly forced through some kind of slavery — has been the lot of humanity. Only in the last couple of centuries, when labour became attached to machines propelled by energy other than wind, water, or muscle, did mankind's freedom from labour become a possibility. Over that period, capitalism has demonstrated repeatedly its amazing ability to coordinate production and consumption, so that virtually the whole of the planet is involved in working to serve popular demand, and for wages that enable the expression of individual demand for a selection of that product. But now as humans slowly escape the ancient curse of labour's necessity, the problem arises: How will social product be allocated? Without work and wages, the basic instruments of allocation developed over millennia now vanish. Yet the basic choice — between trading and raiding — remains, now restated more starkly. Not even private property is secure — that is, property secured by the fruits of labour. Ours is not the only society to cope with this: the leading classes of the ancient world had no work to go to; they consigned the day-to-day running of their estates to slaves. These leaders devoted their time to the affairs of state. Perhaps this is a plausible solution for us. Leave the work to the "bots" while civil society runs the country. The end of work would make participative democracy possible.

2. **The question of what liberals mean by "freedom":** From the material in this book, it would seem that freedom turns on the quality of civil society, its norms and aspirations. This is a cultural issue for which sociological investigation is critical. In our digital world, to be sure, civil society reports on itself in mountains of data on individual transactions that range from "Likes" on Facebook to texts exchanged on social media or by email. All this is already offered up and discounted for sale by aggregators and analysts looking for the best way to market

a product. However, we argue that these transactions and correlations are only behavioural at best. The insight into what it means to live in civil society at any moment is what liberal sociology requires. To put it in the terms Dilthey used,[3] we need to understand the middle layer between the everyday reality experienced by the subjective individual and the objective reality individuals experience when in the world — the reality made up of one's friends and associates, as well as one's encounters with others as one goes about in society. For that is the source of culture and its morphology.

3. **Most Western political systems are kind to private interests, but pursue much less robustly the obligation to show comparable concern for the whole of civil society.** Giving civil society constitutional status as an active body whose care is government's major responsibility might impose a concern for society's overall well-being beyond just growth rates or income shares, and ensure that policy outcomes balance each other such that society is seen to be fair. As work declines and participation in the sharing or "gig" economy grows, governments will find they need a clear and comprehensive approach to these changes. Probably their approach will include a guaranteed minimum wage, paid from the total social product generated by the robotic production force and its management. A constitutional status for civil society would help ensure that rights are matched by the means to exercise them, a step that will be particularly necessary when earnings from labour become a rarity.[4] Above all, this step would make it more difficult for private power to occlude the public interest.

4. **How to determine status and function without the ordering power of work:** Labour also settles the issue of social rank in liberal societies today, with finance at the top of the food chain, Fortune 500 CEOs and senior officers, university professors, Uber drivers, and others farther down the list. We are ranked according to our work and the place where we do it. From these rankings the population draws conclusions about who you are and what power or authority you have in the sociopolitical set-up. Without work, some new system must be put in its place. To function acceptably, it must be transparent and its rules must promote confidence. Perhaps cultural distinction and its gradations

might serve as a replacement. Instead of jobs, people would sort themselves into voluntary groups undertaking particular sporting or cultural activities: orchestras, theatres, chess clubs, literary circles — perhaps even Ruskin workshops for craftsmen and craftswomen — and vie for ranking through competition. If they do, then the state would have to be prepared to spend on new venues for training and practice, and to ensure that competitions are held fairly. Pericles' Athens ran along these lines to an extent — it spent as much on its drama festivals as it did on the maintenance of its war fleet.

The logical consequence of these examples is that if the liberal state is to have a positive role in the advancement of the condition of its citizens, then it has to be able to intervene at the macro-social level in order to ensure that acceptable living standards are maintained. But in this and similar situations since the 1980s, liberal governments have failed to do so. To be sure, the neoliberal ideology according to which economics is more important than sociology and history plays a large role in that failure. But our historical examples suggest that the ideology is often a convenient excuse for letting a bad situation persist because the will to address it is missing. So what has gone wrong? We might well join John Dunn in asking: Does liberalism work? But it might be a better idea to ask instead: How can we make it work? How can liberal institutions be made more effective?

Dunn notes that liberalism has failed (among other ways) in not responding effectively to the growing social inequality in Western countries. John Gray, another notable English political philosopher, says in his more recent study of liberalism[5] that liberalism cannot work as it is beset with conflicts between incommensurable principles — which underlines the importance of postmodernism and the turn toward technology, and in particular the inability to agree on principles to support a common response to the technological challenge to labour. Yet we know that some versions of liberalism do seem to work, for example those of the Nordic countries and Germany, all of which have adopted a version of liberalism similar to that of Eucken's postwar ordoliberalism, discussed earlier. This version privileges mutual care and active social inclusion over competition and exclusion, which are the drivers of liberalism in most large English-speaking countries.

The French political scientist Pierre Rosanvallon is helpful in unpacking current democratic processes.[6] He makes a distinction between competitive democratic processes, such as elections, nominations, and so forth, and functional democracy, about which he elaborates an argument for a fourth level of sovereignty. That is, he proposes it be recognized that democracies have a fourth power, and by virtue of that power an implicit fourth branch that encompasses the other three in its ability to oversee and report on the condition of the state and its democracy as a whole — a concept reminiscent of Fichte's idea of reviving the ancient Greek ephors. He points out that De Gaulle had something similar in mind when he created France's Conseil d'État (Constitutional Council). Just as the Supreme Court oversees the constitutionality of the law in the United States and Canada, the Conseil d'État in France can oversee government operations to ensure they remain democratic.

Rosanvallon's major point is that competitive processes divide and fragment public attention, diverting it from the comprehensive perspective needed on the state and where it is heading. Without a "fourth power" operating on their behalf, electors will lack the information necessary and can easily be distracted from addressing the national situation. The U.S. constitutional founders put their faith in a free press and in a unified executive branch headed by a president holding the only office with a national mandate. Under a strong president with an informed and coherent view and a program that can garner enough support in Congress, history shows, the system can work to its potential. But absent those conditions, the system can quickly stalemate and pull itself into fragments.

The logical consequence of these examples is that if the liberal state is to have a positive role in advancing the condition of its citizens, then civil society needs a special status in law as a community of needs for which the state is ultimately responsible, as well as a public space — including parliament but not restricted to it — for discussing the affairs of state and the state's future. Markets and market mechanisms are part of any solution. But they must not be the only solution. Why not? Again, Croly's Progressive Era analysis of the big trusts and political machines characteristic of his time should be as instructive for us as it was for the Progressive movement. Without state intervention to preserve or ensure a certain standard or quality of life, the law of least cost prevails, and it is only a matter of time before the country slips under control of the political machine. That is what happens when "we the people" forget that "we" (the many) are the sovereign power of the state. Enhanced status for civil society would, for example, ensure that rights and "values" are matched, such that a right to universal education would be matched by allocating the necessary "value," in the form of sufficient resources to ensure that every citizen has affordable access to education on a continuing basis. That is, rights would be made practical by "values" — to the "value" of the program.[7]

One of the most significant and persistent divisions in liberalism is that between so-called republican or communitarian liberalism and the classic individual liberalism of J.S. Mill and Benjamin Constant. In one of his most celebrated speeches, Constant maintains a sharp contrast between ancient civic republicanism, which he associates with Rousseau, and modern democracy, which he equates to utilitarian individualism similar to that explored by Mill. Constant discusses these in terms of the democracy of the ancient city state and the democracy of the modern nation-state. Rousseau's basic idea was of the general will emerging from the identification of the citizen with the state and its participative democracy. The ancient citizen shared actively in every sovereign decision of the state, Constant points out, whereas modern citizens are free to get on with their private business and only exercise their sovereign power by immediately delegating it to the representative of their choice. Thereafter, they are free again to return to their private concerns while their elected officials deal with state business. Under the rules of the ancient republic, the citizenry actively participated in the running of the state as both soldiers and statesmen; their private affairs could only come second. The moderns, then, are doubly favoured by this division of labour in that they can keep an eye on government and, at the same time, pursue their private projects unhindered.

What Constant omits from this contrast is the problem of ensuring that the representatives respect their mandate. Burke's address to the electors of Bristol puts the point clearly: the elected representative is there to judge for himself the best interests of his constituents, taking into account the superior information available to members of the government in contrast to the information available to the private citizen.

It is often forgotten — as Constant seems to have done[8] — that Rousseau's arguments had a powerful effect on Kant and his synthesis of eighteenth-century political thought in his three critiques and other writings on moral principles. In his book on the "Rousseau problem,"[9] Ernst Cassirer — the same philosopher who debated Heidegger in Davos — points out that Kant's basic moral law, a test to see whether a principle can be universalized without causing people harm, is Kant's answer to Rousseau's general will. The sovereign duty of every citizen faced with the loss of democracy is no different from that of the citizen of the ancient city state: the citizen's sovereignty is under attack and the citizen must resist. This is made easier by ensuring that citizens have the right to assemble and protest — recognized as a right not only of individuals but of civil society as an entity.

TECHNOLOGICAL AND FINANCIAL INNOVATION

While Dunn and Gray, among others, call attention to liberal ideas and the problems of making them effective in governance, another critique of liberalism begins with changes to economic organization driven by technology and finance. This point was first driven home by Saint-Simon and later by Comte. Industrialization would inevitably bring to power an oligarchy of technical knowledge and organizational ability. Its competence would lend it both legitimacy and the power to reorganize society in the interests of industry alone. Saint-Simon believed the state had a duty to intervene to assure that the social structure would not disintegrate. His arguments were far-seeing and very influential. In the hands of the French pioneering sociologist Émile Durkheim, they offer a picture of how innovation can drive social change by effectively upsetting the established balance of status and function, and thus generate important misalignments of power and legitimacy.

In this connection, Albert O. Hirschman's suggestion[10] that there is a "Schumpeterian oscillation" between public and private interest priorities in the political life of a country underlines an important social defence mechanism. In that comment, he is referencing Schumpeter's theory of entrepreneurial innovation. It holds that such innovation enables economies to jump from stage to stage via the adoption of new technologies or breakthrough approaches to technical problems that are blocking progress. Schumpeter's theory of innovation explains how a mature economy whose industries are stable and is operating under Pareto-optimal conditions (where an advance by one firm can come only at the expense of another firm) can suddenly progress dramatically via innovation, especially big, systemic innovation that changes the condition of the economy.

Schumpeter was not only an imaginative economist, he was also a competent sociologist, well endowed with what C. Wright Mills called a "sociological imagination." An Austrian, he was also influenced by Schmoller, Sombart, and the historical school, although he was at times critical of it. He made his international reputation in 1942 with *Capitalism, Socialism, and Democracy.*[11] Schumpeter accompanied his economic analysis with a sociological evaluation: innovation is irregular — that is, it comes in bursts. When societies experience the costs of innovation, they generally become quite conservative. Periods of innovation are limited because there are costs to disruption; beyond a certain point, people are capable of turning to politics to block innovation altogether. Prolonged periods of innovation are, then, not sustainable, owing to social resistance to change. The social and political pushbacks pile up as innovation progresses. Therefore, he said, capitalism is always under threat from extreme socialism or fascism, or populism, as entrepreneurs push the limits of public tolerance of innovation.

Hirschman borrows from Schumpeter's analysis, in part, to develop his own perception of an oscillation in society around rates of innovation, seen as a cycle of alternating private and public emphases. In his work *Shifting Involvements,* Hirschman agrees with Schumpeter, but offers a different analysis linked to the consumption of goods and services rather than their production under competitive capitalism.[12] Either way, it seems, there is a cycle in Western society that from time to time sweeps away constraints on private interests in the process of laying the material basis of a new society. This is followed after a time by new constraints that blunt the sharp edges and soften the conflicts of the "self-organized" design, thereby creating new institutions needed for the flourishing of organized social life.[13]

This is perhaps the wave that seems to be building now, reflecting a certain buyer's remorse regarding the "total costs of ownership" of globalization under unrestricted competitive capitalism. However, at present, what is worth keeping and what needs repair and shoring up has received very little serious examination.

As a matter of record, too, Schumpeter was mistaken about socialism (as social democracy): first, because social democracy does accept capitalism, subject to the right to correct its flaws; and second, because it can promote innovation across society. Schumpeter seems to have missed the point that social democracy would save capitalism by curbing its destructiveness while preserving and enhancing its benefits. To be fair, however, the socialism he discusses in *Capitalism, Socialism, and Democracy* is that of a central planning state with no markets at all, the social tolerance of entrepreneurship having been thoroughly corroded by capitalism's innate instability.[14]

In fact, it turns out that technological innovation was never higher than during the thirty years of the postwar social democratic economy. The period saw an enormous expansion of every nation's research capacity in the social and natural sciences, and the creation of university laboratories to take on the applied research problems now too big for industry to solve in its company labs. Leaps forward based on the painstaking work of thousands of researchers produced cures for tuberculosis and polio, and a vastly greater understanding of heart disease and cancer, while opening up whole new territories for scientific exploration in genomics and microbiology — to name just some of the successes. Perhaps the biggest and most interesting game-changers were the revolutions in electronics — the microchip revolution and the creation of the internet — and ultimately the browser, which transformed the internet into the highway and bazaar that it has become. (Wherever possible, private sector companies have moved in to commercialize and improve what public spending invented and established. Even neoliberals recognize the importance of that partnership, although they claim to believe that progress will be enhanced if more public money goes to the private sector rather than continuing the partnership as before.) The explanation is clear: social democracy offers the security necessary to minimize costs from disruptive industrial change.

Measurement and performance evaluation are nevertheless the core of the controversy about what constitutes innovation and how it should be funded. The political controversy is around the purpose of innovation and the management of disruptive innovation. These are not issues for a "watchman state" or a "government for hire." Governments must have or acquire the expertise to evaluate innovation and its deployment. The human and environmental health aspects are clear. Perhaps less clear is the importance of full employment if a state is to be a major innovator. Full employment enables people to take on new challenges and test new organizational arrangements, secure that the disruption they take on can be absorbed at minimum social cost and maximum net social benefit. Workers' status as citizens within the plant irrespective of their specific function can be protected in large organizations by facilitating structures in which workers and managers participate in decision-making — that is, a system of co-determination — and by facilitating co-operative structures among smaller organizations.

So the question then becomes: What kind of social science will be the most helpful? It's a large question. An answer that respects liberal values, including a duty of care to promote quality and defend the vulnerable, might be given along the following lines: People's behaviour is shaped by the transformation of the world around them. This is ground zero for politics; liberalism has to start by connecting to how people really live. Working the other way around — from the abstract general to the assumed particular, from the top to the bottom — is to give in to the temptation to dominate. It is imposing abstraction on a concrete reality rather than letting the general picture emerge in the conscious minds of those who share a "lifeworld." When liberalism works that way, it needs no justification. If it helps people understand their situation the better to deal with it, and get on with their life project, then liberalism is doing what liberalism is supposed to do best.

Getting there, however, is fatally obstructed by ideologies that divide and obscure. Democracy succeeds because people can assemble and exchange ideas and have conversations, not so-called candidates' debates that amount to shouted slogans hurled across a crowded room. Democracy needs salons, coffee shops, and other places like the good old American neighbourhood diner — and a free press that deals with the issues. If liberalism is understood not only as a unique form of government but also as a process of sociopolitical development, then it becomes clearer that any social science investigation will have to take into account historical development, including the history of meanings behind the actions and institutions being researched. Organigrams and Gantt charts and other products of behavioural research are important for a portrait of operations. A quantitative score may be desirable. But in every human endeavour the content — the motivations and ideas of those involved — are also significant and need to be considered. Quality matters in its own right and because it can overcome alienation. Who doesn't want to be associated with something significant?

RECOVERING LIBERALISM IN PHILOSOPHY

There remains the philosophical issue haunting liberalism — the challenge of postmodernism and its variations: Effectively, how can liberalism pretend to offer a formula for human freedom when all it has to offer concretely is class power and market domination? That is perhaps a correct formulation of neoliberalism. Liberalism, what Peter Gay called "the science of freedom," is not that, although for much of the nineteenth and early twentieth centuries that criticism would have been justified. The difference is that liberalism — like society itself — is capable of learning, and thus what constitutes the liberal paradigm is capable of change based on experience.

Consider an example such as the New Deal, which became a template for the postwar welfare state. Its key advances over its predecessors are that (1) it no longer believed in market fundamentalism; (2) it proved itself ready to act to overcome people's actual, concrete needs; and (3) it has subsequently learned how to disaggregate people's needs and to address them one by one, or case by case, wherever that is appropriate to the particular circumstances of those involved. Social democracy is not the one-size-fits-all program some of its critics think.

Most important, sitting at the heart of the issue and undisturbed by economic models and concepts, is Kant's understanding that, as freedom does not exist in nature, it therefore must be created, based on imagination and reason. His argument was that political freedom could be achieved with ideas that link natural science and human values through reason's discovery of what he termed the moral law, or the categorical imperative: that is, whatever is proposed must be universally valid to be acceptable — that a law for one person must be a law for all, and it is immoral for humans to be instrumentalized by others without consent. Kant's ideas highlighted the importance of a public morality underpinning rational institutions in addition to conforming to scientific principles.

Kant's arguments stood up for most of the century until the 1870s, and indeed, until the First World War. In the late nineteenth century, though, we have to mark a break with Kant: the work of Nietzsche. Until Nietzsche, philosophy was rational and reason kept it on rails supportive of human progress. Nietzsche opened the door to the idea that modernism might reveal itself to be "a fatal adventure for mankind." In his work, he identified the "will to power" — not reason — as the mainspring of human conduct. He denounced history, and effectively argued that if the rule of the strongest is inevitable, than the strongest would have to surpass the ancient heroes in their human capacities — like Zarathustra — if mankind was to flourish. Nietzsche's originality undercut both Marxism and positivism, although his views of the future aligned with their warnings of what lay ahead for European civilization.

As material progress developed, from virtually every quarter came cultural pressure to move away from idealism toward materialism and positivism.[15] The main theatre for this battle in the nineteenth century was Germany. It spread to North America by the 1930s and flared up again in the 1960s. As history shows, the stakes are surprisingly high: philosophy is not as unimportant as many people seem to think.

The ideas grounding liberalism — the ideas of freedom, of human dignity, and government of the people, by the people, and for the people; the concept of rights protection, rule of law, and the role of reason — all these values are underpinned by philosophical idealism. In Kantian language, they are *noumena*, which, when translated into action, demonstrate their truth, which becomes a "synthetic" blend of values and accomplished fact. Kant's categorical imperative of a universal moral law is an example. Liberalism is rooted in those ideas: there is little to no material or positive evidence to suggest that liberalism performs better or is more efficient, say, than enlightened despotism or competent technocracy as a system of governance. There is only a powerful ideology that has been a Western ideal since the ancient Greeks (although subsequently much modified) that human nature craves freedom: we are born to be free.

FROM HEIDEGGER TO HABERMAS

Heidegger's debate with Cassirer in Davos in 1929 confronted Kant's system directly, in contrast to positivist nibbling at the validity of his "thing in itself." Defenders of Kant against positivism make a sharp distinction between natural sciences and moral sciences — the first submitting to the logical realm of positivism and experimentation. For the cultural or moral sciences, however, the underlying problem is not natural forces so much as the human forces of historical development. The key to understanding lies in the "facts of consciousness" or "inner experience." In other words, in contrast to the positive truths of natural science, social phenomena can be understood only as subjective meaning, which could best be discovered in hermeneutic interpretation of lifeworlds of experience and belief.[16] Heidegger took Dilthey's work to an entirely new level by reducing meaning to the fact of existence, a pre-political engagement with the world in which mankind is unable to transcend its existential reality as a mortal being with limited capacities for action. From this position, every meta-argument, every general message about human destiny, every emancipatory message, from Hegel's Absolute Spirit to liberalism's promise of freedom, becomes bogus. Indeed, at the end of the 1970s, the French philosopher Jean-François Lyotard announced this new development as the essence of postmodernism.[17]

Cassirer's defence links mankind's social development to its growing ability to manipulate reality by means of symbolic codes, such as language and mathematics. Heidegger, in contrast, emphasizes mankind's existence as primary, with its ability to form relationships limited by the available tools. Critics of Heidegger (such as Hannah Arendt) point to Heidegger's reduced scope for public action.[18] For Heidegger, mankind's capacity for representation amounts to the capacity for domination.[19] No longer the rounded individual citizen of the *polis*,[20] the political community, the individual human is now just a creature of homogenous groups subjugated by the *polis* as a tool of self-innovating technology and/or a metaphysical ideology. As for history, Heidegger claims that "history attacks from in front" — that is, our interest in history is limited to our understanding of those events or ideas that shed light on the present condition of our *Dasein* — the specificity of our individual existence.

In opposition to Heidegger's pre-political bleakness, Hannah Arendt offers the life of action, especially political action in the public square, which presents the possibility of self-affirmation and participation in the construction of the political community,[21] a position close to Sartre's existentialism.

More recently, the eminent German philosopher Jürgen Habermas has come to dominate this discussion with his defence of Kant by repositioning idealism along the lines of John Dewey's pragmatism. Habermas rejects Heidegger's inward turning of philosophy, but in his concept of reasoned political speech also returns us to a world of individuals in groups divided only by value frameworks — akin to Husserl's lifeworlds. It may sound like relativism, but for Habermas it is a sign that political universality is possible, even if there are also universally accepted standards for the concept of "reasonableness." With Gerald Gaus, Habermas agrees that differing parties can agree on a process while disagreeing about outcomes, or agree on outcomes while differing about the process for reaching them — it is still productive agreement.[22] Habermas's argument may be correct, but will be unconvincing to many with deeply held beliefs on one subject or another. Does Habermas also open the door to the neoliberal postulate that commercial values are sufficiently universal to constitute the basis of human association? To be sure, that can constitute a beginning. But its further development is compromised by the logic of competition, a position adopted by Kant and Hegel together. In short, co-operation and complementarity are both essential for solidarity to emerge. Heidegger is not saying that people can't figure out how to live together — only that society must be based on a prior agreement to accept each other's specificity as legitimized by existence. That, one might agree, is the central problem of liberalism today.

SOME TAKEAWAYS

A number of points emerge from the foregoing that I think ought to be remembered if liberalism is to be reconstructed:

1. The world needs a caring, sympathetic, and supportive liberalism. It does not need another hard-edged ideology incapable of understanding the lifeworlds of others.

2. Liberalism is intrinsically unstable and socially divisive. It needs to be encased in a caring polity to achieve its goals of individual freedom with social justice.

3. A rules-based liberalism without a results-based government will fail.

4. If liberalism can be designed to work successfully, that is, without destructive instability, it must pay attention to the "law of requisite variety" (Ashby's Law: there must be enough variety to absorb variety for a system to be stable[23]). Inclusiveness is worth the cost to get right because it affirms the principle of human equality, a value essential to sustainable communities. Results must be shared in such a way to enable full participation in society.

5. In a functioning, developed modern society, public consciousness requires information, not just arguments: social science research can verify whether politics is adequately addressing the issues most closely related to society's purpose — a challenge that the human sciences are better suited to meet than the natural sciences alone.

6. The ideology of positivism is too narrow to permit an understanding of the human and social condition by itself. It may be able to explain a situation, but it cannot understand it — because positivism lacks the human quality of sympathy. Without such understanding, technology rules by presenting as a *fait accompli* what *can* be done before we understand what *should* be done. The moral purpose of liberal society is always to maintain and expand human freedom while advancing the human condition — including sustaining the Earth as a safe place for humans.

7. Liberalism needs a vigilant electorate. Empowering the electorate with rights of petition and recall, as in Switzerland, will raise the stakes and help keep people interested between elections.

8. Ensuring that ordinary people have convenient and inexpensive access to legal tribunals for everyday disputes is essential to ensuring respect for the law. The law must never become a tool that uniquely serves a single class against the rest.

If we accept these points, then I think the inference is obvious: we need to conduct our political discussions in the light not only of economic indicators and the capabilities of technology, but also an understanding of the social and environmental challenges we need to meet. This in turn suggests the need for a redefinition of optimality: inclusion of all — not just "the greatest number" — as the greatest good, and enhancing social quality, not just personal enrichment, as the test of policy. Research, not dogma, is the answer to most of the operating differences in free societies.[24] Resuscitating the idea of the public good in a liberal society has to begin with recovering the concept of a free society, accepting that the freedom of each depends on the freedom of all, and vice versa.

RESSENTIMENT

We are not finished, unfortunately, with the downside of liberalism. *Ressentiment* is the antithesis of Kantian reason in a doubly negative alienation: hatred of oneself and of one's lifeworld. It is the crystallization of despair and futility, with regret and self-loathing lumped in. A feature of *ressentiment* is a desire to strike violently at the other as an enemy and even to blow up the enemy other together with oneself, to go out with a pyrotechnic flash as a stunning end to a life condemned by injustice to insignificance and pain.[25] Next to climate change, it is probably the most serious threat to liberal societies today.

RECOVERING THE LIBERALISM OF "THE LONG REVOLUTION"

Historically, liberalism is the champion of "the long revolution" of modern human emancipation from the superstitions and binding traditions of church, state, and feudal society of the period 1600–1800, and thereafter the promoter of parliamentary democracy and national emancipation.[26] Toward the end of the nineteenth century, however, as the industrial economies needed more and more institutional capital to expand and secure natural resources, liberalism also became the underwriter of what was effectively a financial takeover of Africa, Latin America, and, later, the Middle East. In Africa in particular, it meant the imposition of national boundaries across the reality of tribal links. In the Middle East, it meant the imposition of client governments on the remnants of the Ottoman Empire. Since then, the suffering has hardly ever ceased.

Liberalism has yet to confront its contribution to this record. Yet the tools for this are actually at hand and have been for some time, in the U.N. declarations and the Allied war aims of the Second World War. Statesmen may have been fighting for new national boundaries and spheres of influence. The ordinary Joes and Janes were fighting for the Four Freedoms, including freedom from fear and freedom from want. It's never too late to address what has been neglected for far too long.

In other words, rebuilding liberalism must go beyond getting economics and social sciences to work as a complementary whole. It must also reinvigorate the U.N. organizations and end the horror shows of civil war, ethnic cleansing, and dictatorship at the edges of the Western world. The best way to do that is to follow the successful Asian development models that, in turn, are based upon those of List, Rodbertus, and Schmoller in the German Empire, although, happily, many of them also developed into stronger democracies than that of Bismarck's Germany.

As a reminder of what liberalism was like at the end of the Second World War, I attach the following text. These excerpts are from Roosevelt's fourth State of the Union address conveyed to Congress in January 1944, just before his death and when Allied victory was only dimly in sight and by no means assured:

> This Republic had its beginning, and grew to its present strength, under the protection of certain inalienable political rights — among them the right of free speech, free press, free worship, trial by jury, freedom from unreasonable searches and seizures. They were our rights to life and liberty.
>
> As our Nation has grown in size and stature, however — as our industrial economy expanded — these political rights proved inadequate to assure us equality in the pursuit of happiness.
>
> We have come to a clear realization of the fact that true individual freedom cannot exist without economic security and independence. "Necessitous men are not free

men." People who are hungry and out of a job are the stuff of which dictatorships are made.

In our day these economic truths have become accepted as self-evident. We have accepted, so to speak, a second Bill of Rights under which a new basis of security and prosperity can be established for all regardless of station, race, or creed.

Among these [rights] are:

The right to a useful and remunerative job in the industries or shops or farms or mines of the Nation;

The right to earn enough to provide adequate food and clothing and recreation;

The right of every farmer to raise and sell his products at a return which will give him and his family a decent living;

The right of every businessman, large and small, to trade in an atmosphere of freedom from unfair competition and domination by monopolies at home or abroad;

The right of every family to a decent home;

The right to adequate medical care and the opportunity to achieve and enjoy good health;

The right to adequate protection from the economic fears of old age, sickness, accident, and unemployment;

The right to a good education.

All of these rights spell security. And after this war is won we must be prepared to move forward, in the implementation of these rights, to new goals of human happiness and well-being.

America's own rightful place in the world depends in large part upon how fully these and similar rights have been carried into practice for our citizens. For unless there is security here at home there cannot be lasting peace in the world.[27]

For those of us who still believe liberalism can be rebuilt, let us note some of the salient features of the foregoing text: its sympathetic capture of the economic insecurity of the average man and woman of the time — the concept of the "necessitous" man — and the program to ensure by right a living standard that preserves individual freedom and choice, despite the competitive economic forces driving the nation as a whole. This is what it means to use politics to move forward the good life of a people. It is a stark contrast to the neoliberal concepts of popular subordination to economic forces in the name of "efficiency" or "productivity." Rather, it promises a fair reward for each individual's contribution to those things as well as a secure place from which to make those contributions. It is not contrary to economic science; rather, it is respectful of its potential to improve the life of the average citizen. It is also respectful of a vision of a caring community united by a rights-based constitution in a civil society rather than just a network of prices, buyers and sellers, contracts and transactions. These are the liberal principles that must inform the world ahead as it is transformed by technology to remove from mankind the necessity of labour and open the door to the general participation in a humane and creative civilization.

ACKNOWLEDGEMENTS

RESEARCHING THIS BOOK — like every research project — was a journey of discovery and rediscovery. The sources for the work are generally the works of the generations of scholars and writers who lived through the eras described and who participated in the debates of those times. As a general rule, these scholars — who would have been the contemporaries of my great-grandparents or older — worked tirelessly and published prolifically on the subjects that concerned them. What they may have lacked in methodological expertise according to today's standards, they made up for in culture and erudition. Although most of their works are now out of print, they are available online from such preserves as Project Gutenberg and the Internet Archive or Google Books, and from national library digital services such as that of Gallica, of France's Bibliothèque Nationale. Still others are stocked in online book clubs like Scribd, the Online Library of Liberty, and the Ludwig von Mises Institute. I also benefited from the online capabilities of the Walter Eucken Institut at Freiburg University and the interlibrary arrangements between the University of Montreal and McGill University. The amount of learning preserved by the digital copying initiatives is priceless, and my thanks are due to those university libraries that make their holdings available for digital copying and the technicians who ensure the flawless operation of the services.

Many people helped me with this work. The book's dedication, in addition to my children and grandchildren, is to my first professor in political philosophy, who generously agreed to read early drafts and to provide some helpful direction. My former co-author Dian Cohen offered consistently positive support, read every draft, and provided helpful suggestions and reflections. Jean Kitchen provided technical editing of some early drafts, thereby clarifying the writing challenge. Others especially helpful include Professor Gilles Paquet of the University of Ottawa, who also let me try out some ideas in *Optimum*, a reviewed online publication then at the university's Centre on Governance, while I was a senior fellow; Tony Deutsch, professor emeritus of the McGill Department of Economics; Professor Roger Hall, historian at the University of Western Ontario and fellow of Massey College; and Michael Saykaly, former head of Optima, a public opinion research firm known for its qualitative research. Nicole Morgan, a professor emeritus of political philosophy at Royal Military College of Canada, Kingston, and her online Sardines group including E. Craig Wilson, a retired Canadian foreign service officer with many years in Asia, tackled a number of pertinent issues. Their helpfulness should not imply agreement (or disagreement, for that matter) with any of the ideas in the text.

There were also those who enriched my thinking through their knowledgeable conversations about public affairs. Thanks in this category are due to the Wednesday Night Westmount Salon, including the late David Nicholson, his wife Diana, the late Kimon Valaskakis, and the late John Ciaccia, among other anglophone and francophone participants at what has become something of an institution; and to Paul de Grandmont and his group of long-standing friends during his generously hosted events in Saint-Lazare. The lively and original discussions at WN and those with Paul and his *compagnons de route* during this project helped me understand better what I was trying to do. My wife, Yvette Biondi, who has spent a lifetime in Quebec provincial and municipal politics, patiently tolerated my research and writing, and, whenever the subject came up, underlined that politics is a human experience and a vehicle for improving the lives of the vulnerable and oppressed. My three children — now grown up to be lawyers — also took time to clarify my thinking. Again, this in no way should imply either approval or disapproval of the ideas in this text.

I consider myself fortunate to have had a committee of readers so steeped in both the theoretical and the practical questions of liberal democratic politics. Turning a manuscript into a book also required a team: thanks are particularly due to the editorial and production team at Dundurn Press. Thanks are also due an anonymous reviewer at Palgrave Macmillan who suggested a useful reorientation of an early version. After this extraordinary level of assistance, such errors as may remain are mine alone.

AN ABBREVIATED LITERATURE REVIEW

IT IS ONLY IN RECENT YEARS that liberal scholars have begun probing the intellectual sources of the welfare state.[1] Only recently has scholarship re-examined its links with the political differences among the leading *philosophes* of the French Revolution.[2] General histories of liberalism have also been notable mainly by their absence, although there has recently been a spurt of activity.[3] Generally, we have to go back to the interwar period to find them: Ruggiero's *History of European Liberalism* (1927); Russell's *Freedom and Organization* (1934); Laski's *Rise of European Liberalism* (1936). Dominating postwar examples are the more narrowly focused anti-Keynesian works produced by the Austrians, especially Mises and Hayek, and the use of rational choice economics as a tool of political analysis by the public choice school, such as Downs's *An Economic Theory of Democracy* (1957). Political theory textbooks, such as Sabine, *A History of Political Theory* (1963), and Wolin, *Politics and Vision* (2006), offer summaries of liberalism's theoretical development, largely without critique. Comprehensive studies such as Arblaster's *The Rise and Decline of Western Liberalism* (1984) are rare.

For readers of French, the works of Pierre Manent, *Les Libéraux* (2001) and *Histoire intellectuelle du libéralisme* (2012), and earlier, Raymond Aron,

Les Étapes de la pensée sociologique (1967) are valuable anthologies and analyses. Manent (2001) in particular treats aspects of the "canon" — liberal thinkers, such as Hobbes, Locke, J.S. Mill, and others. Audard, *Qu'est-ce que le libéralisme?* (2009), offers a comprehensive history. Pierre Rosanvallon has produced a stream of useful books on the subjects raised here.[4] He combines eminence as a historian of liberalism with emergence as a wise voice of liberal reconstruction. For German readers, Jürgen Habermas's thorough and comprehensive examination of liberalism's many twists and turns extends over the span of his brilliant career and stands out like a beacon of enlightenment. If anyone can be said to have attempted the cultural reconstruction work required for a robustly political and humanist liberalism, it is he. Perhaps his most comprehensive work is his *Theory of Communicative Action* (1985).

One should also mention the work of the Walter Eucken Institut at Freiburg University. Eucken's ordoliberalism as well as the social philosophies of others in his circle, such as Wilhelm Röpke, amply met the postwar challenge of a non-Keynesian liberal revival, based on a clear understanding of the failures of Weimar and the need for a strong social agenda to offset the destructive effects of competition and innovation. In France, the regulation school of economists evolved a version of ordoliberalism suitable for that country. Neither of these currents of thought has received (in my opinion) adequate attention by English-speaking liberals.

More recent academic attention has been focused on nuanced discussions of certain questions of public ethics among liberals of various shades. One example of a comprehensive examination of liberalism is the collection of essays by Alan Ryan, *The Making of Modern Liberalism* (2012). The dates of Ryan's sources suggest that the discussions continue in an orderly fashion without any recent years of particular effervescence. The latest reference in Ryan's collection is to public opinion polls from the year 2000. The issues covered are those well-plowed furrows familiar to students of the academic literature on liberalism. Works that are genuinely challenging to the fundamentals of liberalism, such as Foucault's lectures on biopolitics (1978–79);[5] Carl Schmitt, *The Concept of the Political* (1996); and Agamben's fusion of Schmitt and Foucault, *Homo Sacer* (1998) are not within the scope of Ryan's considerations, well researched and well argued though they are. Harvey, *A Brief History of Neoliberalism* (2007), in contrast analyzes neoliberalism and warns of its longer-term implications, underlining the importance of a political route to a more just alternative — without, however, finding one.

Later works, such as Toula Nicolacopoulos, *The Radical Critique of Liberalism* (2008), lists a half dozen references from the twenty-first century. They deal with the conflicts between classical and communitarian liberalism. There is nothing that challenges directly the key components of liberal foundations from within the liberal frame, that is, whether liberalism is capable of adequately critiquing itself. An even more recent work on liberal political philosophy, Gerald Gaus, *The Order of Public Reason* (2011), references some fifty publications after 2000 in a probing account of a rules-based liberal social order. It more than adequately takes on the challenges of game-theoretic and logical analysis of liberal propositions — but unfortunately never gets down to actual cases. Foucault, Lyotard, even Heidegger are never mentioned in the work, as they are outside its scope even as they challenge the pertinence of its approach.

It should be recorded that these works on liberalism are fine works of scholarship. But they do not address the issues addressed here. For example: how the hegemony of English ideas got in the way of liberalism's self-understanding and thus the ability of English liberals to resist the decline and banalization of Western liberal political philosophy before the German exception took hold; the "fatal abstraction" of positive economics; the empty self-referentiality of postmodernism. Some postmodernist critics of liberalism and writers on social theory, such as Baudrillard, *Le Système des objets* (1968), and Lyotard, *La Condition postmoderne* (1979), open the door to such exploration. Excellent anthologies in the area of social theory are Jenkins, *The Postmodern History Reader* (1997), and Seidman and Wagner, *Postmodernism and Social Theory* (1992). But these critiques are in the main destructive. If they seek to rehabilitate parts of liberalism, they undertake it under a different name with different, unspecified, goals. It is no accident that a large proportion of sources in my bibliography are works from the nineteenth and early twentieth centuries, most of them made accessible by the internet. The historical richness and universal access of the internet-linked sources is an amazing contemporary achievement, a stunning act of faith in the principles of a free society. The building blocks and pillars of our literary and philosophical culture are available there for all to consult and consider. *Vive la liberté!*

NOTES

INTRODUCTION

1. North America, Western Europe including Germany, Austria, the succession states of the Austro-Hungarian Empire, Poland, and Greece. Clearly, this is a narrow subset of the robust democracies in the world, which, for example, would include India and Japan, among others. One might just as accurately say the Western Roman Empire (without Egypt and North Africa), Scandinavia, and North America. The key is having a nineteenth- and twentieth-century history in which liberalism was important. Russia is not in the list because it is not a liberal country, despite its attempts, particularly between 1905 and 1917, to become one. The Baltic succession states of the Petrine Russian Empire are now in the liberal camp.

2. Alfred Schutz, *The Phenomenology of the Social World,* trans. George Walsh and Frederick Lehnert (Evanston, IL: Northwestern University Press, 1967).

3. Andrew Shonfield, *Modern Capitalism: The Changing Balance of Public and Private Power* (London: Oxford University Press, 1965), 3:

"It is hard for us to believe that the bleak and squalid system which we knew [in the 1930s] could, in so short a time, have adapted itself, without some covert process of total destruction and regeneration, to achieve so many desired objectives." Jürgen Habermas analyzes the persistent problems of legitimacy raised by the welfare state in *Communication and the Evolution of Society,* trans. Thomas McCarthy (Boston: Beacon Press, 1976).

4. John Micklethwait and Adrian Wooldridge, *The Fourth Revolution: The Global Race to Reinvent the State* (New York: Penguin, 2014).

5. John Rawls, *Political Liberalism* (New York: Columbia University Press, 1996).

6. Edward Skidelsky, *Ernst Cassirer: The Last Philosopher of Culture* (Princeton: Princeton University Press, 2011), 308.

7. Henry Hazlitt, James Burnham, and Ayn Rand, and of course Friedrich von Hayek, among others.

8. E.g., George Monbiot, *The Age of Consent: A Manifesto for a New World Order* (New York: The New Press, 2003).

9. Notably, in his book of the same name.

10. H. Stuart Hughes, *Consciousness and Society* (New York: Vintage, 1958).

11. Thorstein Veblen, *The Theory of Business Enterprise* (New York: Scribners, 1904).

12. Adolf Berle and Gardiner Means, *The Modern Corporation and Private Property* (New York: Transaction, 1932).

13. John Kenneth Galbraith, *The New Industrial State* (New York: Houghton Mifflin, 1967).

14. Werner Jacob Cahnman, *Weber and Tönnies* (New York: Transaction, 1995), 10–11.

15. As predicted by Peter Drucker. See his *Concept of the Corporation,* rev. ed. (New York: John Day, 1972), 148, 149–73.

16. Adam Smith, *The Wealth of Nations*, in vol. 39 of *Great Books of the Western World* (Chicago: University of Chicago Press, 1952), book 1.

17. Friedrich von Hayek, *Law, Legislation and Liberty*, vol. 1, *Rules and Order* (Chicago: University of Chicago Press, 1973), 39–51.

18. Eric D. Beinhocker, *The Origin of Wealth: The Radical Remaking of Economics and What It Means for Business and Society* (Boston: Harvard Business Review, 2007), chap. 3.

19. Emil Lask, *Die Logik der Philosophie und die Kategorienlehre: Eine Studie über den Herrschaftsbereich der logischen Form* (Tübingen: J.C.B. Mohr, 1993), 21.

20. Ayn Rand, *Capitalism: The Unknown Ideal* (New York : Signet, 1967).

21. James M. Buchanan, *The Limits of Liberty* (Chicago: University of Chicago Press, 1975); John Rawls, *A Theory of Justice* (Cambridge, MA: Harvard University Press, 1971), and *Political Liberalism* (New York: Columbia University Press, 1996).

22. Isaiah Berlin, *Four Essays on Liberty* (Oxford: Oxford University Press, 1969), 118–72.

23. Friedrich A. Hayek, *The Constitution of Liberty*, ed. Ronald Hamowy, vol. 17 of *The Collected Works of F.A. Hayek* (Chicago: University of Chicago Press, 1960; Kindle edition, 2011).

24. Plato, *Dialogues of Plato, The Republic*, Book 1, trans. Benjamin Jowett, in vol. 7 of *Great Books of the Western World* (Chicago: University of Chicago, 1952).

25. See, e.g., Joseph E. Stiglitz, *Globalization and Its Discontents* (New York: Norton, 2002); Jeffrey D. Sachs, *The End of Poverty* (New York: Penguin, 2005); and Thomas Piketty, *Le Capital au XXIe siècle* (Paris: Éditions du Seuil, 2013).

26. C. Wright Mills, *The Sociological Imagination* (New York: Oxford University Press, 1959), 8–9.

27. A crucial point about North American industrial organization made as long ago as the 1940s by Peter Drucker in *Concept of the Corporation*. The superior Japanese solution to this question is one of the ingredients of the Japanese model's stunning productivity gains whose impact struck North America in the 1970s.

CHAPTER 1: CLASSICAL LIBERALISM'S FAILURE

1. Steve Pincus, *1688: The First Modern Revolution* (New Haven, CT: Yale University Press, 2009). He calls it "the first modern revolution."

2. The work of T.H. Marshall in expanding the idea of citizenship to include social and economic rights for all social classes coincided with the end of the Second World War and the establishment of the

welfare state in Britain and the Dominions; see T.H. Marshall and Tom Bottomore, *Citizenship and Social Class* (London: Pluto, 1992). This was a high point of liberal political evolution. The consensus came unglued in the 1970s as I discuss in chapter 3. Adam B. Seligman in *The Idea of Civil Society* (New York: Free Press, 1992) argues that the universalization of citizenship opened the door to further issues of the alternative lifestyles and identities that form a core of liberal discussion now, alongside the other discussions on divisive questions such as communitarianism, libertarianism, republicanism, and so forth. Civil society, he contends, is unable to reconcile the range of tendencies that now divide it. John Gray agrees; see his *Liberalism,* 2nd ed. (Minneapolis: University of Minnesota Press, 1995).

3. Hannah Arendt, *Qu'est-ce que la philosophie de l'existence suivi de L'existentialisme français et de Heidegger le renard* (Paris: Payot et Rivages, 2002), 39–41.

4. Benedetto Croce, *What Is Living and What Is Dead of the Philosophy of Hegel,* trans. Douglas Ainslie (New York: Russell and Russell, 1969), 110.

5. *The Social Contract,* book 4, chap. 1, 204–5; see Jean-Jacques Rousseau, *The Basic Political Writings,* trans. Donald A. Cress (Indianapolis: Hackett, 1987). Rousseau solves the problem of its persistence with his romantic view of sincere human "simplicity," while Hegel demands a higher political consciousness. For Benjamin Constant's contrast of Rousseau's "republicanism" with "modern" democracy, see his *Écrits politiques* (Paris: Gallimard, 1997), 137.

6. Johann Gottlieb Fichte, *Grundlage des Naturrechts nach Principien der Wissenschaftslehre* (Jena and Leipzig: Christian Ernst Gabler, 1797).

7. See Georg Wilhelm Friedrich Hegel, *Natural Law: The Scientific Ways of Treating Natural Law, Its Place in Moral Philosophy, and Its Relation to the Positive Sciences of Law,* trans. T.M. Knox (Philadelphia: University of Pennsylvania, 1975). In his introduction to the work, H.B. Acton discusses Hegel's "organic" alternative of a higher social consciousness to Fichte's faith in a "mechanical" sum of individual interests, together with an overarching "ephorate" (echoing the ephors of ancient Sparta) to provide an overview of the whole body of legislation and to make adjustments — essentially the idea

of a constitutional supreme court. This same dilemma is touched upon again in the conclusion (p. 136): Rosanvallon's "fourth" branch of government.

8. Dardot and Laval (2009) discuss Foucault's ideas about utlilitarianism as a basis for neoliberal society.

9. Anonymous, review of *Carlyle and Mill*, by Emery Edward Neff, *Columbia Spectator* 47, no. 173 (June 18, 1924): 3. The paragraph shocks the reader with the tear in the "balanced" constitutional fabric of British life as imagined by the Romantic writers of the late eighteenth and early nineteenth century.

10. James Mill (1773–1836). It is presented in a supplement to the 4th, 5th, and 6th editions of the *Encyclopaedia Britannica* (Edinburgh, 1824), vol. 4, 491–505, and reprinted in James Mill, *The Political Writings of James Mill: Essays and Reviews on Politics and Society, 1815–1836*, ed. David M. Hart (Indianapolis: Liberty Fund, 2013; Online Library of Liberty).

11. Pierre Rosanvallon, *Le Capitalisme utopique*, 4th ed. (Paris: Éditions de Seuil, 1999), especially the new introduction and pp. 28–32, argues that at this point economics becomes the new politics. The book provides a thorough examination of antecedents and implications of Adam Smith's *Wealth of Nations*, of which Bentham's legislative ideas were an echo. The preface to Pierre Manent's anthology *Les Libéraux* (Paris: Gallimard, 2001) critiques the idea of individual economic calculation as a sufficient basis of politics owing to the inevitable emergence of class and sector interests.

12. The excerpt is from Lord Macaulay's *Miscellaneous Writings and Speeches,* vol. 2, *Mill on Government* (London, 1829), 80. Thomas Babington Macaulay (1800–59) was a British Whig politician, a renowned historian, and a ferocious opponent of utilitarianism. Macaulay was a philosophical descendant of Edmund Burke (1729–97), a distinguished Whig MP from Ireland, whose *Reflections on the French Revolution* and other writings emphasize the benefits of continuous, organic change over disruptive breaks with tradition on purely rational grounds. Lord Acton regarded them both, along with Gladstone, as the greatest liberals of their age.

13. R.H. Coase, "The Nature of the Firm," reprinted in *The Firm, The Market and the Law* (Chicago: University of Chicago Press, 1988), 33–55.

14. Brian Inglis, *Men of Conscience* (New York: Macmillan, 1971), 380–403, examines the flaws of economic reasoning during the early industrial period.

15. Perhaps an example of correlation rather than causation. The population of England increased substantially during the Napoleonic years. G.D.H. Cole and Raymond Postgate, in *The Common People, 1746–1946* (London: Methuen, 1971), present a census population chart (p. 128) showing a population increase from 10.5 million in 1801 to 14.1 million in 1821, and continued growth at about the same rate or faster thereafter to 44.8 million in 1931. Their explanation for the rapid growth in the early years is a falling infant mortality rate owing to better and more readily available midwifery and hospitalization, beginning in the mid-eighteenth century (p. 138).

16. Wilhelm Roscher, *Zur Geschichte der englischen Volkswirtschaftslehre* (Leipzig, 1854), 3–4.

17. Thomas Robert Malthus, *Principles of Political Economy* (New York: Augustus M. Kelley, 1922), book 2, chap.1, sect. 10, 413–83; especially 480–81.

18. *The Philosophy of Right,* trans. T.M. Knox, in vol. 46 of *Great Books of the Western World* (Chicago: University of Chicago Press, 1952), 277 (para. 245).

19. Matthew Arnold, *Culture and Anarchy* (New York: Dover, 1978), 185.

20. John Stuart Mill, *Autobiography* (New York: Houghton Mifflin/Riverside, 1969), 41.

21. Ibid., 42.

22. John Bowring, introduction to *The Complete Works of Jeremy Bentham,* ed. John Bowring (Edinburgh: William Tait, 1843), xv.

23. Alan Ryan, *The Making of Modern Liberalism* (Princeton: Princeton University Press, 2012), chap. 29. See also Jeremy Bentham, *Introduction to the Principles of Morals and Legislation,* Hafner Library of Classics (New York: Hafner, 1963), 209, 227–29, 235n2.

24. John Stuart Mill, *Autobiography*, 81.

25. Robert Owen, *A New View of Society: Essays on the Principle of the Formation of Human Character and the Application of Principle to Practice* (London, 1813; Internet Archive, 2007), archive.org/details/anewviewsociety00owengoog/page/n4; and *Observations on the Effect of the Manufacturing System* (London: Longman, Hurst, Rees, Orme and Brown, 1817).

26. Owen, *Observations,* 5–6.

27. John Stuart Mill, *Principles of Political Economy,* 6th ed. (London: Longmans, Green, 1911), 465.

28. The grim struggle at the level of municipal reform and the new poor law that ended "outdoor relief" in the teeth of a depression is related in Cole and Postgate, *The Common People,* chap. 23; the charter presented to parliament in 1839 is reproduced in Sydney Jackman, ed., *The English Reform Tradition* (Englewood Cliffs, NJ: Prentice-Hall, 1965), 73–80.

29. John Morley, *The Life of Richard Cobden* (London: Unwin, 1896), 149.

30. Sidney and Beatrice Webb, *The History of Trade Unionism, 1666– 1920,* rev. ed. (printed by the authors for the Trade Unionists of the United Kingdom, 1920), especially chap. 4; Cole and Postgate, *The Common People*, 347.

31. S.E. Finer, *The Life and Times of Sir Edwin Chadwick* (London: Routledge, 2016), chap. 1.

32. Finer, *Life and Times,* chap. 1, part 3.

33. Michel Foucault, *The Birth of Biopolitics: Lectures at the Collège de France, 1978–1979* (New York: Picador/Palgrave, 2004), 357; also Pierre Dardot and Christian Laval, *La Nouvelle Raison du monde: Essai sur la société néolibérale* (Paris: La Découverte, 2010), 14. Giorgio Agamben, in *Homo Sacer* (Stanford: Stanford University Press, 1998), does not mention Bentham or utilitarianism, but his concept of "bare life" is surely little different from Bentham's concept of mankind as a being limited to a binary response (pleasure/pain) to stimulus of any sort. Chadwick in a sense redeemed himself with his campaign against typhus and cholera by promoting the cleanup of urban cesspools and the building of effective sewer systems. This led to the first Public Health Act in Britain (1848),

which acknowledged government responsibility for public health ("Edwin Chadwick," Wikimedia Foundation, en.wikipedia.org/wiki/Edwin_Chadwick).

34. Louis Cazamian, *Le Roman social en Angleterre (1830–1850)* (Paris : Société nouvelle de Librairie et d'Édition,1904).

35. François Guizot, *Sir Robert Peel* (Paris: Didier, 1856), 53; also Joseph Hamburger, *James Mill and the Art of Revolution* (Westport, CT: Greenwood Press, 1963), chap. 6.

36. For Tennyson's "Maud," see *The Victorian Web*, James R. Kincaid, "Maud," victorianweb.org/authors/tennyson/kincaid/ch6.html.

37. Élie Halévy, *Histoire du socialisme européen* (Paris: Gallimard, 1974), 42–43. The full title of Hodgskin's 1825 book is *Labour Defended Against the Claims of Capital, or The Unproductiveness of Capital, Proved with Reference to the Present Combinations Among Journeymen, by a Labourer* (London, 1825).

38. See Cazamian's introduction to his *Le Roman social* for a discussion of the sociohistorical setting of these novels and their contribution to middle class understanding of the condition of England as experienced by industrial workers.

39. Arnold, *Culture and Anarchy*, 212.

40. Elizabeth S. Haldane, *George Eliot and Her Times* (London: Hodder & Stoughton, 1922), 230.

41. George Eliot, "Address to Working Men, by Felix Holt [by "X"]," in *The Essays of George Eliot, Complete*, ed. Nathan Sheppard (Whitefish, MT: Literary Licensing, 2014), Kindle edition, location 4581.

42. Austin Harrison, *Frederic Harrison: Thoughts and Memories* (London: Heinemann, 1926), 4. Harrison's "Victorian Preamble," from which this citation is taken, is a brilliant survey of Victorianism from the standpoint of the son of a famous Comtean positivist, a difficult position in a country that instinctively resisted all "foreign" or "Continental" utopian ideas. One must acknowledge with him that we remain even now to an astonishing extent the children of the Victorian epoch.

43. Peter Gay, *Schnitzler's Century: The Making of Middle Class Culture 1815–1914* (New York: Allen Lane, 2001), 27.

44. Vida D. Scudder, *Social Ideals in English Literature* (New York: Houghlin Mifflin, 1898), 276–78.

45. Émile Durkheim, *Socialism* (New York : Collier Books, 1962), chap. 6, especially pp. 142–43.

46. Émile Levasseur, *Les Sciences sociales sous la restauration: Saint-Simon et le Saint-Simonisme, Fourier et Fouriérisme* (Paris: V. Giard et E. Brière, 1902), 21. The point is also made in *L'Organisateur,* première lettre, reprinted in Juliette Grange, ed., *Saint-Simon: Écrits politiques et économiques, anthologie critique* (Paris: Pocket, 2005), 230–35.

47. John Stuart Mill, *Autobiography,* 100.

48. Harrison, *Frederic Harrison,* contains many insightful passages on the English reception of Comte and Darwin by what was still, to an extent difficult to imagine today, a society ordered by religion and religious ideals.

49. Just after the Second World War, as the Cold War against Soviet Russia was getting under way, Hayek launched an attack on the tyranny — real and potential — of central economic planning, tracing its roots back to Saint-Simon. See his *The Counter-Revolution of Science: Studies on the Abuse of Reason* (Glencoe, IL: Free Press, 1955), first published 1952. I take up this theme later in this chapter. The power of technocracy as a "new class" became an important element of the discussion of liberalism and Soviet Communism alike up until the Soviet collapse.

50. Pierre-Simon Laplace, *A Philosophical Essay on Probabilities*, as quoted in "Pierre-Simon Laplace," Wikimedia Foundation, wikipedia.org/wiki/Pierre-Simon_Laplace.

51. Élie Halévy, "Saint-Simonian Economic Doctrine" and summary *The Era of Tyrannies* (New York: Doubleday Anchor, 1965).

52. Rosanvallon, *Le Bon Gouvernement* (Paris: Éditions de Seuil, 2015), 386.

53. Barthélémy-Prosper Enfantin with S.A. Bazard, Hippolyte Carnot, Henri Fournel, and Charles Duveyrier, *Doctrine de Saint-Simon: Exposition*, première année, 1828–1829 (1830), (Paris: Bureau de l'organisateur, 1831).

54. Enfantin, *Doctrine de Saint-Simon,* 129–27 and 237–38.

55. Henry George, *Progress and Poverty* (New York: Walter J. Black, 1941), especially book 7 and book 10, chap. 5.

56. Piketty, *Le Capital,* especially chap. 11.

57. I have in mind the debate about modern banking and monetary policy, particularly around the rediscovery of Hyman Minsky. For a review, see levyinstitute.org/.

58. Émile Durkheim, *The Division of Labour in Society* (Glencoe, IL: Free Press, 1933); also his *Le Suicide: Étude de sociologie* (Paris: Presses universitaires de France, 1967).

59. Rosanvallon addresses this point in his conclusion to *Le Bon Gouvernement,* especially p. 386.

60. Charles Maurras (1868–1952), thought leader of Action Française, a monarchist, anti-parliamentary, anti-Semitic far-right movement in the Third Republic.

61. Frederick Engels, *Herr Eugen Dühring's Revolution in Science (Anti-Dühring),* trans. Emile Burns, Marxist-Leninist Library (London: Martin Lawrence, 1934), 286.

62. Raymond Aron, *Les Étapes de la pensée sociologique* (Paris: Gallimard, 1967), 122.

63. James Mill, "Government," in *Political Writings of James Mill,* 505. For a discussion of the Radicals' political strategy in the run-up to the Great Reform Act of 1832 and the constitutional issues at stake, see Hamburger, *James Mill and the Art of Revolution.* Mill's argument about the middle class is not unlike the argument used by Georg Lukacs on behalf of working class revolution in *History and Class Consciousness*, almost a century later — effectively an argument for its "virtual representation" of the rest.

64. John Maynard Keynes, *The Economic Consequences of the Peace* (New York: Harcourt, Brace and Howe, 1920), 6.

65. John Maynard Keynes, "The End of Laissez-faire," in *Transformations of Capitalism: Economy, Society, and the State in Modern Times,* ed. Harry F. Dahms (New York: New York University Press, 2000), 105.

66. Frédéric Bastiat (1801–50), French classical liberal theorist.

67. Keynes, "The End of Laissez-faire," 110–111.

CHAPTER 2: THE GERMAN HISTORICAL SCHOOL

1. Keynes, "End of Laissez-faire."

2. Murray Milgate and Shannon C. Stimson, *Ricardian Politics* (Princeton: Princeton University Press, 2014); Halévy, *Histoire du socialisme européen,* chap. 1.

3. Quoted by Charles Gide in Gustav von Schmoller, *Die Entwicklung der deutschen Volkswirtschaftslehre im neunzehnten Jahrhundert: Gustav Schmoller zur siebenzigsten Wiederkehr seines Geburtstages, 24. Juni 1908* (Leipzig: Duncker & Humblot, 1908), 715n2. (Cited hereafter as Schmoller, *Festschrift.*)

4. The customs union (*Zollverein*) was based on treaties completed in 1833, coming into effect January 1, 1834.

5. M. Aycard, *Histoire du Crédit Mobilier* (Paris: Librairie Internationale, 1867).

6. Schmoller, *Festschrift*, chap. 14, 1–43.

7. Schmoller, *Festschrift,* 645.

8. Henry Michel, *L'Idée de l'état* (Paris: Hachette, 1898), introduction, chaps. 1 and 2; Charles Andler, *Les Origines de socialisme d'état en Allemagne* (Paris: Félix Alcan, 1897), introduction.

9. For a convenient introduction to nineteenth- and twentieth-century historical economics, see Gonçalo L. Fonseca, "The German Historical School," The History of Economic Thought, hetwebsite.net/het/schools/historic.htm.

10. Martin Swales, *The German Bildungsroman from Wieland to Hesse* (Princeton: Princeton University Press, 1978), chap. 1.

11. Keith Tribe, "Historical Schools of Economics: German and English" (Keele Economics Research Paper, University of Keele, Keele, U.K., 2002).

12. For a brief account, see Eric Roll, *A History of Economic Thought* (London: Faber & Faber, 1978), 302–10. For a comparison of the German school with English economics, see Tribe, "Historical Schools."

13. *Basic Plan of Lectures About National Economics According to the Historical Method.*

14. Paul Krugman, *The Self-Organizing Economy* (London: Blackwell, 1991), and *Geography and Trade* (Cambridge, MA: MIT Press, 1996);

and Masahisa Fujita, Paul Krugman, and Anthony J. Venables, *The Spatial Economy* (Cambridge, MA: MIT Press, 2001).

15. Andler, *Les Origines de socialisme d'état,* introduction, 4, affirms the powerful influence of Rodbertus, whose ideas Andler discusses in detail; see also Halévy, *Histoire du socialisme européen,* part 4, chap. 1, section 1, 223ff.

16. Hajo Holborn, *A History of Modern Germany, 1840–1945* (London: Eyre and Spottiswoode, 1969), 221–29, discusses Bismarck's political challenges in completing the federation. He notes that when the Prussian king was presented with the imperial crown for the second time (in the Versailles Hall of Mirrors), it was the aristocracy backed by the military who offered it, in contrast to the failed liberal offer in 1848. J.H. Clapham, *Economic Development of France and Germany, 1815–1914* (Cambridge: Cambridge University Press, 1961), 346–8, discusses Bismarck's railway policy following the annexation, amounting to thirty years of railway acquisition between 1876 and 1909.

17. For example, Thorstein Veblen, *Imperial Germany and the Industrial Revolution* (Ann Arbor: University of Michigan Press, 1968), 179.

18. Tribe, "Historical Schools," 10.

19. Holborn, *History of Modern Germany*, 269–70, discusses Bismarck's early economic policy; pp. 270–97 trace his subsequent policy to his dismissal.

20. Bismarck's social insurance scheme in the end helped improve working conditions. But it did not detach working class support from the Social Democrats as Prussian leadership hoped. The ideas behind the program were developed by the historical school, led by Schmoller's *Verein für Sozialforschung.* The creation of the German *Sozialstaat* was a progressive innovation that complemented the new country's military power with social programs designed to ensure that the working class was accepted as an integral part of the new Germany. As such, it became a model of progressive policy for every modern Western country. It was Germany's success in apparent contrast to the economic oppression in "liberal" societies that put "social" into the normal political vocabulary of liberals hitherto unconcerned with any other frame of reference but economic. But persistent questions surrounded the meaning of the term "social."

21. Germany's economic development strategy after unification was certainly influenced by the economic thinking of the *Verein*. But it was driven over the same period by a dramatic rise in industrial scale and in finance, in part fuelled by the French indemnity for the Franco-Prussian war, and the vertiginous expansion of banking, which ended ultimately in the significant consolidation of that sector under the Reichsbank. These developments were part of a general trend in the industrializing countries. See J.A. Hobson, *The Evolution of Modern Capitalism: A Study of Machine Production* (London: George Allen & Unwin, 1949), chaps. 7, 8, and 9; Herbert Feis, *Europe: The World's Banker 1870–1914*, Publications of the Council on Foreign Relations (New Haven, CT: Yale University Press, 1930), chaps. 3 and 6.

22. Keith Tribe, *Strategies of Economic Order: German Economic Discourse, 1750–1950* (Cambridge: Cambridge University Press, 1995), 45–55, weighs the thesis that List's ideas were inspired by the German economist Adam Müller in his *Die Elemente der Staatskunst*, 3 vols. (Berlin, 1809) against the view put forward by C.P. Neill that List was inspired by the American lawyer and economist Daniel Raymond. See Charles Patrick Neill, *Daniel Raymond: An Early Chapter in the History of Economic Theory in the United States* (Baltimore: Johns Hopkins, 1897).

23. Halévy, *Histoire du socialisme européen,* 223–30.

24. Friedrich List, *Système national d'économie politique,* trans. Henri Richelot (Paris: Gallimard, 1998) book 2, chaps. 1–3. On suppressive competition, List noticed that Napoleon's counter-blockade of England, known as the Continental System, had helped German industries achieve an early stage of industrialization. But when England adopted free trade and overturned the laws protecting its wheat production to specialize in industrial exports, Germany's new companies folded, to be replaced by agricultural output once again. Indeed, List accused the English of compelling other states to sign free trade agreements with Britain as a way of suppressing local industrial competition in favour of British exporters.

25. Andler, in *Les Origines de socialisme d'état,* discusses Rodbertus in each chapter.

    Rodbertus's volume on capital is a compilation of his writings organized by Theophil Kozak, under the supervision of Adolph Wagner, a celebrated financial economist at the University of Berlin and a member of the Schmoller group. Wagner thought highly of Rodbertus, considering him "the Ricardo of socialism": Karl Rodbertus-Jagetzow, *Das Kapital,* ed. Adolph Wagner and Theophil Kozak (Berlin: Puttkammer & Mühlbrecht, 1884).

H. Dietzel, in his *Karl Rodbertus: Darstellung seines Lebens und seiner Lehre* (Berlin: Gustav Fischer, 1886), places Rodbertus and his ideas in the flow of events and personalities of his time, with good discussions of his social program and his relations with Lassalle. My text draws mostly on Andler's and Robertus's volumes.

26. Rodbertus's argument is similar to that of Henry George in *Progress and Poverty,* which first appeared in 1879. George argues that the general rise in urban values was undeservedly rewarding unimproved land and sees a single tax on land as the solution to poverty. The enormous success of his book led to the now general practice of taxing unimproved land in private hands.

27. Marx and Engels, in their *Capital,* critiqued Rodbertus's theory of overproduction, but found other points to approve in his analysis of capitalism. See "Johann Karl Rodbertus," Marxists Internet Archive, marxists.org/reference/subject/economics/rodbertus/index.htm. The Marxist critique is sometimes rephrased by classical economics as the relationship between fixed and circulating capital, which contemporary economics in turn rephrases as the discount relationship between short- and long-term capital, an issue that continues to provoke controversy.

28. Insisting that the wage bill must cover a household's minimum needs is sufficient.

29. Rodbertus-Jagetzow, *Das Kapital.* This quoted passage and the following are my translations taken from the French version of this work, published as Carl Rodbertus-Jagetsov, *Le Capital,* trans. E. Chatelain (Paris: V. Giard et E. Brière, 1904). (The book preserves the original pagination of the individual letters that comprise the main text. Hence the page numbers for the quoted passages are 13, 14, and 18 in the French text, and 5 and 6 in the German text. The actual pages that include the respective introductions are 65 and 66 in the French text, and 31 and 32 in the German text.)

30. Ibid.

31. The entrepreneur borrows to cover his costs, including workers'
    pay for the first round of production. If workers' pay is adequate to
    absorb that product, the entepreneur will recoup his costs, but he
    still has his overdraft to reimburse, and then he must borrow again to
    finance another round of production. In effect, just matching salary
    to productivity fails to make the enterprise fully self-sustaining.

32. In effect, the same conclusion as Saint-Simon.

33. Or, alternatively, apply the productivity to exports, to gain abroad
    the sales that cannot be gained at home, and with perhaps a similar
    suppressive effect on local industries in the importing countries. To
    be sure, the resulting "specialization" in the importing country further
    adds to bilateral productivity increases, but its effect on employ-
    ment is apt to be negative in the absence of government transitional
    assistance — which is likely, in that liberal ideology denies that such
    assistance is routinely necessary.

34. From *Grundriss zu Vorlesungen über die Staatswirtschaft nach geschichtli-
    cher Methode* (1843), 12–14. Translation is taken from W.J. Ashley, "Ro-
    scher's Programme of 1843," *The Quarterly Journal of Economics* 9, no.
    1 (October 1894): 99–105. See also Tribe, *Strategies of Economic Order,*
    68–70. Tribe argues that most of Roscher's *Grundriss* ideas were either
    restatements or extensions of ideas current in the Germany of his time,
    except perhaps for his alignment of economic-historical research with
    the research of Savigny's legal-historical school's search for constitutional
    principles. Note, however, Roscher also prefers Malthus to Ricardo for
    the purposes of national economics — as did J.M. Keynes (introduction
    to *Grundriss*, v). Ashley, a supporter of the historical method, presents the
    text in a more favourable light, including a full translation of the preface
    to the *Grundriss*, subsequently known as Roscher's manifesto of 1843.

35. For example, Fernand Braudel, *Civilisation matérielle, économie et
    capitalisme, XVᵉ–XVIIIᵉ siècles,* 3 vols. (Paris: Armand Colin, 1979).

36. See G.P. Gooch, *History and Historians in the Nineteenth Century*
    (Boston: Beacon Press, 1959) for Ranke (p. 72ff.), Acton (pp. 354–
    67), and Buckle (pp. 534–35). Braudel's *The Mediterranean and the
    Mediterranean World in the Age of Philip II* is mentioned in Gooch's
    introduction (p. xvi) as being as much sociology as history, which in

effect confirms my comment. The Annales school begun by Braudel, Marc Bloch, and Lucien Febvre before the war is not mentioned.

37. Gustav von Schmoller, *Zur Literaturgeschichte der Staats- und Sozial- wissenschaften* (Leipzig: Duncker & Humblot, 1888), 150.

38. Gustav von Schmoller, *The Mercantile System and Its Historic Signif- icance,* Economic Classics, ed. W.J. Ashley (New York and London: Macmillan, 1914), 31.

39. Ibid., 40.

40. Ibid., 48–51.

41. Ibid., 54.

42. It is more than a point of interest that the World Trade Organiza- tion (WTO), the successor organization to the post–Second World War General Agreement on Tariffs and Trade (GATT), is the highest implementation of that system to date, although it finds itself under severe pressure from so-called regional trade agreements designed as instruments of compulsion in the interests of hegemonic economic strategies. Thus, the North American Free Trade Agreement (NAFTA) was put together to encourage the European Union to sign on to the WTO. The Trans-Pacific Partnership (TPP) was originally designed to group China's regional neighbours in an arrangement with its trans-Pacific (Western hemisphere) trade partners, mainly to boost the price China would have to pay for a trade deal with them.

43. Schmoller, *Mercantile System,* 78.

44. Ibid., 80.

45. As, indeed, trade theory since his time has evolved to show, in par- ticular with the replacement of the Ricardian free-trade model based on comparative advantage by the Krugman trade model based on industrial organization and strategy.

46. Joseph Schumpeter, *Ten Great Economists* (London: Unwin, 1966), 298–301, provides a portrait of von Wieser.

47. Karl Knies, *Die politische oekonomie vom Standpunkte der historischen Methode* (1853), *Der Telegraf als Vehrkerhsmittel* (1857), and *Die Sta- tistik als selbstanständige Wissenchaft* (1850).

48. E.g., "The Construction of the Historical World in the Human Stud- ies," in Wilhelm Dilthey, *Dilthey: Selected Writings,* ed. H.P. Rickman (Cambridge: Cambridge University Press, 1976).

49. Ferdinand Tönnies (1855–1936) was a German sociologist. His principal ideas are contained in his *Gemeinschaft und Gesellschaft: Abhandlung des Communismus und des Socialismus als empirisches Culturformen* (Berlin: Fues, 1887).

50. Schumpeter, *Ten Great Economists*, 80–90, offers a portrait of Menger, his contribution to economic theory, and a brief discussion of the *Methodenstreit.*

51. Menger explored in some detail the issues in economic methodology of his time in his *Methodenstreit* with Schmoller. His reflections are set out at length in his *Investigations into the Method of the Social Sciences, with Special Reference to Economics,* ed. Louis Schneider, trans. Francis J. Nock (New York: New York University Press, 1985). The point noted in the text is made clearly in Appendix 3, 203 passim.

52. Carl Menger, *Principles of Economics* (Auburn, AL: Ludwig von Mises Institute, 1976).

53. See the essays by Gide and Ashley in Schmoller, *Festschrift*, on the flight from classical economics in the 1870s.

54. Carl Menger, *Die Irrthümer des Historismus in der deutschen Nationalökonomie* (Vienna: Alfred Hölder, 1884). See, for example, Menger's defence of his view of statistics in the seventh letter. It was Walter Eucken's contribution at the end of the Second World War to solve the Great Antinomy between the historical German and analytical Austrian schools in what became ordoliberalism, as discussed earlier.

55. However, one of his students, Friedrich von Wieser, who became one of Hayek's dissertation supervisors, built on Menger's theories to develop a more complete theory of value as well as a sociological theory of power in economics and the structure of society. See in particular Friedrich von Wieser, *Social Economics,* trans. A. Ford Hinrichs (New York: Adelphi, 1927).

56. See the discussion of the Great Antinomy below.

57. Vol. 1, 70. It is also cited in the appendix to the eighth edition: "Appendix on the Growth of Economic Thought." See also the citation in T.W. Hutchison, *A Review of Economic Doctrines 1870–1929* (New York: Oxford University Press, 1953), 146n1.

58. For a brief but illuminating discussion of the study of history as a part of English economics and of Ashley's contribution to the discipline, see Tribe, "Historical Schools."

59. W.J. Ashley, *Surveys, Historic and Economic* (New York: Longmans Green, 1900).

60. Viktor J. Vanberg, *The Freiburg School: Walter Eucken and Ordoliberalism,* Freiburger Diskussionspapiere zur Ordnungsökonomik 04/11 (Freiburg: Walter Eucken Institut, 2004). For a parsing of the tendencies and influences, see Sally Razeen, "Ordoliberalism and the Social Market: Classical Political Economy from Germany," in Patricia Commun, ed., *L'Ordolibéralisme allemande* (Cergy-Pontoise: CIRAC, 2003, 2017), 31–36. Gerhard Schnyder and Mathias Siems summarize much of the currently available research in "The 'Ordoliberal' Variety of Neo-liberalism," in *Banking Systems in the Crisis: The Faces of Liberal Capitalism*, ed. Suzanne J. Konzelmann and Marc Fovargue-Davies (Abingdon, U.K.: Routledge, 2013), 250–68.

61. Walter Lippmann, *The Good Society* (New York: Grosset and Dunlap, 1943), 186.

62. Explored in Sylvain Broyer, "Ordnungstheorie et ordolibéralisme," in Commun, *L'Ordolibéralisme allemande,* 79–100. See also Tribe, *Strategies of Economic Order,* chap. 1.

63. Buchanan, *Limits of Liberty,* chap. 3, "Post-Constitutional Contract." See also James M. Buchanan, *The Collected Works of James M. Buchanan*, ed. Geoffrey Brennan, vol. 10, *The Reason of Rules: Constitutional Political Economy* (Indianapolis: Liberty Fund, 1985; Online Library of Liberty). Ordoliberalism achieves a similar effect in one step.

64. Walter Eucken, *Die Grundlagen der Nationalökonomie*, in *Enzyklopädie der Rechts- und Staatswissenschaft,* 9th ed., Abteilung Staatswissenschaft (Berlin: Springer, 1989), especially chap. 2 and chap. 6, sections 13–18. The argument is pursued in the last chapter of this book.

65. Quoted at the close of the last chapter of the book.

66. H.C. Simons (1899–1946) — now generally remembered for his monetarism — was also a staunch advocate of state intervention to maintain competition and the breakup of monopolies as a guarantee of individual consumer freedom. See his 1934 essay *A Positive Program*

for Laissez-faire (Chicago: University of Chicago Press). He was the first economist to teach in the University of Chicago law faculty.

67. Eucken, *Die Grundlagen der Nationalökonomie.*

68. Eric Dehay, "L'Indépendence de la banque central en Allemagne: Des principes ordolibéraux à la pratique de la Bundesbank," in Commun, *L'Ordolibéralisme allemande,* 255–64.

69. Its postulate of a single, unchanging demand for money is incorrect. For a post-Keynesian stock-flow-consistent critique, see Wynne Godley and Marc Lavoie and *Monetary Economics: An Integrated Approach to Credit, Money, Income, Production and Wealth* (London: Palgrave Macmillan, 2007).

70. Jean-Daniel Weisz, "L'Intérêt pour une approche régulationniste du détour par l'ordolibéralisme," in Commun, *L'Ordolibéralisme allemande,* 49–66.

71. Christian Schröppel and Mariko Nakajima describe the Japanese "flying geese" development model, inspired by the German historical school. See "The Changing Interpretation of the Flying Geese Model of Economic Development," in *Japanstudien 14. Japan als Fallbeispiel in den Wissenschaften* (Munich: Iudicium-Verlag, 2002), 203–36.

72. Gerald Gaus, *The Order of Public Reason* (Cambridge: Cambridge University Press, 2011), and *Justificatory Liberalism* (Oxford and New York: Oxford University Press, 1996).

73. Schnyder and Siems, "The 'Ordoliberal' Variety of Neo-liberalism," 6.

74. Michael Wohlgemuth, *The Boundaries of the State,* Freiburger Diskussionspapiere zur Ordnungsökonomik 11/3 (Freiburg: Walter Eucken Institut, 2011). Also Michael Wohlgemuth and Jörn Sideras, *Globalisability or Universalisability? How to Apply the Generality Principle and Constitutionalism Internationally,* Freiburger Diskussionspapiere zur Ordnungsökonomik 04/7 (Freiburg: Walter Eucken Institut, 2004); and Vanberg, *The Freiburg School.* Buchanan's two-stage constitutional argument is also a basic theme; see his *Limits of Liberty.*

75. Alberto Alesina and Enrico Spolaore, *The Size of Nations* (Cambridge, MA: MIT Press, 2003).

76. Marcus Marktanner, "Addressing the Marketing Problem of the Social Market Economy," in *60 Years of Social Market Economy — Formation, Development and Perspectives of a Peacemaking Formula,* ed.

Christian L. Glossner and David Gregosz (St. Augustine and Berlin: Konrad-Adenauer-Stiftung, 2010), 170–88. Foucault, in *Birth of Biopolitics*, underlines the differences between ordoliberalism and the "anarcho-liberalism" of Friedman and the Chicago school (p. 218).

CHAPTER 3: THE RISE AND FALL OF THE WELFARE STATE

1. Holborne, *A History of Modern Germany 1839–1945*, chap. 8, 374–91; Fritz Stern, *Gold and Iron* (New York: Vintage, 1977), Part 1, chap. 4 and 5; Feis, *Europe: The World's Banker*, chap. 3.

2. Moise Ostrogorsky, *Democracy and the Organization of Political Parties,* trans. Frederick Clark, 2 vols. (New York: Macmillan, 1902); Robert Michels, *Political Parties* (New York: Free Press, 1968).

3. Thomas Carlyle (1795–1881), brilliant Victorian writer and philosopher, influenced by German idealism.
   Sir Walter Scott (1771–1832), celebrated Scottish romantic novelist; a jurist by profession. His Waverley novels were read as relief from the bleak utilitarianism of the 1830s. Richard Wagner (1813–83) revolutionized German opera and music, projecting the new Germany's *Kultur* worldwide: his image is still marred for many by his strong association with racism and Hitler's favouring of Wagner's music.

4. Important reflections on this period are to be had in Jacques Barzun, *From Dawn to Decadence: 1500 to the Present* (New York: Harper Collins, 2000), 593ff. Barzun portrays what was in retrospect a civilization sleepwalking toward self-destruction.

5. Jeanne Morefield, *Covenants Without Swords* (Princeton: Princeton University Press, 2005), 69–72.

6. Sidney Webb, "Social Movement," in *The Cambridge Modern History,* ed. Lord Acton et al., vol. 10, *The Latest Age* (Cambridge: Cambridge University Press, 1910), 732. This seeming inevitability conceals the immense struggle around the Lloyd George budget and its impact, ultimately diminishing the powers of the British House of Lords and marking a downturn in the subsequent fortunes of the British Liberal Party. See Dangerfield, *Strange Death,* chap. 2.

7. Woodrow Wilson, *The New Freedom* (New York: Doubleday, 1913), Kindle edition, location 45–52.

8. James T. Kloppenberg, *Uncertain Victory: Social Democracy and Progressivism in European and American Thought 1870–1920* (New York: Oxford University Press, 1986), Kindle edition, location 5052–5144.

9. Herbert Croly, *The Promise of American Life* (New York: Macmillan, 1912), especially chaps. 5 and 6.

10. Ibid., 104.

11. Ibid., 105.

12. Alexis de Tocqueville (1805–59), especially noted for his warnings about the "tyranny of the majority" (vol. 1, chap. 15) and the emergence of an aristocracy of American managers (vol. 2, p. 171), in his *Democracy in America,* 2 vols., trans. Francis Bowen (New York: Vintage, 1960).

13. A small group of financiers who combined to control the railroads, the subject of a Congressional investigation in 1907. Louis D. Brandeis, *Other People's Money and How the Bankers Use It* (New York: Frederick A. Stokes, 1914).

14. Hilaire Belloc, *The Servile State* (Indianapolis: Liberty Fund, 1977), "written to maintain the thesis that industrial society as we know it will tend towards the re-establishment of slavery." He argued that "reformers" and "reformed" were both driving toward the "servile state."

15. Walter Lippmann, *Drift and Mastery* (Englewood Cliffs, NJ: Prentice-Hall, 1966), 82–83.

16. Kloppenberg, *Uncertain Victory* (1986), Kindle edition, location 117 and n68.

17. Kloppenberg, *Uncertain Victory*. I accept Kloppenberg's discussion of James and Dewey but am omitting his points of comparison with Dilthey and the German debate about historicism, culminating in Weber's sociology.

18. Jacques Bainville, *Les Conséquences politiques de la paix* (Paris: Gallimard, 1920).

19. Keynes, *Economic Consequences of the Peace.*

20. John Patrick Diggins, *The Promise of Pragmatism: Modernism and the Crisis of Knowledge and Authority* (Chicago: University of Chicago Press, 1994), especially chapter 8; Kloppenberg, *Uncertain Victory,* especially chap. 8.

    Richard Rorty, in the introduction to his *Essays on Heidegger and*

Others, vol. 2 (Cambridge: Cambridge University Press, 1991), underlines Nietzsche's influence on subsequent European thinkers in preparing the terrain for pragmatism, referring the reader to the following passage: "There exists neither 'spirit,' nor reason, nor thinking, nor consciousness, nor soul, nor will, nor truth: all are fictions that are of no use.… Knowledge works as a tool of power." See Friedrich Nietzsche, *The Will to Power,* trans. Walter A. Kaufmann (New York: Vintage, 1968), sections 480–544 (March–June 1888). Cf. William James's 1905 essay, "La Notion du conscience," which argues that consciousness is an illusion-masking experience, thus attacking Kantian dualism in the name of lived sensations and anticipating Heidegger's attack on Kant and neo-Kantianism. The essay — a summary of a professional presentation to psychologists — is reprinted in James, *Essays in Radical Empiricism* (Cambridge, MA: Harvard University Press, 1912).

21. Phenomenology is the study of conscious experience from the first-person point of view, bracketing any preconceived ideas. Heidegger's version adds "being in the world," expanding the hermeneutic procedure of "knowing the world." See David Woodruff Smith, "Phenomenology," Stanford Encyclopedia of Philosophy, last modified December 16, 2013, plato.stanford.edu/entries/phenomenology/. See also Gina M. Reiners, *Understanding the Difference Between Husserl's (Descriptive) and Heidegger's (Interpretive) Phenomenological Research* (2010; available from Google Books).

22. Edmund Husserl, *La Crise des sciences européennes et la phénoménologie transcendentale* (Paris: Gallimard, 1976), especially chap. 1, "La Crise des sciences comme expression de la crise radicale de la vie dans l'humanité européenne."

23. There are many discussions of this meeting, a powerful symbol of the break between Enlightenment and post-Nietzsche Western philosophy. This account relies on Skidelsky, *Ernst Cassirer,* chap. 8; Ernst Cassirer, *The Myth of the State* (New Haven, CT: Yale University Press, 1946), 292–98; and Martin Heidegger, *Kant et le problème de la métaphysique* (Paris: Gallimard, 1953), especially section 4.

24. From Rorty, *Essays,* 11. The term is Hilary Putnam's. Heidegger preferred "the mathematical," or formalization of what is already known.

25. Martin Heidegger, *Letter on Humanism,* in *Martin Heidegger: Basic Writings from* Being and Time *(1927) to* The Task of Thinking *(1964),* ed. David Farrell Krell (New York: Harper & Row, 1977), 189–242. Sartre's own 1946 essay was titled *L'Existentialisme est un humanisme.*

26. Jean-Paul Sartre, *L'Existentialisme est un humanisme* (Paris: Gallimard, 1996).

27. Cassirer, *Myth of the State.*

28. It is perhaps too often forgotten that while the Germans are an ancient European people, they came late to established nationhood. The *"völkisch"* attempt to define a cultural nationality was rooted in the ideas of Johann Gottfried Herder (1744–1803) and applied by Savigny (see chapter 3), who strongly influenced the new Germany's civil code. From Savigny it also took root in the German historical school of economics (drawing criticism from Weber) and became a definite element of Wilhelmine Germany. The challenge of national reassertion after the Versailles Treaty propelled the concept of *Volk* to become an integral and racist part of a catastrophic concept of nationhood as racial superiority. Liberals developed a contrasting version of nationalism over the late nineteenth century, concluding that nations are made up of people who follow the same law, irrespective of their ethnic or cultural backgrounds; see, e.g., Lord Acton, "Nationality," *The Home and Foreign Review*, No. 1 (July 1862): 1–25. panarchy.org. For a discussion of Herder as an anti-Enlightenment thought leader of nationalism, see Zeev Sternhell, *Les Anti-Lumières* (Paris: Folio/histoire, 2010), especially chap. 6, and Isaiah Berlin, *Against the Current: Essays in the History of Ideas* (Harmondsworth: Penguin, 1982).

29. George Steiner, *Martin Heidegger* (Chicago: University of Chicago Press, 1978), chap. 2.

30. Until the "struggle for life" was rendered as *"Kampf ums Dasein"* in Darwin's German translation, *Dasein* was just a synonym for *Anwesenheit*, or "being present." Thereafter it became associated exclusively with human beings as beings that understand their own Being. See David Farrell Krell, "The Question of Being," introduction to Heidegger, *Martin Heidegger: Basic Writings,* note to p. 48.

31. Albert Camus, *Le Mythe de Sisyphe* (Paris: Gallimard, 1942), 40–41. Cited by Krell in his introduction to *Martin Heidegger: Basic Writings*, 24.
32. Heidegger, *Kant.*
33. John Dewey, *Reconstruction in Philosophy* (New York: Mentor, 1949), originally published in 1920.
34. More recently, some notebooks were found in which, among other things, he expressed a disturbing level of anti-Semitism, including references to the "World Jewry" Nazi stereotype. So grave were his comments that a distinguished German philosopher, Professor Gunter Figal of Freiburg University, took it upon himself to resign from his post as chair of the Heidegger Society: "As chairman of a society, which is named after a person, one is in certain way a representative of that person. After reading the *Schwarze Hefte* [*Black Notebooks*], especially the antisemitic passages, I do not wish to be such a representative any longer. These statements have not only shocked me, but have turned me around to such an extent that it has become difficult to be a co-representative of this." Quoted in Justin Weinberg, "Germany's Heidegger Society Chair Resigns," the *Daily Nous*, January 19, 2015, dailynous.com/2015/01/19/germanys-heidegger-society-chair-resigns/.
35. Steiner, *Martin Heidegger.*
36. Foucault, in his *Birth of Biopolitics,* chap. 6, 132–35, discusses its significance for neoliberalism. A public account of the colloquium in French available at fr.wikipedia.org/wiki/Colloque_Walter_Lippmann#Article_connexe. See also the Mont Pelerin Society website: montpelerin.org/montpelerin/index.html.
37. Behind the victory lay a sustained propaganda campaign whose organization began shortly after the establishment of the Mont Pelerin Society. See Lewis Lapham, "Tentacles of Rage: The Republican Propaganda Mill — a Brief History," *Atlantic* 309, no. 1852 (September 2004); also Nicole Morgan, *La Haine froide: A quoi pense la droite américaine?* (Paris: Éditions de Seuil, 2012), part 2; and Sidney Blumenthal, *The Counter-Establishment: From Conservative Ideology to Political Power* (New York: Harper & Row, 1988).
38. Galbraith, *New Industrial State.*

39. John Kenneth Galbraith, *The Affluent Society* (Harmondsworth: Penguin, 1958).

40. This contradiction is explored by Michael Ignatieff, *The Needs of Strangers* (New York: Penguin, 1986), and Patricia Springborg, *The Problem of Human Needs and the Critique of Civilization* (London: George Allen & Unwin, 1981).

41. *A Theory of Justice.*

42. This discussion draws upon ideas from rational choice theory, which emerged from government service after the Johnson administration to fill a vacuum in postmodern, post-Parsons thinking about politics. See Sonja M. Amadae, *Rationalizing Capitalist Democracy: The Cold War Origins of Rational Choice Liberalism* (Chicago: University of Chicago Press, 2003), especially chap. 8.

43. Friedrich A. Hayek, "The Use of Knowledge in Society," *American Economic Review* 35, no. 4 (September 1945): 519–30.

44. The quotation is from Hayek, *Constitution of Liberty,* Kindle edition, location 1220.

45. Ibid., Kindle edition, location 1930–31.

46. This is imprecise, although it is Hayek's point. The theory of the firm stated by British economist Ronald Coase (1910–2013) explains that markets do not in fact coordinate the production of complex products. Entrepreneurs and firms exist to take on the risks and coordinate the stages of product design, production, and marketing, "internalizing" the costs of doing so in the expectation of benefit from the subsequent market uptake of the product. Hayek's broader point is that the knowledge that exists has to be assembled, and that competitive markets, enforceable contracts, and property rights enable the process. What these theories do not say is that law is needed to keep markets competitive. See Brandeis, *Other People's Money,* for an account of the origins and operations of the Money Trust in the United States as the railway age grew to maturity.

47. Ronald Coase received a Nobel Prize for economics in 1991 for his work on the nature of the firm and social costs. His theorem holds that firms arise when entrepreneurs internalize the costs of overcoming market failures — that is, when the transaction costs of

assembling an organization are lower than the expected value of its markets. See R.H. Coase, *The Firm, The Market and the Law* (Chicago: University of Chicago Press, 1988), especially chap. 2.

48. Mancur Olson, *The Rise and Decline of Nations* (New Haven, CT: Yale University Press, 1982).

49. Peter Aranson, *American Government: Strategy and Choice* (Cambridge, MA: Winthrop, 1981), 491.

50. Adam Smith, *The Theory of Moral Sentiments* (Indianapolis: Liberty Classics, 1976).

51. Carolyn Webber and Aaron Wildavsky, *A History of Taxation and Expenditure in the Modern World* (New York: Simon & Schuster, 1986), 528–34, shows the U.S. income tax system in this period as "mildly redistributive" and difficult to change because of its wide range of preferences, which make it a "paradigm of democratic responsiveness."

52. Berlin, *Four Essays on Liberty*.

53. David Hume, *A Treatise of Human Nature* (1738–40; Project Gutenberg eBook, 2010), 304: "It is not contrary to reason to prefer the destruction of the whole world to the scratching of my little finger. It is not contrary to reason for me to chuse [*sic*] my total ruin, to prevent the least uneasiness of an Indian or person wholly unknown to me."

54. Hegel believed that a successful state must be supported by a population whose self-understanding transcends their individual situations enough to relate to the concerns of their fellow citizens. Indeed, his whole philosophical project concerned the development of human consciousness to the point where it grasped the fundamental force of the Reason that drives the created universe, which he termed the Absolute Spirit. Attaining this level of transcendant self-consciousness, Hegel believed, was the purpose of mankind's trajectory through the dialectic of history. He outlines the growth process in his first major work, *The Phenomenology of Mind* (first published in 1807), of which one section is devoted to an exploration of the master-slave relation and how, through labour, the slave comes to realize that he is a being equal to the master. But before the master will recognize that, the slave must overcome his fear and confront the master as an equal, an act that may cost him his life. Nevertheless, it is by rejecting a state of mind that knowingly accepts life under a falsehood and adopting

a state of mind that asserts Reason's truth that mankind advances to ever higher planes of knowledge and consciousness. Such is the power of this section that under the influence of a Marxist specialist on Hegel — Alexandre Kojève — it became a major theme in Marxist interpretations of Hegel after the Second World War, in support of the Marxist argument for eventual replacement of bourgeois civilization by a working class that has acquired the consciousness necessary to assume political power and end its exploitation by capital.

55. Fred Hirsch, *Social Limits to Growth,* Twentieth Century Fund Study (Cambridge, MA: Harvard University Press, 1976).

56. Christopher Lasch, *The Culture of Narcissism* (New York: Warner Books, 1979).

57. Daniel Bell, *The Cultural Contradictions of Capitalism* (New York: Harper Torchbooks, 1976).

58. Heidegger, *Letter on Humanism,* 189–242.

59. André Gorz, *Critique of Economic Reason* (London: Verso, 1989), 59–66.

60. Jacques Rancière, "May '68 Reviewed and Corrected," in *Moments politiques: Interventions 1977–2009,* trans. Mary Foster (Montreal: Lux, 2014).

61. Louis Althusser (1918–90), influential French Marxist philosophy professor whose innovative insights revived interest in Marxism. He characterized student uprisings in May 1968 as "infantile leftism." He remained at the École Normale Supérieure until tragedy struck: in 1980, after a period of recurring severe mental disturbance, he killed his wife. He died in an asylum. His work after 1980 — including an autobiography recounting the events leading to the death of his wife — was published posthumously. See chapter 19 of his *L'Avenir dure longtemps* (Paris: Flammarion, 2013).

62. Bernard Bosanquet, *The Philosophical Theory of the State* (Kitchener, ON: Batoche Books, 2001), and especially his analysis of Hegel's view of society as a system of social ethics (chap. 10).

63. Norman Mackenzie and Jeanne Mackenzie, *The Fabians* (New York: Touchstone-Simon & Schuster, 1977), 203, underlines the conflict between the trade union–oriented Fabians and the Liberal Hegelians like D.G. Ritchie.

64. Richard Sennett, *The Fall of Public Man* (New York: Vintage, 1978), chap. 11, explores the historical roots of a cultural shift away from a public to a private social focus.

65. Pierre Rosanvallon discusses the significance of *civitas* in "How to Create a Society of Equals," *Foreign Affairs* (January/February 2016): 22.

66. Interesting in this connection is the almost total neglect in public discourse of the British Hegelian ethical theories, which so inspired early twentieth-century idealism — in particular, T.H. Green — despite the examples of the civil rights activists and the early hopes for the U.S. Peace Corps in the 1960s. By the mid-1970s, even in Britain, the British Hegelians were forgotten.

67. This is obviously in part a euphemism for the "white rage" that informed Republican political strategies from the Southern strategy to the Tea Party attack on the "administrative state." See Carol Anderson, *White Rage* (New York: Bloomsbury, 2016).

68. Some might see this as a variation on a theme famously identified by Richard Hofstadter in *The Paranoid Style in American Politics and Other Essays* (Cambridge, MA: Harvard University Press, 1964).

69. Charles Reich, *The Greening of America,* rev. and ed. Jesse Kornbluth (Head Butler, 2012, online).

70. John Kenneth Galbraith, *Economics and the Public Purpose* (New York: Houghton Mifflin, 1973), especially chap. 8.

CHAPTER 4: REBUILDING LIBERALISM

1. Blumenthal, *The Counter-Establishment;* Morgan, *La Haine froide,* part 2.

2. Marshall and Bottomore, *Citizenship and Social Class.*

3. John Dunn, *Western Political Theory in the Face of the Future* (Cambridge: Cambridge University Press, 1980), especially his preface, p. vii.

4. Particularly in his essay "The Construction of the Historical World in the Human Studies," and especially the section "The Procedure Through Which the Mind-Constructed World Is Given," *Gesammelte Schriften,* vol. 7, 79–88, translated by H.P. Rickman in *Dilthey: Selected Writings*, especially 186–89.

5. This may seem excessively statist to some. But civil society and

the state are mutual creations; the one requires the other if liberal juridical and institutional concepts are to function and to evolve democratically. Recent literature on civil society is less optimistic about this: e.g., Seligman, *Idea of Civil Society*, and Jean L. Cohen and Andrew Arato, *Civil Society and Political Theory* (Cambridge, MA: MIT Press, 1994). It should be remembered, however, that liberalism requires a strong centre able to negotiate in three dimensions — and to be effective thereafter as a skilled professional public service.

6. Gray, *Liberalism.*

7. Pierre Rosanvallon, *Le Bon Gouvernement* (Paris: Éditions du Seuil, 2015), 384–86.

8. David Abraham, *The German Duality of State and Society* (Miami: University of Miami School of Law, Institutional Repository, 1996).

9. Benjamin Constant, *De la Liberté des anciens comparée a celle des modernes,* in his *Écrits politiques*, 591–619.

10. Ernst Cassirer, *Le Problème Jean-Jacques Rousseau*, (Paris: Pluriel, 2010).

11. Albert O. Hirschman, *Shifting Involvements: Private Interest and Public Action* (Princeton: Princeton University Press, 1982), 3–4.

12. Joseph Schumpeter, *Capitalism, Socialism, and Democracy* (New York: Harper & Row, 1942), 84–85, introduces the process of creative destruction.

13. Hirschman, *Shifting Involvements,* 55–56.

14. Schumpeter, *Capitalism, Socialism, and Democracy,* 134–42, describes the elimination of the "protecting strata" that supported the precapitalist economy.

15. Ibid., passim.

16. For a brilliant short history, see Leszek Kolakowski, *The Alienation of Reason: A History of Positivist Thought* (Garden City, NY: Anchor Books, 1969).

17. *Dilthey: Selected Writings,* especially introduction 5, "Methodology"; "Construction of the Historical World in the Human Studies," especially 1; and "The Delimitation of Human Studies," 170–84.

18. Jean-François Lyotard, *La Condition postmoderne* (Paris: Éditions de Minuit, 1979). See also Steiner, *Martin Heidegger.*

19. Dana R. Villa, *Arendt and Heidegger: The Fate of the Political*

(Princeton: Princeton University Press, 1996), chap. 7.

20. Heidegger, *Basic Writings*, chap. 7, "The Question Concerning Technology."

21. As established in philosophy since Plato. See also Heidegger, *Letter on Humanism*.

22. Sylvie Courtine-Denamy, *Hannah Arendt* (Paris: Hachette, 1997), especially chap. 3.

23. Gaus, *Order of Public Reason.*

24. Stafford Beer, *Designing Freedom*, Massey Lectures (Toronto: Anansi, 1974), 11–17.

25. For example, in Canada a pressing perennial question is the endangerment of the minority official language, French. It ought to be obvious that French can survive as a creative force in the midst of an "Anglo-Saxon sea" (the English-speaking majorities in Canada and the United States) only if it can achieve a self-sustaining existence that also imparts a sense of pride in achievement to those for whom its use is an everyday reality. It is also obvious, as Henri Bourassa, founder of *Le Devoir,* stated, that "federalism is not a suicide pact." Thus, there is a shared interest across the country for supporting and enhancing French language and culture, to say nothing of the broader national interest these serve in opening the door as a lifeworld partner with other French-speaking nations. Understanding the linguistic situation thus is, or ought to be, a priority for continual sociological investigation, discussion, and, where necessary, supportive action. Yet it is a surprisingly thorny matter. Besides all the everyday implications for people across the country who are not French speakers, there is the belief held by many English speakers that optimality requires unilingualism. So thorny is this that the issue is neglected between crises — which means it lurks unresolved until it can surge up again. Building public understanding of long-standing difficult problems is not a trivial challenge — but it is a requirement if liberal government is to become immune to many of its potential pathologies.

26. Max Scheler, *Ressentiment: Das Ressentiment im Aufbau der Moralen*, trans. Louis Coser (Milwaukee, WI: Marquette University Press, 1998.

27. Explored by, among others, Raymond Williams with respect to

Britain. See his *The Long Revolution* (Harmondsworth: Penguin, 1961).

AN ABBREVIATED LITERATURE REVIEW

1. For example, Kloppenberg, *Uncertain Victory;* also Jonathan Israel, *A Revolution of the Mind: Radical Enlightenment and the Origins of Modern Democracy* (Princeton: Princeton University Press, 2010).
2. Jonathan Israel, *Democratic Enlightenment: Philosophy, Revolution and Human Rights 1750–1790* (Oxford: Oxford University Press, 2011).
3. For example, Catherine Audard, *Qu'est-ce que le libéralisme?* (Paris: Gallimard, 2009); Edmund Fawcett, *Liberalism: The Life of an Idea* (Princeton: Princeton University Press, 2014); and Micklethwait and Wooldridge, *The Fourth Revolution.*
4. In particular, Pierre Rosanvallon, *Le Libéralisme économique* (Paris: Éditions de Seuil, 1989), and *Democratic Legitimacy: Impartiality, Reflexivity, Proximity,* trans. Arthur Goldhammer (Princeton and Oxford: Princeton University Press, 2011).
5. *The Birth of Biopolitics* and some derivative books by his students, such as Dardot and Laval, *La nouvelle raison du monde.*

BIBLIOGRAPHY

Abraham, David. *The German Duality of State and Society*. Miami: University of Miami School of Law, Institutional Repository, 1996.

Acton, Lord (John Emerich Edward Dalberg-Acton). *The History of Freedom and Other Essays*. London: Macmillan, 1907.

———. "The Study of History" (Inaugural Lecture as Regius Professor of Modern History at Cambridge University, 1865). *Essays in the Study and Writing of History* (*Selected Writings of Lord Acton*), edited by J. Rufus Fears, 504–55. Indianapolis: Liberty Classics, 1986.

Acton, Lord, A.W. Ward, G.W. Prothero, and Stanley Leathes, eds. *The Latest Age*. Vol. 10 of *The Cambridge Modern History*. Cambridge: Cambridge University Press, 1910.

Adams, Charles F., Jr., and Henry Adams. *Chapters of Erie and Other Essays*. New York: Henry Holt, 1886.

Adams, Henry. *The Education of Henry Adams*. Project Gutenberg eBook, 2011. First published 1905.

Agamben, Giorgio. *Homo Sacer*. Stanford: Stanford University Press, 1998.

Aghion, Philippe, and Peter Howlitt. *Endogenous Growth Theory*. Cambridge, MA: MIT Press, 1998.

Alesina, Alberto, and Enrico Spolaore. *The Size of Nations*. Cambridge, MA: MIT Press, 2003.

Amadae, Sonja M. *Rationalizing Capitalist Democracy: The Cold War Origins of Rational Choice Liberalism*. Chicago: University of Chicago Press, 2003.

Anderson, Carol. *White Rage*. New York: Bloomsbury, 2016.

Andler, Charles. *Les Origines de socialisme d'état en Allemagne*. Paris: Félix Alcan, 1897.

Apuleius "Africanus," Lucius. *The Golden Ass*. Translated by William Adlington, 1566, rev. ed. 1639. Project Gutenberg eBook, 2013.

Aranson, Peter. *American Government: Strategy and Choice*. Cambridge, MA: Winthrop, 1981.

Arblaster, Anthony. *The Rise and Decline of Western Liberalism*. London: Blackwell, 1984.

Arendt, Hannah. *La Condition de l'homme moderne*. Paris: Calmann-Lévy, 1983. First published 1961.

———. *On Revolution*. Harmondsworth: Penguin, 1965.

———. *Les Origines du totalitarisme — Eichmann à Jérusalem*. Paris: Quarto/Gallimard, 2002.

———. *Qu'est-ce que la philosophie de l'existence suivi de L'existentialisme français et de Heidegger le renard*. Paris: Payot et Rivages, 2002.

———. *Qu'est-ce que la politique?* Paris: Éditions de Seuil, 1995.

Aristotle. *Aristotle I*. Vol. 8 of *Great Books of the Western World*. Chicago: University of Chicago Press, 1952.

———. *Aristotle II*. Vol. 9 of *Great Books of the Western World*. Chicago: University of Chicago Press, 1952.

Arnold, Matthew. *Culture and Anarchy*. New York: Dover, 1978. First published 1869.

Aron, Raymond. *Les Étapes de la pensée sociologique*. Paris: Gallimard, 1967.

———. *La Philosophie critique de l'histoire*. Paris: J. Vrin, 1969.

Arrow, Kenneth J. *Social Choice and Individual Values*. 2nd ed. New Haven, CT: Yale University Press, 1963.

Arthur, W. Brian. *Increasing Returns and Path Dependence in the Economy.* Ann Arbor: University of Michigan Press, 1994.

———. *The Nature of Technology: What It Is and How It Evolves.* New York: Free Press, 2009.

Ashley, W.J. "Roscher's Programme of 1843." *Quarterly Journal of Economics* 9, no. 1 (October 1894): 99–105. jstor.org/stable/1883638.

———. *Surveys, Historic and Economic.* New York: Longmans, Green, 1900.

Audard, Catherine. *Qu'est-ce que le libéralisme?* Paris: Gallimard, 2009.

Aycard, M. *L'Histoire du Crédit Mobilier.* Paris: Librairie Internationale, 1867.

Bagehot, Walter. *The English Constitution.* Oxford: Oxford World's Classics, 2001. First published 1867.

Bainville, Jacques. *Les Conséquences politiques de la paix.* Paris: Gallimard, 1920. First published 1920.

Bambach, Charles R. *Heidegger, Dilthey, and the Crisis of Historicism.* Ithaca, NY: Cornell University Press, 1995.

Barash, Jeffrey Andrew, ed. *The Symbolic Construction of Reality: The Legacy of Ernst Cassirer.* Chicago: University of Chicago Press, 2008.

Baudrillard, Jean. *Le Système des objets.* Paris: Gallimard, 1968.

Beale, Linda M. "In the Wake of Financial Crisis." *International Monetary Fund (IMF), Current Developments in Monetary and Financial Law* 5 (2010); Wayne State University Law School Research Paper No. 10–07. ssrn.com/abstract=1681577.

Beer, Stafford. *Designing Freedom.* Massey Lectures. Toronto: Anansi, 1974.

Beinhocker, Eric D. *The Origin of Wealth: The Radical Remaking of Economics and What It Means for Business and Society.* Boston: Harvard Business Review, 2007.

Bell, Daniel. *The Cultural Contradictions of Capitalism.* New York: Harper Torchbooks, 1976.

Belloc, Hilaire. *The Servile State.* Indianapolis: Liberty Fund, 1977. First published 1912.

Beniger, James R. *The Control Revolution.* Cambridge, MA: Harvard University Press, 1986.

Bentham, Jeremy. *Introduction to the Principles of Morals and Legislation.* Hafner Library of Classics. New York: Hafner, 1963.

Bentley, Arthur F. *The Process of Government: A Study of Social Pressures.* Chicago: University of Chicago Press, 1908.

Berle, Adolf, and Gardiner Means. *The Modern Corporation and Private Property.* New York: Transaction, 1932.

Berlin, Isaiah. *Against the Current: Essays in the History of Ideas.* Harmondsworth: Penguin, 1982.

———. *Four Essays on Liberty.* Oxford: Oxford University Press, 1959.

———. *Russian Thinkers.* Harmondsworth: Penguin, 1981.

———. *The Sense of Reality: Studies in Ideas and Their History.* New York: Farrar, Straus and Giroux, 1996.

Bernstein, Richard. *The Restructuring of Social and Political Theory.* New York: Harcourt, Brace, Jovanovich, 1976.

Bertier de Sauvigny, G. de. *La Restauration.* Paris: Flammarion, 1955.

Binder, Sarah A. *Stalemate: Causes and Consequences of Legislative Gridlock.* Washington, DC: Brookings Institution Press, 2003.

Blumenthal, Sidney. *The Counter-Establishment: From Conservative Ideology to Political Power.* New York: Harper & Row, 1988.

Boeckh, August. *Encyklopädie und Methodologie der philologischen Wissenschaften.* Leipzig: Ernst Bratuscheck, 1877.

Bonefeld, Werner. "Ordoliberalism and the Crisis of the Neo-Liberal Political Economy: On the Social Market, the Free Economy and the Strong State." *New Public Economy* (January 2013).

Bosanquet, Bernard. *The Philosophical Theory of the State.* Kitchener, ON: Batoche Books, 2001. First published 1899.

Bourdieu, Pierre. *Langage et pouvoir symbolique.* Paris: Fayard, 1991.

Bowring, John. Introduction to *The Complete Works of Jeremy Bentham.* Edited by John Bowring. Edinburgh: William Tait, 1843.

Brandeis, Louis D. *Other People's Money and How the Bankers Use It.* New York: Frederick A. Stokes, 1914.

Broyer, Sylvain. "Ordnungstheorie et ordolibéralisme." In Commun, *L'Ordolibéralisme allemande,* 79–100.

Buchanan, James M. *The Limits of Liberty.* Chicago: University of Chicago Press, 1975.

———. *The Reason of Rules: Constitutional Political Economy.* Vol. 10 of

The Collected Works of James M. Buchanan, edited by Geoffrey Brennan. Indianapolis: Liberty Fund, 1985. Online Library of Liberty.

Buchanan, James M., and Gordon Tullock. *The Calculus of Consent.* Ann Arbor, MI: Ann Arbor Paperbacks, 1962.

Buchanan, James M., and Richard E. Wagner. *Democracy in Deficit: The Political Legacy of Lord Keynes.* Indianapolis: Liberty Fund, 1977. Online Library of Liberty.

Burke, Edmund. *Reflections on the French Revolution and Other Essays.* In vol. 3 of *The Complete Works of the Right Honourable Edmund Burke.* Project Gutenberg eBook, 2005. New York: J.M. Dent, 1935. First published 1790.

———. *Selected Writings and Speeches.* Edited by Peter J. Stanlis. New York: Anchor, 1963.

———. *Thoughts on the Cause of the Present Discontents.* 1797. In vol. 1 of *The Complete Works of the Right Honourable Edmund Burke.* Project Gutenberg eBook, 2010.

———. *Vindication of Natural Society: Inquiry into the Origin of Our Ideas of the Sublime and the Beautiful.* 1797. In vol. 1 of *The Complete Works of the Right Honourable Edmund Burke.* Project Gutenberg eBook, 2010.

Burkhardt, Jacob. *Judgments on History and Historians.* Translated by Larry Zohn. Indianapolis: Liberty Fund, 1999. First published 1929.

Cahnman, Werner Jacob. *Weber and Toennies.* New York: Transaction, 1995.

Caird, Edward. *The Critical Philosophy of Immanuel Kant.* 2 vols. Glasgow: James Maclehose & Sons, 1909.

———. *Hegel.* Philadelphia: J.B. Lippincott, 1886.

———. *Individualism and Socialism: Being the Inaugural Address to the Civic Society of Glasgow.* Glasgow: James Maclehose & Sons, 1897.

———. *The Social Philosophy and Religion of Comte.* Glasgow: James Maclehose & Sons, 1885.

Camus, Albert. *Le Mythe de Sisyphe.* Paris: Gallimard, 1942.

Cassirer, Ernst. *Das Erkenntnisproblem in der Philosophie und Wissenschaft der neuren Zeit.* 3 vols. Berlin: Bruno Cassirer, 1922.

———. *An Essay on Man.* New York: Doubleday Anchor, 1944.

———. *Freiheit und Form: Studien zur deutschen Ideengeschichte.* Berlin: Bruno Cassirer, 1918.

———. *The Myth of the State*. New Haven, CT: Yale University Press, 1946.

———. *Le Problème Jean-Jacques Rousseau*. Paris: Pluriel, 2010. First published 1932.

———. *Substance and Function and Einstein's Theory of Relativity*. Translated by William Curtis Swabey and Marie Collins Swabey. Chicago: Open Court, 1923.

Castels, Manuel. *The Rise of the Network Society*. Vol. 1. London: Blackwell, 1999.

Cazamian, Louis. *Le Roman social en Angleterre (1830–1850)*. Paris: Société nouvelle de Librairie et d'Édition, 1904.

Chandler, Alfred D., Jr. *Scale and Scope*. Cambridge, MA: Belknap/Harvard University Press, 1990.

Cho, Dong-Sung, and Hwy-Chang Moon. *From Adam Smith to Michael Porter: Evolution of Competitiveness Theory*. Singapore: World Scientific, 2005.

Clapham, J.H. *Economic Development of France and Germany, 1815–1914*. Cambridge: Cambridge University Press, 1961.

Clark, Kenneth. *Ruskin Today*. Harmondsworth: Penguin, 1982.

Coase, R.H. *The Firm, The Market and the Law*. Chicago: University of Chicago Press, 1988.

Cohen, Jean L., and Andrew Arato. *Civil Society and Political Theory*. Cambridge, MA: MIT Press, 1994.

Cole, G.D.H., and Raymond Postgate. *The Common People, 1746–1946*. London: Methuen, 1971.

Collins, J. Churton. *Voltaire, Montesquieu and Rousseau in England*. London: Eveleigh Nash, Fawside House, 1908.

Commun, Patricia, ed. *L'Ordolibéralisme allemande*. Cergy-Pontoise: CIRAC, 2003, 2017.

Connolly, William E. *The Fragility of Things*. Durham, NC: Duke University Press, 2013.

———. *Political Theory and Modernity*. Ithaca, NY: Cornell University Press, 1993.

Constant, Benjamin. Écrits politiques. Paris: Gallimard, 1997.

Cooley, Charles Horton. *Social Organization: A Study of the Larger Mind*. New York: Charles Scribner's Sons, 1910.

Cournot, Augustin. *Researches into the Mathematical Principles of the Theory of Wealth.* Translated by Nathanial T. Bacon. New York and London: Macmillan, 1897.

Courtine-Denamy, Sylvie. *Hannah Arendt.* Paris: Hachette, 1997.

Croce, Benedetto. *History of Europe in the Nineteenth Century.* London: Unwin, 1965. First published 1934.

———. *The Philosophy of Giambattista Vico.* Translated by R.G. Collingwood. London: Howard Latimer, 1913.

———. *What Is Living and What Is Dead of the Philosophy of Hegel.* Translated by Douglas Ainslie. New York: Russell and Russell, 1969.

Croly, Herbert. *Progressive Democracy.* 1914. Amazon Digital Services LLC. Online.

———. *The Promise of American Life.* New York: Macmillan, 1912.

Cropsey, Joseph. *Polity and Economy: With Further Thoughts on the Principles of Adam Smith.* South Bend, IN: St. Augustine's Press, 2001.

Cusset, François. *French Theory: Foucault, Derrida, Deleuze & Cie et les mutations de la vie intellectuelle aux États-Unis.* Paris: La Découverte, 2005. First published 2003.

Dahms, Harry F., ed. *Transformations of Capitalism: Economy, Society, and the State in Modern Times.* New York: New York University Press, 2000.

Dangerfield, George. *The Strange Death of Liberal England.* London: Constable, 1935.

Dardot, Pierre, and Christian Laval. *La Nouvelle Raison du monde: Essai sur la société néolibérale.* Paris: La Découverte, 2010.

Darwin, Charles. *The Origin of the Species, or The Preservation of Favoured Races in the Struggle for Life.* Harmondsworth: Penguin, 1981. First published 1859.

Debord, Guy. *La Société de spectacle.* Les Classiques des sciences sociales. 1992. Classiques uquac.ca. Online.

Dehay, Eric. "L'Indépendance de la banque central en Allemagne: Des principes ordolibéraux à la pratique de la Bundesbank." In Commun, *L'Ordolibéralisme allemande*, 255–64.

De Ruggiero, Guido. *The History of European Liberalism.* Boston: Beacon Press, 1966. First published 1927.

Dewey, John. *German Philosophy and Politics.* New York: Henry Holt, 1915. Project Gutenberg eBook.

———. *Individualism Old and New.* Amherst, NY: Prometheus Great Books in Philosophy, 1999.

———. *Reconstruction in Philosophy.* New York: Mentor, 1949.

Dietzel, H. *Karl Rodbertus: Darstellung seines Lebens und seiner Lehre.* Berlin: Gustav Fischer, 1886.

Diggins, John Patrick. *The Promise of Pragmatism: Modernism and the Crisis of Knowledge and Authority.* Chicago: University of Chicago Press, 1994.

Dilthey, Wilhelm. *Dilthey: Selected Writings.* Edited by H.P. Rickman. Cambridge: Cambridge University Press, 1976.

Downs, Anthony. *An Economic Theory of Democracy.* New York: Harper & Row, 1957.

Drucker, Peter. *Concept of the Corporation.* Rev. ed. New York: John Day, 1972. First published 1946.

Dunn, John. *Western Political Theory in the Face of the Future.* Cambridge: Cambridge University Press, 1980.

Durkheim, Émile. *The Division of Labour in Society.* Glencoe, IL: Free Press, 1933. First published 1893.

———. *Socialism.* New York: Collier Books, 1962. First published 1928.

———. *Le Suicide: Étude de sociologie.* Paris: Presses universitaires de France, 1967. First published 1897.

Ebenstein, Alan. *Friedrich Hayek: A Biography.* Chicago: University of Chicago Press, 2001–3.

Eksteins, Modris. *Rites of Spring: The Great War and the Birth of the Modern Age.* Toronto: Lester & Orpen Dennys, 1989.

Enfantin, Barthélémy-Prosper. *Doctrine de Saint-Simon: Exposition.* 1830. BNF-Gallica. Online.

Engels, Frederick. *Herr Eugen Dühring's Revolution in Science (Anti-Dühring).* Translated by Emile Burns. Marxist-Leninist Library. London: Martin Lawrence, 1934.

Eucken, Walter. *Die Grundlagen der Nationalökonomie.* In *Enzyklopädie der Rechts- und Staatswissenschaft.* 9th ed. Abteilung Staatswissenschaft. Berlin: Springer, 1989.

Fawcett, Edmund. *Liberalism: The Life of an Idea*. Princeton: Princeton University Press, 2014.

Feis, Herbert. *Europe: The World's Banker 1870–1914*. Publications of the Council on Foreign Relations. New Haven, CT: Yale University Press, 1930.

Ferguson, Niall. *The Cash Nexus: Money and Power in the Modern World 1700–2000*. New York: Basic Books, 2001.

Fichte, Johann Gottlieb. *Grundlage des Naturrechts nach Principien der Wissenschaftslehre*. Jena and Leipzig: Christian Ernst Gabler, 1797.

Finer, S.E. *The Life and Times of Sir Edwin Chadwick*. London: Methuen, 1952.

Fischer, David Hackett. *The Great Wave: Price Revolutions and the Rhythm of History*. Oxford and New York: Oxford University Press, 1996.

Foucault, Michel. *The Birth of Biopolitics: Lectures at the Collège de France, 1978–1979*. New York: Picador/Palgrave, 2004.

Freeden, Michael. *Liberal Languages: Ideological Imaginations and Twentieth Century Political Thought*. Princeton: Princeton University Press, 2005.

Friedman, Michael. *A Parting of the Ways: Carnap, Cassirer, and Heidegger*. Chicago: Open Court, 2007.

Friedman, Milton. *Capitalism and Freedom*. Chicago: University of Chicago Press, 1962.

Freud, Sigmund. *The Major Works of Sigmund Freud*. In vol. 54 of *Great Books of the Western World*. Chicago: University of Chicago Press, 1952.

Fujita, Masahisa, Paul Krugman, and Anthony J. Venables. *The Spatial Economy*. Cambridge, MA: MIT Press, 2001.

Galbraith, John Kenneth. *The Affluent Society*. Harmondsworth: Penguin, 1958.

———. *Economics and the Public Purpose*. New York: Houghton Mifflin, 1973.

———. *The New Industrial State*. New York: Houghton Mifflin, 1967.

Gaucher, Marcel. *La Crise du libéralisme*. Paris: Gallimard, 2007.

Gaus, Gerald. *Justificatory Liberalism*. Oxford and New York: Oxford University Press, 1996.

————. *The Order of Public Reason.* Cambridge: Cambridge University Press, 2011.

Gay, Peter. *Schnitzler's Century: The Making of Middle Class Culture 1815–1914.* New York: Allen Lane, 2001.

George, Henry. *Progress and Poverty.* New York: Walter J. Black, 1941. First published 1879.

Gerth, H.H., and C. Wright Mills. *From Max Weber: Essays in Sociology.* Oxford: Oxford University Press, 1946.

Gilding, Paul. *The Great Disruption: Why the Climate Crisis Will Bring On the End of Shopping and the Birth of a New World.* New York: Bloomsbury, 2011.

Gillespie, Michael Allen. *Hegel, Heidegger and the Ground of History.* Chicago: University of Chicago Press, 2015.

Godley, Wynne, and Marc Lavoie. *Monetary Economics: An Integrated Approach to Credit, Money, Income, Production and Wealth.* London: Palgrave Macmillan, 2007.

Goldschmidt, Nils. *Gibt es eine ordoliberalische Entwicklungsidee? Walter Euckens Analyse des gesellschaftlichen und wirtschaftlichen Wandels.* Freiburger Diskussionspapiere zur Ordnungsökonomik 12/03. Freiburg: Walter Eucken Institut, 2012.

Goldschmidt, Nils, and Jan-Otman Hesse. *Eucken, Hayek and the Road to Serfdom.* Freiburger Diskussionspapiere zur Ordnungsökonomik 12/4. Freiburg: Walter Eucken Institut, 2012.

Goldschmidt, Nils, and Hermann Rauchenschwandtner. *The Philosophy of the Social Market Economy: Michel Foucault's Analysis of Ordoliberalism.* Freiburger Diskussionspapiere zur Ordnungsökonomik 07/4. Freiburg: Walter Eucken Institut, 2007.

Gooch, G.P. *History and Historians in the Nineteenth Century.* Boston: Beacon Press, 1959.

Gordon, Peter. *Weimar Thought: A Contested Legacy.* Princeton: Princeton University Press, 2007.

Gorz, André. *Critique of Economic Reason.* London: Verso, 1989.

Grampp, William D. *Economic Liberalism.* Vols. 1 and 2. Indianapolis: Liberty Fund, 1965.

Gray, J. Glenn. *G.W.F. Hegel on Art, Religion, Philosophy.* New York: Harper Torchbooks, 1970.

Gray, John. *Liberalism.* 2nd ed. Minneapolis: University of Minnesota Press, 1995.

Green, Thomas Hill. *Lectures on the Principles of Political Obligation.* Kitchener, ON: Batoche Books, 1999. First published 1885.

———. *Prolegomena to Ethics.* Oxford: Clarendon Press, 1906.

Greider, William. *Secrets of the Temple: How the Federal Reserve Runs the Country.* New York: Simon & Schuster, 1987.

Groethuysen, Bernard. *Anthropologie philosophique.* Paris: Gallimard Édition électronique, 2014. Online. First published 1953.

———. *Origines de l'esprit bourgeois en France.* Paris: Gallimard, 1927.

———. *Philosophie et histoire.* Paris: Albin Michel, 1995.

Guizot, François. *Historical Essays and Lectures.* Edited by Stanley Mellon. Chicago: University of Chicago Press, 1972. First published 1828.

———. *Des Moyens de gouvernement.* Paris: Belin, 2009. First published 1821.

———. *Sir Robert Peel.* Paris: Didier, 1856.

Guyer, Paul. *Kant's Critique of the Power of Judgment.* Lanham, MD: Rowman and Littlefield, 2003.

Habermas, Jürgen. *Communication and the Evolution of Society.* Translated by Thomas McCarthy. Boston: Beacon Press, 1979.

———. *Connaissance et intérêt.* Paris: Gallimard, 1976. First published 1968.

———. *Raison et légitimité.* Paris: Petite Bibliothèque Payot, 2012.

———. *The Structural Transformation of the Public Sphere.* Translated by Thomas Burger with Frederick Lawrence. Cambridge, MA: MIT Press, 1991.

———. *La Technique et la science comme idéologie.* Paris: Denoël, 1973. First published 1968.

———. *Theory and Practice.* Boston: Beacon Press, 1973.

———. *Theory of Communicative Action.* 2 vols. Boston: Beacon Press, 1985.

Haldane, Elizabeth S. *George Eliot and Her Times.* London: Hodder & Stoughton, 1922.

Halévy, Élie. *The Era of Tyrannies.* New York: Doubleday Anchor, 1965. First published 1938.

———. *The Growth of Philosophic Radicalism.* Translated by Mary Morris. London: Faber & Faber, 1939. First published 1928.

———. *Histoire du socialisme européen.* Paris: Gallimard, 1974. First published 1948.

Hamburger, Joseph. *James Mill and the Art of Revolution.* Westport, CT: Greenwood Press, 1963.

Hamilton, Alexander, James Madison, and John Jay. *The Federalist.* In vol. 43 of *Great Books of the Western World.* Chicago: University of Chicago Press, 1952.

Harvey, David. *A Brief History of Neoliberalism.* Oxford and New York: Oxford University Press, 2007.

Harrison, Austin. *Frederic Harrison: Thoughts and Memories.* London: Heinemann, 1926.

Hayek, Friedrich A. *The Constitution of Liberty.* Vol. 17 of *The Collected Works of F.A. Hayek*, edited by Ronald Hamowy. Chicago: University of Chicago Press, 1960. Kindle edition, 2011.

———. *The Counter-Revolution of Science: Studies on the Abuse of Reason.* Glencoe, IL: Free Press, 1955.

———. *Law, Legislation and Liberty.* 3 vols. Chicago: University of Chicago Press, 1973–79.

———. *The Pure Theory of Capital.* London: Routledge & Kegan Paul, 1950.

———. *The Road to Serfdom.* London: George Routledge & Sons, 1944.

———. "The Use of Knowledge in Society." *American Economic Review* 35, no. 4 (September 1945): 519–30.

Hegel, G.W.F. *Lectures on the History of Philosophy.* 3 vols. Translated by E.S. Haldane. London: Routledge & Kegan Paul, 1968.

———. *Natural Law: The Scientific Ways of Treating Natural Law, Its Place in Moral Philosophy, and Its Relation to the Positive Sciences of Law.* Translated by T.M. Knox. Philadelphia: University of Pennsylvania, 1975.

———. *The Phenomenology of Mind.* Translated by J.B. Baillie. New York: Harper Torchbooks, 1967.

———. *The Philosophy of History.* Translated by J. Sibree. In *Georg Wilhelm Friedrich Hegel.* Vol. 46 of *Great Books of the Western World.* Chicago: University of Chicago Press, 1952.

———. *The Philosophy of Right.* Translated by T.M. Knox. In *Georg Wilhelm Friedrich Hegel.* Vol. 46 of *Great Books of the Western World.* Chicago: University of Chicago Press, 1952.

Heidegger, Martin. *Basic Writings from* Being and Time *(1927) to* The Task of Thinking *(1964)*. Edited by David Farrell Krell. New York: Harper & Row, 1977.

———. *Being and Time.* Translated by John Maquarrie and Edward Robinson. New York: Harper & Row, 1962.

———. *Kant et le problème de la métaphysique.* Paris: Gallimard, 1953.

———. "Letter on Humanism." In *Martin Heidegger: Basic Writings from* Being and Time *(1927) to* The Task of Thinking *(1964)*, edited by David Farrell Krell, 189–242. New York: Harper & Row, 1977, 189–242.

Henrich, Dieter. *Between Kant and Hegel.* Cambridge, MA: Harvard University Press, 2003.

Hildebrand, Bruno. *Die Nationalökonomie der Gegenwart und Zukunft und andere Schriften.* Jena: Gustav Fischer, 1922. First published 1848.

Himmelfarb, Gertrude. *Victorian Minds.* New York: Alfred A. Knopf, 1968.

Hirsch, Fred. *Social Limits to Growth.* Twentieth Century Fund Study. Cambridge, MA: Harvard University Press, 1976.

Hirschman, Albert O. *The Passions and the Interests.* Princeton: Princeton University Press, 1977.

———. *Shifting Involvements: Private Interest and Public Action.* Princeton: Princeton University Press, 1982.

Hobbes, Thomas. *Leviathan.* In vol. 23 of *Great Books of the Western World.* Chicago: University of Chicago Press, 1952.

Hobhouse, L.T. *Liberalism.* Home University Library. London: Oxford University Press, 1911.

Hobson, J.A. *The Evolution of Modern Capitalism: A Study of Machine Production.* London: George Allen & Unwin, 1949.

Hofstadter, Richard. *The Paranoid Style in American Politics and Other Essays.* Cambridge, MA: Harvard University Press, 1964.

Holborn, Hajo. *A History of Modern Germany, 1840–1945.* London: Eyre and Spottiswoode, 1969.

Hollander, Samuel. *Classical Economics.* Toronto: University of Toronto Press, 1992.

Hudson, Michael. *Killing the Host: How Financial Parasites and Debt Bondage Destroy the Global Economy.* Petrolia, CA: CounterPunch Books, 2015. CounterPunch eBook.

Hughes, H. Stuart. *Consciousness and Society.* New York: Vintage, 1958.

Hume, David. *An Enquiry Concerning Human Nature.* In vol. 35 of *Great Books of the Western World.* Chicago: University of Chicago Press, 1952. First published 1748.

———. *Hume's Moral and Political Philosophy.* Edited by Henry D. Aiken. Hafner Library of Classics. New York: Hafner, 1948.

———. *A Treatise of Human Nature.* 1738–40. Project Gutenberg eBook, 2010.

Huntington, Samuel P. *The Third Wave: Democratization in the Late Twentieth Century.* Carl Albert Centre, University of Oklahoma Julien J. Rothbaum Distinguished Lecture Series. Norman: University of Oklahoma Press, 1989–90.

Husserl, Edmund. *The Cartesian Meditations.* Translated by Dorion Cairns. The Hague: Martinus Nijhoff, 1982. First published 1960.

———. *La Crise des sciences européennes et la phénoménologie transcendentale.* Paris: Gallimard, 1976. First published 1936.

———. *Idées directrices pour une phénoménologie.* Paris: Gallimard, 1950. First published 1926.

Hutchison, T.W. *A Review of Economic Doctrines 1870–1929.* New York: Oxford University Press, 1953.

Iggers, George G. *The German Conception of History: The National Tradition of Thought From Herder to the Present.* Middletown, CT: Wesleyan University Press, 1968.

Ignatieff, Michael. *The Needs of Strangers.* New York: Penguin, 1986.

Inglis, Brian. *Men of Conscience.* New York: Macmillan, 1971.

Israel, Jonathan. *Democratic Enlightenment: Philosophy, Revolution and Human Rights 1750–1790.* Oxford: Oxford University Press, 2011.

———. *A Revolution of the Mind: Radical Enlightenment and the Origins of Modern Democracy.* Princeton: Princeton University Press, 2010.

Jackman, Sydney, ed. *The English Reform Tradition.* Englewood Cliffs, NJ: Prentice-Hall, 1965.

Jácome, Luis Ignacio, Marcela Matamoros-Indorf, Mrinalini Sharma, and Simon Baker Townsend. "Central Bank Credit to the Government: What Can We Learn from International Practices?" IMF Working Paper 12/16 (2012).

James, William. *Essays in Radical Empiricism.* Cambridge, MA: Harvard University Press, 1912.

———. *Pragmatism and Other Essays.* New York: Washington Square Press, 1963.

———. *The Principles of Psychology.* In vol. 53 of *Great Books of the Western World.* Chicago: University of Chicago Press, 1952.

Jay, Martin. *The Dialectical Imagination: A History of the Frankfurt School and the Institute of Social Research.* New York: Little, Brown, 1973.

Jefferson, Thomas. *The Portable Jefferson.* Edited by Merrill D. Peterson. New York: Penguin, 1975.

Jenkins, Keith. *The Postmodern History Reader.* London: Routledge, 1997.

Kant, Immanuel. *Kant: The Critiques and Other Writings.* In vol. 42 of *Great Books of the Western World.* Chicago: University of Chicago Press, 1952.

Kelly, Kevin. *What Technology Wants.* New York: Viking, 2010.

Keynes, John Maynard. *Les Conséquences économiques de la paix.* Paris: Gallimard, 1920.

———. *The Economic Consequences of the Peace.* New York: Harcourt, Brace and Howe, 1920.

———. "The End of Laissez-faire." In *Transformations of Capitalism: Economy, Society, and the State in Modern Times,* edited by Harry F. Dahms, 101–20. New York: New York University Press, 2000.

———. *The General Theory of Employment, Interest and Money.* Vol. 7 of *The Collected* Writings. London: Royal Economic Society, 1976.

Kloppenberg, James T. *Uncertain Victory: Social Democracy and Progressivism in European and American Thought 1870–1920.* New York: Oxford University Press, 1986. Kindle edition.

Kojève, Alexandre. *Introduction à la lecture de Hegel.* Paris: Gallimard, 1947.

Kolakowski, Leszek. *The Alienation of Reason: A History of Positivist Thought.* Garden City, NY: Anchor Books, 1969.

Körner, Heiko. *Soziale Marktwirtschaft: Versuch einer pragmatischen Begründung.* Freiburger Diskussionspapiere zur Ordnungsökonomik 07/7. Freiburg: Walter Eucken Institut, 2007.

Koslowski, Peter, ed. *The Social Market Economy: Theory and Ethics of the Economic Order.* Berlin: Springer, 1998.

Krugman, Paul. *Geography and Trade.* Cambridge, MA: MIT Press, 1996.

———. *The Self-Organizing Economy.* London: Blackwell, 1991.

Kuhn, Thomas S. *The Structure of Scientific Revolutions.* 2nd ed. *International Encyclopedia of Unified Science.* Chicago: University of Chicago Press, 1970.

Kymlika, Will. *Contemporary Political Philosophy: An Introduction.* New York: Oxford University Press, 2002.

Labrousse, Agnès, and Jean-Daniel Weisz, eds. *Institutional Economics in France and Germany: German Ordoliberalism Versus the French Regulation School.* Berlin: Springer, 2001.

Lapham, Lewis. "Tentacles of Rage: The Republican Propaganda Mill — a Brief History." *Atlantic* 309, no. 1852 (September 2004).

Lasch, Christopher. *The Culture of Narcissism.* New York: Warner Books, 1979.

———. *The World of Nations.* New York: Vintage Books, 1974.

Lask, Emil. *Die Logik der Philosophie und die Kategorienlehre: Eine Studie über den Herrschaftsbereich der logischen Form.* Tübingen: J.C.B. Mohr, 1993.

Lefebvre, Henri. *The Critique of Everyday Life.* London and New York: Verso, 2014. First published 1958.

Levasseur, Émile. *Les Sciences sociales sous la restauration: Saint-Simon et le Saint-Simonisme, Fourier et Fouriérisme.* Paris: V. Giard et E. Brière, 1902.

Levine, Emily J. *Dreamland of Humanists: Warburg, Cassirer, Panofsky, and the Hamburg School.* Chicago: University of Chicago Press, 2013.

Lévy, Bernard-Henri. *La Barbarie à visage humain.* Paris: Grasset, 1977.

Lippmann, Walter. *Drift and Mastery.* Englewood Cliffs, NJ: Prentice-Hall, 1966.

———. *The Good Society.* New York: Grosset and Dunlap, 1943.

List, Friedrich. *Système national d'économie politique.* Translated by Henri Richelot. Paris: Gallimard, 1998. First published 1857.

Locke, John. *An Essay Concerning Human Understanding.* In vol. 35 of *Great Books of the Western World.* Chicago: University of Chicago Press, 1952.

———. *A Letter Concerning Toleration.* In vol. 35 of *Great Books of the Western World.* Chicago: University of Chicago Press, 1952.

———. *Two Treatises of Government.* Edited by Peter Laslett. New York: Mentor, 1965.

Longuenesse, Béatrice. *Kant and the Capacity to Judge.* Translated by Charles T. Wolfe. Princeton and Oxford: Princeton University Press, 2000.

Losurdo, Domenico. *Liberalism: A Counter History.* Translated by Gregory Elliott. London and New York: Verso, 2014.

Lukacs, Georg. *History and Class Consciousness.* Cambridge, MA: MIT Press, 1971. First published 1922.

Lyotard, Jean-François. *La Condition postmoderne.* Paris: Éditions de Minuit, 1979.

Macaulay, T.B. *Mill on Government.* Vol. 2 of *Miscellaneous Writings and Speeches of Lord Macaulay.* London, 1829. Project Gutenberg eBook, 2008.

Mackenzie, Norman, and Jeanne Mackenzie. *The Fabians.* New York: Touchstone-Simon & Schuster, 1977.

Malthus, Thomas Robert. *Essai sur le principe de population.* Translated by P. Prevost and G. Prevost. Paris: GF Flammarion, 1992.

———. *Principles of Political Economy.* New York: Augustus M. Kelley, 1922.

Manent, Pierre. *Histoire intellectuelle du libéralisme.* Paris: Pluriel, 2012.

———. *Les Libéraux.* Paris: Gallimard, 2001.

Marktanner, Marcus. "Addressing the Marketing Problem of the Social Market Economy." In *60 Years of Social Market Economy — Formation, Development and Perspectives of a Peacemaking Formula,* edited by Christian L. Glossner and David Gregosz, 170–88. St. Augustine and Berlin: Konrad-Adenauer-Stiftung, 2010.

Marshall, Alfred. *Industry and Trade.* 4th ed. Reprints of Economic Classics. New York: Augustus M. Kelley, 1923.

———. *Money, Credit and Commerce.* London: Macmillan, 1923.

———. *Principles of Economics.* 8th ed. London: Macmillan, 1949.

Marshall, T.H., and Tom Bottomore. *Citizenship and Social Class.* London: Pluto, 1992.

Marx, Karl. *Capital.* In vol. 50 of *Great Books of the Western World.* Chicago: University of Chicago Press, 1952. First published 1867.

———. *Grundrisse: Foundations of the Critique of Political Economy.* Translated by Martin Nicolaus. London: Pelican, 1973. First published in 1953.

Marx, Karl, and Friedrich Engels. *Das Kapital.* 3 vols. Frankfurt: Ullstein, 1972. First published 1872.

———. *Manifesto of the Communist Party*. In vol. 50 of *Great Books of the Western World*. Chicago: University of Chicago Press, 1952. First published 1848.

Mathias, Peter. *The First Industrial Nation: An Economic History of Britain 1700–1914*. New York: Charles Scribner's Sons, 1969.

Mayer, Arno. *La Persistance de l'ancien régime*. Paris: Flammarion, 1983.

Mayer, Martin. *The Bankers: The Next Generation*. New York: Plume, 1997.

Mayer, Thomas, James S. Duesenberry, and Robert Z. Aliber. *Money, Banking, and the Economy*. 2nd ed. New York: Norton, 1981.

McKaern, M., B.S. Phillips, and Robert Cohen. *Georg Simmel and Contemporary Sociology*. Berlin: Springer, 2012.

Meinecke, Friedrich. *The German Catastrophe*. Translated by Sidney Fay. Boston: Beacon Press, 1964.

Menand, Louis. *The Metaphysical Club*. New York: Farrar, Straus and Giroux, 2001.

Menger, Carl. *Investigations into the Methods of the Social Sciences, with Special Reference to Economics*. Edited by Louis Schneider. Translated by Francis J. Nock. New York: New York University Press, 1985. First published 1884.

———. *Die Irrthümer des Historismus in der deutschen Nationalökonomie*. Vienna: Alfred Hölder, 1884.

———. *On the Origins of Money*. Auburn, AL: Ludwig von Mises Institute, 2009. First published 1892.

———. *Principles of Economics*. Auburn, AL: Ludwig von Mises Institute, 1976. First published 1871.

Michel, Henry. *L'Idée de l'état*. Paris: Hachette, 1898.

Michels, Robert. *Political Parties*. New York: Free Press, 1968. First published 1915.

Micklethwait, John, and Adrian Wooldridge. *The Fourth Revolution: The Global Race to Reinvent the State*. New York: Penguin, 2014.

Milgate, Murray, and Shannon C. Stimson. *Ricardian Politics*. Princeton: Princeton University Press, 2014.

Mill, James. *The Political Writings of James Mill: Essays and Reviews on Politics and Society, 1815–1836*. Edited by David M. Hart. Indianapolis: Liberty Fund, 2013. Online Library of Liberty.

Mill, John Stuart. *Auguste Comte and Positivism*. 1865. Project Gutenberg eBook, 2005.

———. *Autobiography.* New York: Houghton Mifflin/Riverside, 1969. First published 1874.

———. *An Examination of Sir William Hamilton's Philosophy.* London: Longmans, Green, 1865.

———. *On Bentham and Coleridge.* New York: Harper Torchbook, 1950. First published 1838.

———. *On Liberty and Other Essays.* Oxford and New York: Oxford University Press, 1991. First published 1859.

———. *Newspaper Writings.* December 1822–December 1824. Vol. 22 of *The Collected Works of John Stuart Mill.* Indianapolis: Liberty Fund. Online Library of Liberty.

———. *Newspaper Writings.* August 1831–July 1832. Vol. 23 of *The Collected Works of John Stuart Mill.* Indianapolis: Liberty Fund. Online Library of Liberty.

———. *Principles of Political Economy.* 6th ed. London: Longmans, Green, 1911.

———. *A System of Logic and Ratiocination.* Vols. 1 and 2. 1843. Project Gutenberg eBook, 2011.

Mills, C. Wright. *The Sociological Imagination.* New York: Oxford University Press, 1959.

Mirowski, Philip, and Dieter Plehwe, eds. *The Road from Mont Pèlerin.* Cambridge, MA, and London: Harvard University Press, 2009.

Montesquieu, Charles de Secondat et Baron de la Brède et de. *De l'Esprit des lois.* Paris: GF Flammarion, 1979. First published 1748.

———. *Lettres persanes.* Paris: Gallimard, 1973. First published 1758.

———. *Of the Spirit of the Laws.* In vol. 38 of *Great Books of the Western World.* Chicago: University of Chicago Press, 1952.

Morefield, Jeanne. *Covenants Without Swords.* Princeton: Princeton University Press, 2005.

Morgan, Nicole. *La Haine froide: À quoi pense la droite américaine?* Paris: Éditions de Seuil, 2012.

Morley, John. *The Life of Richard Cobden.* 2 vols. London: Unwin, 1896.

Mosca, Gaetano. *The Ruling Class.* Translated by Hannah D. Kahn. New York: McGraw-Hill, 1939.

Mueller, Dennis C. *Public Choice*. Cambridge: Cambridge University Press, 1979.

Neill, Charles Patrick. *Daniel Raymond: An Early Chapter in the History of Economic Theory in the United States*. Baltimore: Johns Hopkins, 1897.

Neumann, Franz. *Behemoth: The Structure and Practice of National Socialism*. New York: Harper Torchbook, 1966. First published 1944.

Nietzsche, Friedrich. *On the Advantage and Disadvantage of History for Life*. Indianapolis: Hackett, 1980.

———. *The Philosophy of Nietzsche*. The Modern Library. New York: Random House, 1954.

———. *The Will to Power*. Edited by Walter A. Kaufmann. New York: Vintage, 1968.

Nobile, Philip, ed. *The Con III Controversy: The Critics Look at the Greening of America*. New York: Simon & Schuster Pocket Books, 1971.

Nonaka, Ikujiro. "The Knowledge-Creating Company." *Harvard Business Review on Knowledge Management* (1991). Boston: Harvard Business School Publishing, 1998.

OECD. *OECD Economic Surveys: United States 2012*. Paris: OECD Publishing, 2012. oecd-ilibrary.org/economics/oecd-economic-surveys-united-states-2012_eco_surveys-usa-2012-en.

———. *OECD at 50: OECD Economic Outlook*. Vol. 2011/1. Paris: OECD Publishing, 2012. oecd.org/eco/outlook/48010330.pdf.

Olson, Mancur. *The Rise and Decline of Nations*. New Haven, CT: Yale University Press, 1982.

Onfray, Michel. *L'Eudémonisme social*. Paris: Grasset, 2008.

Ostrogorsky, Moise. *Democracy and the Organization of Political Parties*. Translated by Frederick Clark. 2 vols. New York: Macmillan, 1902.

Owen, Robert. *A New View of Society: Essays on the Principle of the Formation of Human Character and the Application of Principle to Practice*. London, 1813; Internet Archive, 2007. archive.org/details/anewviewsociety00owengoog/page/n4.

———. *Observations on the Effect of the Manufacturing System*. London: Longman, Hurst, Rees, Orme and Brown, 1817.

Oz-Salzberger, Fania, ed. Introduction to *Ferguson: An Essay on the History of Civil Society*. Cambridge: Cambridge University Press, 2001.

Park, Robert E., and Ernest W. Burgess. *Introduction to the Science of*

Sociology. Chicago: University of Chicago Press, 1921.

Parsons, Talcott. *Societies: Evolutionary and Comparative Perspectives*. Foundations of Modern Sociology. Edited by Alex Inkeles. Englewood Cliffs, NJ: Prentice-Hall, 1966.

———. *The Structure of Social Action*. New York: Free Press, 1949.

Parsons, Talcott, and Neil J. Smelser. *Economy and Society*. New York: Free Press, 1965.

Parsons, Talcott, and Edward A. Shils, eds. *Towards a General Theory of Action*. New York: Harper Torchbooks, 1962.

Peck, Jamie. *Constructions of Neoliberal Reason*. Oxford and New York: Oxford University Press, 2010.

Piketty, Thomas. *Le Capital au XXIe siècle*. Paris: Éditions du Seuil, 2013.

Pincus, Steve. *1688: The First Modern Revolution*. New Haven, CT: Yale University Press, 2009.

Pinkard, Terry. *German Philosophy 1760–1860: The Legacy of Idealism*. Cambridge: Cambridge University Press, 2002. First published 1840.

Plato. *Dialogues of Plato, The Republic*, Book 1. Translated by Benjamin Jowett. In *Great Books of the Western World*. Chicago: University of Chicago, 1952.

Plihon, Dominique. *Le Nouveau Capitalisme*. Paris: Dominos/Flammarion, 2001.

Pomeranz, Kenneth. *The Great Divergence: China, Europe and the Making of the Modern World Economy*. Princeton: Princeton University Press, 2000.

Popper, Karl R. *The Open Society and Its Enemies*. Rev. ed. Princeton: Princeton University Press, 1966.

Postan, M.M., D.C. Coleman, and Peter Mathias. *The Industrial Economies: Capital, Labour and Enterprise*. The Cambridge Economic History Of Europe. Part 2. Cambridge: Cambridge University Press, 1978.

Prigogine, Ilya. *The End of Certainty: Time, Chaos and the New Laws of Nature*. New York: Free Press, 1996.

Proudhon, Pierre-Joseph. *De la Capacité politique des classes ouvrière*. Paris: E. Dentu, 1865. BNF-Gallica. Online.

———. *Les Confessions d'un révolutionnaire pour servir à l'histoire de février*. Paris, 1849. BNF-Gallica. Online.

———. *Qu'est-ce que c'est la propriété?* Paris: Garnier-Flammarion, 1966. First published 1840.

Ptak, Ralf. "Neoliberalism in Germany: Revisiting the Ordoliberal Foundations of the Social Market Economy." In *The Road from Mont Pèlerin,* edited by Philip Mirowski and Dieter Plehwe, 98–138. Cambridge, MA, and London: Harvard University Press, 2009.

———. *Vom Ordoliberalismus zum sozialen Marktwirtschaft: Stationen des Neoliberalismus in Deutschland.* Berlin: Springer Fachmedien, 2004.

Raiffa, Howard. *The Art and Science of Negotiation.* Cambridge, MA: Belknap/Harvard University Press, 1982.

Rancière, Jacques. *Moments politiques: Interventions 1977–2009.* Translated by Mary Foster. Montreal: Lux, 2014.

———. *Nights of Labour: Workers' Dream in Nineteenth Century France.* Translated by David Fernbach. London and New York: Verso, 2012.

Rand, Ayn. *Capitalism: The Unknown Ideal.* New York : Signet, 1967.

Rawls, John. *Political Liberalism.* (New York, NY: Columbia University Press, 1996).

———. *Political Liberalism.* New York: Columbia University Press, 1996.

———. *A Theory of Justice.* Cambridge, MA: Harvard University Press, 1971.

Razeen, Sally. "Ordoliberalism and the Social Market: Classical Political Economy from Germany." In Commun, *L'Ordolibéralisme allemande,* 31–36.

Reich, Charles. *The Greening of America.* Revised and edited by Jesse Kornbluth. Head Butler, 2012. Online.

Renan, Ernest. *Qu'est-ce qu'une nation? et autres essais politiques.* Paris: Presses Pocket, 1962. First published 1882.

Ricardo, David. *The Principles of Political Economy and Taxation.* London: Everyman's Library, 1973.

Richards, John. *Retooling the Welfare State.* Policy Study 31. Toronto: C.D. Howe Institute, 1997.

Rickert, Heinrich. *Die Grenzen der naturwissenschaftlichen Begriffsbildung.* Tübingen: J.C.B. Mohr, 1896.

Ritchie, David G. *Hegel and Darwin with Other Philosophical Studies.* London: Swan Sonnenschein, 1893.

———. *Natural Rights: A Criticism of Some Political and Ethical Conceptions.* London: Swan Sonnenschein, 1903.

———. *Plato.* New York: Charles Scribner's Sons, 1902.

———. *The Principles of State Interference.* London: Swan Sonnenschein, 1891.

Rodbertus-Jagetzow, Karl. *Das Kapital.* Edited by Adolph Wagner and Theophil Kozak. Berlin: Puttkammer & Mühlbrecht, 1884.

Rodrick, Dani. *One Economics, Many Recipes.* Princeton: Princeton University Press, 2007.

Roepke, Wilhelm [Wilhelm Röpke]. *The Moral Foundation of Civil Society.* Translated by C.S. Fox. New Brunswick, NJ: Transaction, 2002.

———. *The Social Crisis of Our Time.* New Brunswick, NJ: Transaction, 2017.

Roll, Eric. *A History of Economic Thought.* London: Faber & Faber, 1978.

Rorty, Richard. *Essays on Heidegger and Others.* Vol. 2. Cambridge: Cambridge University Press, 1991.

———. *Philosophy and the Mirror of Nature.* Princeton: Princeton University Press, 1979.

Rosanvallon, Pierre. *Le Bon Gouvernement.* Paris: Éditions du Seuil, 2015.

———. *Le Capitalisme utopique.* 4th ed. Paris: Éditions de Seuil, 1999.

———. *Democratic Legitimacy: Impartiality, Reflexivity, Proximity.* Translated by Arthur Goldhammer. Princeton and Oxford: Princeton University Press, 2011.

———. "How to Create a Society of Equals." *Foreign Affairs*, January/February 2016.

———. *Le Libéralisme économique.* Paris: Éditions de Seuil, 1989.

Roscher, Wilhelm. *Zur Geschichte der englischen Volkswirtschaftslehre.* Leipzig, 1854.

———. *Grundriss zu Vorlesungen* über *die Staatswirtschaft nach geschichtlicher Methode.* Göttingen: Verlag der Dietrichschen Buchhandlung, 1843.

———. *Principles of Political Economy.* Translated by John J. Lalor. 2 vols. New York: Henry Holt, 1878.

Rothschild, Emma. *Economic Sentiments: Adam Smith, Condorcet and the Enlightenment.* Cambridge, MA: Harvard University Press, 2001.

Rousseau, Jean-Jacques. *The Basic Political Writings.* Translated by Donald A. Cress. Indianapolis: Hackett, 1987.

Ruitenbeek, Hendrik M., ed. *Varieties of Classic Social Theory.* New York: Dutton, 1963.

Russell, Bertrand. *Freedom Versus Organization, 1776–1914.* London: Unwin, 1965.

Ryan, Alan. *The Making of Modern Liberalism.* Princeton: Princeton University Press, 2012.

Sabine, George H. *A History of Political Theory.* New York: Holt, Rinehart, Winston, 1963.

Sachs, Jeffrey D. *The End of Poverty.* New York: Penguin, 2005.

———. *The Price of Civilization.* New York: Random House, 2011.

Saint-Simon, Henri de. *Saint-Simon: Écrits politiques et économiques, anthologie critique.* Edited by Juliette Grange. Paris: Pocket, 2005.

Samuelson, Paul. *Foundations of Economic Analysis.* Rev. ed. Cambridge, MA: Harvard University Press, 1983.

Sartre, Jean-Paul. *L'Existentialisme est un humanisme.* Paris: Gallimard, 1996. First published 1945.

———. *L'Être et le néant: Essai d'ontologie phénoménologique.* Paris: Gallimard, 1943.

Scheer, Robert. *The Great American Stickup.* New York: Nation Books, 2010.

Scheler, Max. *Ressentiment: Das Ressentiment im Aufbau der Moralen.* Translated by Louis Coser. Milwaukee, WI: Marquette University Press, 1998. First published 1912–15.

Schmidt, Vivien A., and Mark Thatcher, eds. *Resilient Liberalism in Europe's Political Economy.* Cambridge: Cambridge University Press, 2013.

Schmitt, Carl. *The Concept of the Political.* Chicago: University of Chicago Press, 2007.

Schmoller, Gustav von. *Die Entwicklung der deutschen Volkswirtschaftslehre im neunzehnten Jahrhundert: Gustav Schmoller zur siebenzigsten Wiederkehr seines Geburtstages, 24. Juni 1908.* Leipzig: Duncker & Humblot, 1908.

———. *Grundriss der allgemein Volkswirtschaftslehre.* Vols. 1 and 2. Leipzig: Duncker & Humblot, 1901, 1904.

———. *Zur Literaturgeschichte der Staats- und Sozialwissenschaften.* Leipzig: Duncker & Humblot, 1888.

———. *The Mercantile System and Its Historic Significance.* Economic Classics. Edited by W.J. Ashley. New York and London: Macmillan, 1914.

———. *Politique sociale et économie politique. Classiques des sciences sociales*. 1902. classiques.uqac.ca.

Schnyder, Gerhard, and Mathias Siems. "The 'Ordoliberal' Variety of Neo-liberalism." In *Banking Systems in the Crisis: The Faces of Liberal Capitalism*, edited by Suzanne J. Konzelmann and Marc Fovargue-Davies, 250–68. Abingdon, U.K.: Routledge, 2013.

Schröppel, Christian, and Mariko Nakajima. "The Changing Interpretation of the Flying Geese Model of Economic Development." In *Japanstudien 14. Japan als Fallbeispiel in den Wissenschaften*, 203–36. Munich: Iudicium-Verlag, 2002.

Schopenhauer, Arthur. *Le Monde comme volonté et comme représentation*. Paris: Quadrige, 2004. First published 1818.

Schumpeter, Joseph. *Capitalism, Socialism, and Democracy*. New York: Harper & Row, 1942.

———. *Ten Great Economists*. London: Unwin, 1966.

Schutz, Alfred. *The Phenomenology of the Social World*. Translated by George Walsh and Frederick Lehnert. Evanston, IL: Northwestern University Press, 1967.

Scudder, Vida D. *Social Ideals in English Literature*. New York: Houghlin Mifflin, 1898.

Seidman, Steven. *Liberalism and the Origins of European Social Theory*. Berkeley and Los Angeles: University of California Press, 1983.

Seidman, Steven, and David G. Wagner, eds. *Postmodernism and Social Theory*. London: Blackwell, 1992.

Seligman, Adam B. *The Idea of Civil Society*. New York: Free Press, 1992.

Semmel, Bernard. *The Methodist Revolution*. London: Heinemann, 1974.

Sen, Amartya. Éthique et économie. Paris: PUF Quadrige, 1987.

Senge, Peter, Art Kleiner, Charlotte Roberts, Richard B. Ross, and Bryan J. Smith. *The Fifth Discipline Field Book*. New York: Doubleday, 1994.

Sennett, Richard. *The Fall of Public Man*. New York: Vintage, 1978.

Sheppard, Nathan, ed. "Address to Working Men, By Felix Holt [by 'X']." In *The Essays of George Eliot, Complete*. Whitefish, MT: Literary Licensing, 2014. Kindle edition.

Shonfield, Andrew. *Modern Capitalism: The Changing Balance of Public and Private Power*. London: Oxford University Press, 1965.

Simmel, Georg. *Conflict and the Web of Group Affiliations.* New York: Free Press, 1955.

———. *On Individuality and Social Forms.* Edited by Donald N. Levine. Chicago: University of Chicago Press, 1971.

———. *Philosophie de l'argent.* Paris: PUF Quadrige, 1987. First published 1900.

———. *La Tragédie de la culture.* Paris: Rivages, 1988. First published 1911.

Sismonde de Simondi, John-Charles Leonard. *Nouveaux principes d'économie politique, ou De la Richesse dans ses rapports avec la population.* Paris: Delaunay, Treuttel et Wurtz, 1819.

———. *Political Economy and the Philosophy of Government, Selected Essays.* Translated by M. Mignet. London: George Woodfall and Son, 1847.

Skidelsky, Edward. *Ernst Cassirer: The Last Philosopher of Culture.* Princeton: Princeton University Press, 2011.

Smith, Adam. *The Theory of Moral Sentiments.* Indianapolis: Liberty Classics, 1976. First published 1759.

———. *The Wealth of Nations.* In vol. 39 of *Great Books of the Western World.* Chicago: University of Chicago Press, 1952. First published 1776.

Sombart, Werner. *Socialism and the Social Movement in the Nineteenth Century.* New York: G.P. Putnam's Sons, 1898. Project Gutenberg eBook, 2011.

Spencer, Herbert. *The Principles of Sociology.* London: Williams and Norgate, 1885.

Spengler, Oswald. *The Decline of the West.* New York: Alfred A. Knopf, 1926.

Springborg, Patricia. *The Problem of Human Needs and the Critique of Civilization.* London: George Allen & Unwin, 1981.

Steger, Manfred B., and Ravi K. Roy. *Neoliberalism: A Very Short Introduction.* Oxford and New York: Oxford University Press, 2010.

Steiner, George. *Martin Heidegger.* Chicago: University of Chicago Press, 1978.

Stern, Fritz. *Gold and Iron: Bismarck, Bleichröder and the Building of the German Empire.* New York: Vintage, 1977.

Sternhell, Zeev. *Les Anti-Lumières.* Paris: Folio/histoire, 2010.

Stewart, James. *Huit jours pour sauver la finance.* Paris: Grasset, 2010.

Stigler, George J. *Production and Distribution Theories.* New York: Transaction, 1994.

Stiglitz, Joseph E. *Globalization and Its Discontents.* New York: Norton, 2002.

Strauss, Leo. *Natural Rights and History.* Boston: Beacon Press, 1965.

Strauss, Leo, and Joseph Cropsey. *History of Political Philosophy.* 2nd ed. Chicago: University of Chicago Press, 1981.

Suntum, Ulrich van, Tobias Böhm, Jens Oelgemöller, and Cordelius Ilgmann. "Walter Eucken's Principles of Economic Policy Today." CAWM Discussion Paper 49, University of Münster, Center of Applied Economic Research Münster (CAWM), 2011.

Swales, Martin. *The German* Bildungsroman *from Wieland to Hesse.* Princeton: Princeton University Press, 1978.

Taylor, Charles. *Hegel.* Cambridge: Cambridge University Press, 1977.

———. *A Secular Age.* Cambridge, MA: Belknap/Harvard University Press, 2007.

———. *Les Sources du moi: La Formation de l'identité moderne.* Montreal: Boréal, 1998.

Thompson, William. *An Inquiry into the Principles of Distribution of Wealth Most Conducive to Human Happiness: Applied to the Newly Proposed System of Voluntary Equal Wealth.* London: Longman, Hurst, Rees, Orme, Brown and Green, 1824.

Thünen, J.H. von. *Die Isolierte Staat.* Berlin: Gustav Fischer, 1910.

Tietmayer, Hans. *Soziale Marktwirtschaft in Deutschland: Entwicklungen und Erfahrungen.* Freiburger Diskussionspapiere zur Ordnungsökonomik 10/4. Freiburg: Walter Eucken Institut, 2008.

Tocqueville, Alexis de. *Conversations and Correspondence with Nassau Senior.* 2 vols. Edited by M.C.M. Simpson. London: Henry S. King, 1872. First published 1862.

———. *Democracy in America.* 2 vols. Translated by Francis Bowen. New York: Vintage, 1960.

Tönnies, Ferdinand. *Gemeinschaft und Gesellschaft: Abhandlung des Communismus und des Socialismus als empirisches Culturformen.* Berlin: Fues, 1887.

Toynbee, Arnold. *The Industrial Revolution.* Boston: Beacon Press, 1956. First published 1884.

Trevino, A. Javier. *The Anthem Companion to Talcott Parsons.* New York: Anthem Press, 2016.

———. *Talcott Parsons Today.* Lanham, MD: Rowman & Littlefield, 2001.

Tribe, Keith. "Historical Schools of Economics: German and English." Keele

Economics Research Paper, Keele, University of Keele, U.K., 2002.

―――. *Strategies of Economic Order: German Economic Discourse, 1750–1950*. Cambridge: Cambridge University Press, 1995.

Tucker, Robert C., ed. *The Marx-Engels Reader*. New York: Norton, 1972.

Vaihinger, Hans. *The Philosophy of "As If."* London: Kegan Paul, Trench, Trubner, 1935.

Vanberg, Viktor J. *Föderaler Wettbewerb, Bürgersouveränität und die zwei Rollen des Staates*. Freiburger Diskussionspapiere zur Ordnungsökonomik 13/3. Freiburg: Walter Eucken Institut, 2013.

―――. *The Freiburg School: Walter Eucken and Ordoliberalism*. Freiburger Diskussionspapiere zur Ordnungsökonomik 04/11. Freiburg: Walter Eucken Institut, 2004.

―――. *Privatrechtsgesellschaft und ökonomische Theorie*. Freiburger Diskussionspapiere zur Ordnungsökonomik 07/05. Freiburg: Walter Eucken Institut, 2007.

Vaneigem, Raoul. *The Revolution of Everyday Life*. Translated by Donald Nicholson-Smith. Detroit: Red and Black, 1963–1965. http://theanarchistlibrary.org/library/raoul-vaneigem-the-revolution-of-everyday-life.

Veblen, Thorstein. *The Engineers and the Price System*. New York: Cosimo, 2006. First published 1926.

―――. *Imperial Germany and the Industrial Revolution*. Ann Arbor: University of Michigan Press, 1968. First published 1915.

―――. *The Theory of Business Enterprise*. New York: Scribner's, 1904.

―――. *The Theory of the Leisure Class*. New York: Mentor, 1953. First published 1899.

Vico, Giambattista. *The New Science: Principles of the New Science Concerning the Common Nature of Nations*. 3rd ed. Translated by David Marsh. London: Penguin, 2002. First published 1744.

Villa, Dana R. *Arendt and Heidegger: The Fate of the Political*. Princeton: Princeton University Press, 1996.

Voltaire [François-Marie Arouet de]. *Dictionnaire philosophique*. Paris: GF Flammarion, 1964.

Wallas, Graham. *The Great Society: A Psychological Analysis*. London: Macmillan, 1914.

———. *Human Nature in Politics.* London: Archibald Constable, 1908.

Watson, John. *Schelling's Transcendental Idealism.* Chicago: S.C. Griggs, 1882.

Watt, Richard M. *The Kings Depart, The Tragedy of Germany: Versailles and the German Revolution.* London: Weidenfeld and Nicolson, 1968.

Weaver, Richard M. *Ideas Have Consequences.* Expanded ed. Chicago: University of Chicago Press, 2013.

Webb, Sidney. "Social Movement." In *The Latest Age.* Vol. 10 of *The Cambridge Modern History*, edited by Lord Acton, A.W. Ward, G.W. Prothero, and Stanley Leathes, 730–65. Cambridge: Cambridge University Press, 1910.

Webb, Sidney, and Beatrice Webb. *The History of Trade Unionism, 1666–1920.* Rev. ed. Printed by the authors, for the Trade Unionists of the United Kingdom, 1920.

Webber, Carolyn, and Aaron Wildavsky. *A History of Taxation and Expenditure in the Modern World.* New York: Simon & Schuster, 1986.

Weber, Max. *The Agrarian Sociology of Ancient Civilizations.* Translated by R.I. Frank. London and New York: Verso, 2013. First published 1909.

———. *The City.* Translated by Don Martindale and Gertrude Neuwirth. New York: Free Press, 1958.

———. *Économie et Société.* 2 vols. Paris: Plon, 1971.

———. *Gesammelte Aufsäetze zur Wissenschaftslehre.* Tübingen: J.C.B. Mohr, 1922.

———. *The Protestant Ethic and the Spirit of Capitalism.* Translated by Talcott Parsons. New York: Charles Scribner's Sons, 1958. First published 1904.

Weisz, Jean-Daniel. "L'Intérêt pour une approche régulationniste du détour par l'ordolibéralisme." In Commun, *L'Ordolibéralisme allemande,* 49–66.

West, Cornel. *The American Evasion of Philosophy: A Genealogy of Pragmatism.* Madison: University of Wisconsin Press, 1989.

Wicksell, Knut. *Interest and Prices: A Study of the Causes Regulating the Value of Money.* Translated by R.F. Kahn. London: Macmillan, for the Royal Economic Society, 1926. Reprinted by the Ludwig von Mises Institute, 1962.

———. *General Theory.* Vol. 1 of *Lectures on Political Economy.* Translated by E. Classen. London: Routledge, 1934. Reprinted by the Ludwig von Mises Institute, 1977.

Wieser, Friedrich von. *Social Economics.* Translated by A. Ford Hinrichs. New York: Adelphi, 1927.

Williams, Raymond. *Culture.* London: Fontana, 1981.

———. *The Long Revolution.* Harmondsworth: Penguin, 1961.

———. *Marxism and Literature.* Oxford and New York: Oxford University Press, 1977.

Wilson, Woodrow. *Congressional Government.* New York: Riverside Press, 1985.

———. *The New Freedom.* New York: Doubleday, 1913. Kindle edition.

Wolf, Kurt H., ed. and trans. *The Sociology of Georg Simmel.* Glencoe, IL: Free Press, 1950.

Wohlgemuth, Michael. *The Boundaries of the State.* Freiburger Diskussionspapiere zur Ordnungsökonomik 11/3. Freiburg: Walter Eucken Institut, 2011.

Wohlgemuth, Michael, and Jörn Sideras. *Globalisability or Universalisability? How to Apply the Generality Principle and Constitutionalism Internationally.* Freiburger Diskussionspapiere zur Ordnungsökonomik 04/7. Freiburg: Walter Eucken Institut, 2004.

Wolin, Sheldon. *Politics and Vision.* Princeton: Princeton University Press, 2006.

Wollstonecraft, Mary. *Political Writings: Rights of Men, Rights of Women, French Revolution 1789.* Toronto: University of Toronto Press, 1953.

Wolowski, L. "Essay on the Historical Method in Political Economy." Preface to *Principles of Political Economy*, vol. 1, by Wilhelm Roscher. Translated by John J. Lalor. New York: Henry Holt, 1878.

Wright, Ronald. *A Short History of Progress.* Massey Lectures. Toronto: Anansi, 2004.

Zinn, Howard. *A People's History of the United States.* New York: Harper & Row, 1980.

Zweynert, Joachim. *Die Entstehung ordnungsökonomischer Paradigmen theoriegeschichtliche Betrachtungen.* Freiburger Diskussionspapiere zur Ordnungsökonomik 07/8. Freiburg: Walter Eucken Institut, 2007.

INDEX

Acton, Lord John, 107, 132
alienation, 86–87, 191
Alsace-Lorraine, 97–99
American government, 135
anarchy, 51, 71, 93, 105, 180
ancien régime, 27–29, 43
ancient city state, 186–87
Anti–Corn Law League, 64–65, 108
Arendt, Hannah, 46, 193–94
Aristotle, 24, 35, 48
Arnold, Matthew, 60
Aron, Raymond, 87, 150
Ashley, William, 108, 118

banks, 23, 89, 93, 126, 153
Bentham, Jeremy, 14–15, 51–53,
   56, 60–62, 68–70, 92

utilitarianism, 51, 53, 164
Berlin, 42, 94, 99, 112–13, 116–17
Berlin, Isaiah, 31, 165
Bismarck, 28, 94, 97–99
Böhm, Franz, 120, 122
Bowring, John, 61
Brentano, Franz, 139
British Hegelians, 131
Bryce, Sir James, 135
Buchanan, James, 31, 121
Buckle, Henry Thomas, 107
Burke, Edmund, 186
business, 15, 28, 39, 120, 132,
   134–36, 167, 171–72, 178

cameralism, 28–29
Canada, 4, 32, 155, 170, 185

capital, 33, 36, 48, 64, 79, 83–84, 102–5, 168

capitalism, 17–18, 27, 31, 154–55, 182, 188–89

Carlyle, Thomas, 70–71, 129, 131

Cassirer, Ernst, 138–41, 187, 193

Chadwick, Sir Edwin, 68–69

citizenship, 11, 17, 22, 34, 36, 47, 66, 151, 159, 164, 177–78, 184–87, 190, 198

civilization, 34, 40, 47, 49–50, 70, 75, 78, 107, 111, 145, 151, 156–57

civil society, 10–11, 39–42, 52–55, 59, 64–67, 73–75, 86–88, 110–11, 123–24, 129–30, 163, 182–83, 185–87

importance of, 72, 118

industrial, 41, 94

theory of, 7, 41, 103

classical liberalism, 10, 17, 37, 41, 55, 88, 128, 133, 150, 175, 177

failure, 41, 43, 45, 47, 49, 51, 53, 55, 57, 59, 61, 65, 67, 69, 73

climate change, 14, 19–20, 27, 36, 153, 173, 196

Cobden, Richard, 64–65, 108

Cold War, 18, 20, 26, 31, 130, 168

community, 20, 39, 66, 74, 79, 87–88, 103, 142, 163, 166, 169, 174, 185

political, 110, 126, 147, 179, 193–94

Comte, Auguste, 27, 40, 76–81, 85–88, 94, 113, 131, 187

Course of Positive Philosophy, 79, 85

consciousness, 22, 25, 39, 42–43, 46, 49–52, 136, 139, 143, 147, 160, 165, 168–69

consent, 45, 51, 149, 192

Constant, Benjamin, 186–87

constitution, 16, 22, 28, 42, 74, 97, 136

economic, 120–21

Constitution of Liberty (Hayek), 31

consumers, 59, 124, 157, 167, 173, 180

costs, social, 21, 129, 162, 180, 190

Course of Positive Philosophy (Comte), 79, 85

crisis, 13, 16, 19, 24, 27, 29, 33, 37, 57, 70

critiques, 40, 45, 77–79, 85, 161, 175, 187

public choice, 156, 161

Croly, Herbert, 133, 135, 158

cultural despair, 25–26

culture, 15, 24, 38, 71, 73, 106, 148, 167, 174, 177, 183

Darwin, Charles, 29, 69, 86

Dasein, 115, 140, 143–44, 193

Davos, 138, 140–42, 144, 187, 193

democracy, 17, 19, 34–35, 131, 136, 145, 151, 185–90

democratic politics, 33, 155, 157, 179

destitution, 92, 94, 105, 110, 129, 178

Dewey, John, 144, 147–48, 194

Dilthey, Wilhelm, 113, 131, 183, 193

Dunn, John, 184, 187

Durkheim, Émile, 27, 30, 84, 86, 113, 187

economic analysis, 107, 188

economic competition, 122–24

economic development, 29, 33, 42, 101, 113, 126–27, 175, 178

economic order, 115–16

economic policy, 88, 96–97, 182

economic problems, 23, 33, 116, 135

economics, 19–23, 29, 34–35, 47, 96, 102–3, 107, 111–17, 122–23, 162, 174–75, 177–78
classical, 37, 58, 76, 114, 151

economists, 77, 98, 100, 115

economist-sociologists, 177

economy, 15, 18, 28, 120–22, 124, 127, 153–54, 161–63, 177, 180–81, 183, 187–88

elections, 93, 129, 148, 158, 160, 185, 195

Eliot, George, 71–73, 75, 129

employment, 22, 37, 64, 83, 122, 128, 151, 153, 162, 166–67, 170, 190

Engels, Friedrich, 87

England, 43, 45, 51–52, 54, 59, 61, 65, 70–71, 74–75, 77, 85, 88, 92, 95

English society, 74, 131

enterprise, 105, 180–81

entrepreneurship, 28, 171

Eucken, Walter, 107, 120–22, 127, 139, 149

Europe, 41–43, 78–79, 91, 94, 107, 110, 125–26, 130, 137–39, 149, 151, 155

European liberalism, 140

European Union, 15, 122, 125

factories, 54, 63, 66, 69, 125, 168

fair system, 39

families, 34, 56, 62, 67, 124, 134, 151, 154–55, 166, 172, 198

Ferguson, Adam, 163

Fichte, Johann Gottlieb, 50–51, 86, 96, 185
Grundlage des Naturrechts nach Principien der Wissenschaftslehre, 50, 86

finance, 25, 51, 69, 130, 181, 183, 187

financial markets, 15, 17, 25

financial power, 22, 36

financial system, 23, 181

First World War, 30–31, 91, 110, 114, 118–19, 137, 152, 175, 192

Foucault, Michel, 69

France, 10, 17, 43–45, 69, 76–78, 92–95, 98, 101, 110, 113, 137, 151, 185

Franco-Prussian War, 97

free society, 10, 19, 47, 125, 149, 196

free trade, 15, 58, 60, 101, 111, 122

freedom, liberal, 10, 140
Freiburg University, 120, 127, 144, 149
French Revolution, 18, 45–46, 48, 52, 54, 75, 78, 81
Fukuyama, Francis, 26

Galbraith, John Kenneth, 18, 28, 136, 155, 165, 172
Gay, Peter, 74, 191
George, Henry, 83
German Empire, 97, 197
German historical school, 92–97, 99–101, 103, 105–7, 109, 111–17, 119, 121, 123, 125, 127, 174–75
program, 118
German ordoliberalism, 107, 119
German social market economy, 119
Germany, 40, 42, 98–99, 101, 103, 116, 118–19, 125–27, 129–31, 137, 139, 145, 177–78
new, 98, 131
governance, 9, 13, 15–16, 66, 82, 84, 179, 187, 192
government, 44–45, 55–56, 67–69, 112, 120–23, 151–52, 154–56, 160–62, 172–74, 181, 183, 186, 190
liberal, 120, 148, 184
Gray, John, 184, 187
Great Antinomy, 121–22
Great Britain, 13, 15, 37, 43, 75, 77, 82, 88, 91, 178

Great Depression, 13, 17, 91, 95, 119, 136, 138, 151, 178
Grundlage des Naturrechts nach Principien der Wissenschaftslehre (Fichte), 50, 86

Habermas, Jürgen, 193–94
Hamilton, Alexander, 100–1
Harrison, Frederic, 73–74
Hayek, Friedrich von, 29, 111, 116, 139, 149
Hegel, 26, 46, 48–51, 59, 80, 85–86, 95, 165, 169, 194
alienation, 163
concept of civil society, 94
concept of history, 50
system, 48
Hegelian idealism, 133
left-wing, 145
Hegelian *Rechtsstaat*, 120
Heidegger, Martin, 138–49, 166, 168, 193–94
Hildebrand, Bruno, 97
Hirschman, Albert O., 187–88
historical method, 113
Hobbes, Thomas, 43, 45, 52, 139
Hodgskin, Thomas, 70, 92
human condition, 50, 143–45, 151, 195
human freedom, 16, 46, 191, 195
human mind, 86, 139, 141, 156, 169
human nature, 140
humanism, 70, 140–41, 168
humanity, 10, 21, 35, 38, 40, 71,

76, 79–80, 118, 142, 165, 182

Hume, David, 31, 43, 48, 61, 86, 90, 139, 163, 165

Husserl, Edmund, 121, 138–39

imagination, 39, 42, 62, 80, 140–41, 191
  moral, 47, 52
  sociological, 27, 37, 84, 188

IMF (International Monetary Fund), 15, 181

individual freedom, 18, 21, 47, 112–13, 122, 127, 177, 180, 195, 197, 199

individualism, 14, 50–51, 88, 171

industrial crafts, 66, 120

industrial economies, 127, 130, 196–97

Industrial Revolution, 21, 34, 41, 52

industrial society, 84, 86, 93–94, 99–100, 105, 113, 150

industrialism, 54, 79–80, 82

industrialization, 21, 37, 43, 75, 77, 79, 82–83, 85, 87, 92, 94, 98, 101, 175, 178–80

industry, 23, 28, 58, 63, 73, 86, 105, 109, 123–24, 134, 152, 160, 187–89

inflation, 122, 150, 161, 166

injustice, 23, 35–36, 155, 196

innovation, 35, 106, 181, 187–90

institutions, 30, 50, 86, 100, 106, 110, 117, 141, 175, 177, 191
  liberal, 22, 184

interests, 10, 15, 55, 86–88, 96–98, 109, 111, 119, 122, 142, 145, 148
  common, 123, 134
  economic, 118, 159
  general, 87, 174
  individual, 50–51, 164
  landed, 54, 65
  particular, 36, 42, 65–66
  political, 109, 160
  private, 46, 66, 102, 148, 165, 183, 188

internet, 171, 176, 181, 189

investment, 18, 58, 123, 125, 153, 172

iron triangles, 159–60

James, William, 133, 135–36, 144

Japan, 28, 151

Jefferson, 45

Jevons, Stanley, 115

justice, 10, 14, 18, 22, 31, 34–36, 50, 52, 79, 130, 149, 154, 165, 169

Kant, Immanuel , 26, 32, 39, 45–50, 80, 85, 139–40, 142–43, 187, 192–94
  concept, 47, 139, 141
  ideas, 140, 192

Keynes, John Maynard , 58, 88–90, 122, 137–38
  economics, 24, 172, 179

Keynesians, 18, 124, 166

liberalism, 18, 34

system, 153, 161
welfare state, 153, 155
Knies, Karl, 97
Kojève, Alexandre, 234

labour, 33, 38, 67, 69, 79, 82, 84,
    86, 102–5, 123–24, 132, 134,
    180, 182–84
labour markets, 64, 68
labourers, 64, 72, 88
laissez-faire, 31, 56, 62, 80, 88–89,
    125, 129, 137
language, 29, 46, 52, 89–90, 140,
    146, 193
Lask, Emil, 30
    anomaly, 30, 32
Lassalle, Ferdinand, 103
laws, 20, 22, 47, 56, 65–66, 77, 79,
    81, 103–4, 185–86, 191–92, 195
    individual bankruptcy, 33
    natural, 44
legitimacy, 17, 51, 83, 187
liberal capitalism, 71, 125
liberal democracies, 123, 158
liberal ideas, 10, 51, 174–75, 187
liberalism, 9–10, 13–27, 29, 31–
    35, 37–39, 41–46, 51, 119–20,
    130–31, 147–50, 174–75, 184,
    190–92, 194–98
    communitarian, 186
    contemporary, 85, 180
    industrial, 37, 178
    orthodox, 105–6
    postwar, 19, 27, 167
    roots, 19, 40, 129, 162, 168

liberal mind, 46, 80
liberal paradigm, 93, 191
liberal philosophy, 22, 30
liberal principles, 26, 62, 199
liberal societies, 27–29, 38, 119–
    20, 124, 148, 177, 180, 183,
    195–96
liberal state, 10, 25, 119, 126,
    184–85
liberals, 26, 30, 47, 51, 75, 77, 81,
    89, 91, 97, 169, 175–76, 178,
    180, 182
    classical, 79–80
liberal thinkers, 44, 53
liberty, individual, 31–32, 121–22,
    125
Lippmann, Walter, 121, 135–36,
    139, 150
    colloquium, 121, 139, 149, 172
List, Friedrich, 96, 100–1, 180
Locke, John, 43, 45, 116
Lyotard, Jean-François, 193

Macaulay, Lord Thomas Babing-
    ton, 56
Malthus, Thomas, 53, 58, 68, 129
management, 28, 38–39, 64, 103,
    126, 130, 135, 168, 183, 189
    economic, 167
    estate, 28
    scientific, 136
Manchester, 52, 70
Manchester system, 105
Manchesterism, 51, 63, 82–83,
    92–94, 97–98, 100, 103, 177

marginalist price theory, 29, 116

market competition, 125

market concentrations, 120

market failures, 158

market forces, 50, 53, 75, 103, 178, 180–81

market mechanisms, 185

market performance, 19

market power, 124
  abusive, 123

markets, 10, 14–15, 17, 28–30, 44, 50–51, 109, 111, 114, 122, 124–25, 156–57, 160, 172–73
  competitive, 28, 32, 121, 123
  efficient, 23
  international, 181
  open, 97
  rational, 178

markets and market mechanisms, 185

Marshall, T.H., 117, 178

Marx, Karl, 26, 46, 86–87, 103, 105, 115
  Marxism, 141, 145, 192

material progress, 37, 192

materialism, 85, 192

Menger, Carl, 111–12, 114–16, 118–19

mercantilism, 44, 107–8, 110–11

metaphysics, 47, 78, 85–86, 139, 143

Methodenstreit, 112–14, 118–19

Michels, Robert, 131

middle class, 16–17, 54–55, 57, 69, 129, 152, 164, 177, 179

rule, 55–56, 92

Mill, John Stuart, 38–39, 51, 53, 56, 58, 60–64, 76, 79–80, 85, 87–88, 90, 101, 186

Mills, C. Wright, 27, 188

Mises, Ludwig von, 116, 139, 149

modern democracy, 160, 186

modern liberalism, 43–44

modernism, 51, 131, 192

money, 36, 110, 115–16, 122, 130, 135, 145, 152, 155, 157, 160–62, 172, 176

money trust, 135, 179

Mont Pelerin Society, 150, 172

Montesquieu, Charles-Louis de Secondat, Baron de, 43–44, 83, 95, 132, 169

moral law, 26, 32, 47–48, 139, 191

morality, 22, 47–48, 61

Morley, John, 64

Müller-Armack, Alfred, 120, 122

Napoleon, 42, 49, 55, 77, 81–82, 95

Napoleon III, 93

Napoleonic Wars, 9, 57–58

Nassau Senior, 68

nation, 55, 57, 69, 71–72, 78–79, 86, 100, 102, 104, 108, 197–99

Nazism, 24, 119, 141

neoliberalism, 14, 16, 18–22, 24, 26–27, 35–40, 114, 116, 152, 177, 179

neoliberals, 15–16, 25, 37–38, 152, 175, 181, 189

New Deal, 17, 24, 26, 129, 136, 191
New Liberalism, 17, 131–32, 168
Nietzsche, Friedrich , 33, 46, 77,
    131, 146, 192
North America, 28, 45, 48, 61,
    107, 131, 151, 168, 175, 192

observers, 30, 45, 82, 142, 152,
    163, 165, 168
oppression, 18, 36, 42
    economic, 122
ordoliberalism, 40, 119–27
organizations, 15, 30, 39, 110,
    112, 120, 132, 134, 190, 197
    economic, 102, 187
    industrial, 62, 81, 94
    social, 39, 80, 86, 139
Owen, Robert, 62–63, 70, 80, 92

Paris, 77, 81, 93, 121, 139, 149
Parsons, Talcott, 99
pathologies, 155–56
Peel, Sir Robert, 42
phenomenology, 121, 138–39
philosophers, 29, 57, 138, 141,
    187
philosophical theory, 49
philosophy, 15–16, 25–27, 42, 46,
    48, 95, 131–33, 140, 143–44,
    191–92, 194
Piketty, Thomas, 83
Plato, 24, 139–40, 143, 146
policy, 23, 29, 67–68, 111, 122,
    129, 158, 162, 173, 175, 196
    monetary, 15, 22, 122, 126

political economy, 76, 79, 93,
    115, 117
political freedom, 16, 19, 36, 40,
    62, 88, 91, 124, 180, 191
political machines, 133, 135, 179,
    185–86
political parties, 65, 84, 93, 131, 158
political pathologies, 130, 156
political philosophers, 90, 131
    liberal, 26, 155
political philosophy, 18, 22, 24, 36
political power, 33, 36, 75, 110
political representation, 22, 158
political science, 44, 61, 106, 151
political speech, 124, 194
political systems, 20, 39
political theory, 18, 24, 26, 145,
    148, 165
politicians, 134, 158–59, 172
politics, 22, 26, 35, 44, 135, 145,
    157–58, 188, 190, 199
Poor Law, 54, 67, 69, 92, 132
positive knowledge, 75, 77–78, 81
positivism, 20, 27, 76, 81, 85, 87,
    138, 141–42, 149, 192–93, 195
positivists, 40, 77, 79–80, 86, 92,
    151
postmodernism, 19, 21, 25, 85,
    127, 138, 148, 184, 191, 193
postwar welfare state, 191
poverty, 34, 36, 54, 59, 69, 71, 73,
    100, 102, 154–55, 164–65, 173
power, 17, 19–21, 44–45, 51, 54–55,
    68–69, 81–82, 111, 132, 140–41,
    148–49, 157–61, 185, 187

pragmatism, 136, 148

preservation, 120–21

prices, 23, 52, 57, 104, 111, 114–16, 131, 175, 181, 199

principles, 10–11, 26, 51, 55, 59–61, 63, 104, 184, 187

programs, 60, 100, 154, 161–62, 170, 173, 185–86, 198

   great society, 155, 170

progress, 50, 53, 77, 106, 111, 129, 182, 188–89

progressivism, 133, 136

prosperity, 18, 34, 37, 91, 155, 166–67, 198

   national, 101, 152, 155

Prussia, 42, 93–94, 101

Prussian, 97–99

public goods, 42, 75, 126–27, 161

public interest, 55, 66, 148, 161, 183

public policy, 11, 30, 35, 55, 83, 103

rational voter paradox, 157–58

Rawls, John, 31, 154–55

reason, 25–26, 37, 40, 42, 44–49, 52, 56, 60–61, 138–41, 143, 163, 191–92

reconstruction, liberal, 46

redistribution, 31, 83–84, 123, 166

regimes, liberal, 14, 28

regulations, 17, 25, 27, 63, 108, 124–26, 178

rejection, 64, 71, 75, 133, 141–42, 171

religion, 24, 44, 51, 61, 73, 76, 86, 89–90, 128, 141

rents, 57–58, 102, 104–5, 181

representative government, 65, 140

revolution, 36, 42–43, 62–63, 69, 82, 119, 132, 177, 189

   tech, 20, 22

Ricardo, David, 51, 53, 58, 60, 92, 97, 105, 114–15, 166

rights, 4, 34, 42, 45, 61, 67, 183, 186, 195, 197–98

   human, 22, 34, 37, 122

risks, 22, 28, 30, 32, 36, 110, 122, 141

Ritchie, David, 131

Rodbertus-Jagetzow, Karl, 97, 100, 102–5, 155, 197

Roosevelt, Franklin D., 121–22, 129, 136, 197

Röpke, Wilhelm, 120, 149

Rosanvallon, Pierre, 56, 82, 185

Roscher, Wilhelm, 58, 97, 100, 106–7, 113, 115, 119

Rousseau, 43–45, 50, 83, 186–87

Russell, 138

Rüstow, Alexander, 120, 149

Ryan, Alan, 62

Saint-Simon, Henri de, 27, 77–85, 87–88, 93, 131, 160, 187

Sartre, Jean-Paul , 140–41, 168

Savigny, Friedrich Carl von, 96

Schmoller, Gustav, 95–100, 106–12, 115–19, 188, 197

   defence of mercantilism, 107

Verein für sozialforschung, 37, 96–98, 113

Schumpeter, Joseph, 188–89

Scott, Sir Walter, 70, 131

Scudder, Vida D., 75

Second Empire, 92–93

security, economic, 18, 154, 197

single-issue groups, 25, 159–60

Smith, Adam, 43, 51, 101, 108, 115, 155, 162–63, 165–66

Theory of Moral Sentiments, 162–63

social change, 25, 54, 71, 187

social classes, 54, 57, 61, 72, 74, 84, 87, 91, 134–35, 172, 175, 179, 182

social contract, 56, 62, 126

social democracy, 17, 38, 119, 178, 189, 191

social market economy, 40, 107, 119

social movement, 132

social phenomena, 96, 132, 193

social problems, 54, 57, 86, 173

social programs, 66, 151, 171

socialism, 31, 62, 80, 87, 89, 105, 175, 188–89

sociology, 39–40, 77, 79, 86, 95–96, 113, 124, 148, 162, 164, 174, 178–79, 184

solidarity, 66, 111, 164, 170, 194

solutions, 20, 40, 42, 59, 68–69, 76, 88, 93, 105–6, 113–14, 116, 120, 127, 177, 185

Spengler, Oswald, 145

state, 22–24, 29–30, 51–52, 54, 81–82, 89–90, 99, 105–6, 126–29, 168–69, 176, 178–80, 184–87, 233–36

state socialism, 17, 94, 99, 103, 131, 135, 177

status, 28, 39, 66–67, 80, 84, 86, 118, 124, 148, 151, 183, 187

and function of, 28, 80, 86, 183, 187

Steiner, George, 147

Stephen, Leslie, 70

taxes, 25, 161–62, 172, 176, 181

technological innovation, 82, 123, 151, 189

technology, 20–21, 35, 39, 75–77, 80–81, 83–85, 87, 149, 173, 176, 181, 184, 187, 196, 199

Thatcher, Margaret, 30, 150

theory

economic, 70, 124

social, 55, 146

Theory of Moral Sentiments (Smith), 162–63

Thrasymachus, 35–36

Thünen, Johann Heinrich von, 97

Tönnies, Ferdinand, 95, 113, 131

tools, 19–20, 23, 37–38, 60, 107, 126, 136, 140, 146, 175–76, 181, 193, 195, 197

trade, 15, 106, 110, 115, 134, 198

trade unions, 65–66, 73, 120, 135, 172

transformations, 25, 34, 82, 110,

130–31, 160, 169, 175, 190

Tribe, Keith, 107

tyrannies, 14, 16, 19, 31, 36, 145

United Kingdom, 17, 150

United States, 10, 13–14, 17, 101, 116, 118, 133–34, 136–37, 150–52, 155, 168, 170, 177, 179–80

utilitarianism, 15, 48, 51–52, 56–57, 59, 70, 76, 80, 88, 92, 129, 177

utilitarians, 47, 54–56, 75, 90, 165

values, 14, 25, 38, 57, 104, 111–12, 115–17, 119, 136, 139, 147, 180, 186, 192, 195

liberal, 17, 25, 40, 93, 190

Verein für sozialforschung (Schmoller), 37, 96–98, 113

Victorians, 69–71, 73–74

Vienna, 96, 111–14, 116

Voltaire, 43–44

wages, 13, 57, 59, 67, 83, 86, 102–3, 125, 155, 170, 182

Wagner, Adolph, 131

war, 42, 44, 51, 58, 129, 137–38, 140, 144–45, 150–52, 154–55, 162, 164–65, 170, 175, 177

wealth, 14, 59, 63, 83, 89–90, 112, 179, 181

Weber, Max, 30, 99

welfare state, 16–18, 24–26, 37–38, 40, 128–31, 133, 135–37, 139, 141, 143, 145, 151–57, 161–73, 177–78

Western Europe, 13, 151, 175

Western liberalism, 18

Western philosophy, 144, 147

Western world, 14–16, 18–19, 21, 23–24, 34, 37–38, 130–31, 153, 157

Wieser, Friedrich von, 111–12, 167

Wilson, Woodrow, 133, 136

workers, 28, 38, 57, 62–63, 65–68, 102–6, 112, 157, 177, 190

working class, 41, 55, 58, 69, 73, 83, 87, 103, 119, 129, 131, 145, 152, 175, 178–79

WTO (World Trade Organization), 181

Zollverein, 93